INDEPENDENT SECTOR

INDEPENDENT SECTOR is a coalition of 830 corporations, foundations, and voluntary organizations with national interests in and impact on philanthropy, voluntary action, and other activities related to the educational, scientific, cultural, and religious life, as well as the health and welfare, of the nation.

INDEPENDENT SECTOR is a meeting ground where diverse elements in and related to the sector can come together and learn how to improve their performance and effectiveness.

INDEPENDENT SECTOR is serving the sector through
- education, to improve the public's understanding of the independent sector
- research, to develop a comprehensive store of knowledge about the sector
- government relations, to coordinate the multitude of interconnections between the sector and the various levels of government
- encouragement of effective sector leadership and management, to maximize service to individuals and society, by promoting educational programs for managers and practitioners
- communication within the sector, to identify shared problems and opportunities

The impact of INDEPENDENT SECTOR's effort can be measured by the growth in support of the sector, as manifested by increased giving and volunteering.

For additional information, please contact

INDEPENDENT
SECTOR

1828 L Street, N.W.
Washington, DC 20036
(202) 223-8100

GOVERNING, LEADING, AND MANAGING NONPROFIT
ORGANIZATIONS

Dennis R. Young
Robert M. Hollister
Virginia A. Hodgkinson
and Associates

Foreword by Frances Hesselbein

GOVERNING, LEADING, AND MANAGING NONPROFIT ORGANIZATIONS

ORGANIZATIONS

*New Insights
from Research and Practice*

Jossey-Bass Publishers · San Francisco

For sales outside the United States, contact Maxwell Macmillan
International Publishing Group, 866 Third Avenue, New York,
New York 10022.

Manufactured in the United States of America

 The paper used in this book is acid-free and meets the
State of California requirements for recycled paper
(50 percent recycled waste, including 10 percent
postconsumer waste), which are the strictest guidelines
for recycled paper currently in use in the United States.

10% POST
CONSUMER
W A S T E

Library of Congress Cataloging-in-Publication Data

Young, Dennis R., date.
    Governing, leading, and managing nonprofit organizations : new
insights from research and practice / Dennis R. Young, Robert M.
Hollister, Virginia A. Hodgkinson, and associates.
        p.   cm. — (The Jossey-Bass nonprofit sector series)
    Includes index.
    ISBN 1-55542-490-2 (alk. paper)
    1. Corporations, Nonprofit—Management.   I. Hollister, Robert M.
II. Hodgkinson, Virginia Ann.   III. Title.   IV. Series.
HD62.6.Y678   1992
658′.048—dc20   92-25884
                                                                  CIP

FIRST EDITION
HB Printing   10 9 8 7 6 5 4 3 2 1   *Code 9290*

*The
Jossey-Bass
Nonprofit Sector
Series*

Contents

Foreword

Few nonprofit organizations have funds for comprehensive research and environmental scanning to examine current and future trends as they plan for the 1990s and beyond, yet most managers recognize the danger of flying on untested assumptions as they build and communicate their vision of the organization's future. *Governing, Leading, and Managing Nonprofit Organizations* is a timely contribution to nonprofit boards and staff who are attempting to make governance and management responsive to mission and needs in a volatile decade. Managing in the turbulent 1990s requires a knowledge base, a clear view of major trends, and an understanding of the implications of these trends for the nonprofit enterprise. Nonprofit boards and staff, facing burgeoning demands and stringent budgets, are ever more aware of the importance of research as a basis for planning and the importance of models of innovative practice that can transform the services of their organizations.

Many third sector organizations have adapted appropriate private sector business practices, yet are aware of the need for solid research on management innovation in the nonprofit sector. This new resource will serve well the serious practitioners, researchers, and students for whom it was designed. *Governing, Leading, and Managing Nonprofit Organizations* provides the solid research and basic information so necessary for the responsible third sector organization to carry out its leadership and management accountabilities. There is a great hunger for ideas, direction, and tools singularly designed for the nonprofit board and staff. The chapters of this book highlight innovative management practices unique to the nonprofit world.

This book belongs in the hands of men and women responsible for defining and communicating the vision, managing the mission, and knowing who the customer is and what the customer values. It will strengthen both governance and management and the crucial partnership of board and staff in an affirmative and supportive way.

I encourage the book's authors to see this as just the beginning of a flow of research and support required by today's nonprofit organizations — nonprofit organizations more needed, more recognized, more effective, more significant, and more indispensable than ever before. Today's "social sector" organizations deserve and require their own sector research and resources. This book is a welcome response.

September 1992   Frances Hesselbein
                                    President and CEO
                                    The Peter F. Drucker Foundation
                                    for Nonprofit Management
                                    New York, New York

Preface

People have been managing nonprofit organizations for several centuries. Compared to the nonprofit organization, particularly religious groups and nonprofit associations, such as the Knights of Columbus or the Masons, both the business corporation and the modern government bureaucracy are relative newcomers. However, while managers and administrators in business and government have had access to professional education for a long time, programs tailored for managers in nonprofit organizations have been established only recently. Many colleges include courses specifically in nonprofit organization management in their MBA and MPA programs, and a few institutions, such as the Mandel Center for Nonprofit Organizations at Case Western Reserve University and the Institute for Nonprofit Organization Management at the University of San Francisco, offer degrees exclusively in nonprofit organization and management. The challenge to the professionals who develop these curricula is to design programs based on research on both nonprofit organizations and effective management and leadership practice.

Serious research on nonprofit management began about fifteen years ago when the Program on Nonprofit Organizations was founded at Yale University. What has emerged from research at Yale and at several new academic centers that focus on nonprofit organizations is a set of themes and questions that will probably form the research agenda for the next decade and lead to the development of a knowledge base that will be used to educate nonprofit managers.

Spurred by the spiraling inflation of the 1970s and cutbacks in federal government funding in the 1980s, using resources efficiently and managing more effectively became a priority for nonprofit organizations. However, scholars and practitioners needed to address several questions in order to determine what effective management meant in nonprofit organizations, as compared to business and government. What knowledge about good management practice is common among the three sectors and what is different? How are personnel different? What kind of management practices will effectively recruit and retain volunteers? Do personnel in nonprofit organizations (who generally make less money than those in business and government) have different motivations and expect different rewards than those working for business or government? Since nonprofits are financed differently than business or government, what skills are needed to effectively finance them? How do accounting and financial reporting differ in nonprofits? What are the functions and responsibilities of boards and how do they differ from business and government boards? What are effective board-staff relationships? How does the function of a nonprofit determine its management needs, and how do these needs differ according to function? Are different kinds of management skills and practices needed for small organizations—food kitchens or homes for battered women, for instance—than for large organizations, such as the Girl Scouts, hospitals, and colleges and universities? Are the management needs and board compositions different for large membership organizations than for advocacy organizations or colleges? Is there a difference between nonprofit, public, and for-profit management in hospitals, colleges and universities, and research institutes? Are nonprofits affected or regulated differently than organizations in other sectors? What impact does government regulation have on the management of nonprofit organizations? Scholars and practitioners asked these questions to determine what kind of research was needed to improve nonprofit management and how to include the research in programs on nonprofit management.

The authors of *Governing, Leading, and Managing Nonprofit Organizations* discuss these and other questions. This book grew out of the 1991 Spring Research Forum, cosponsored by IN-DEPENDENT SECTOR, the United Way Strategic Institute, and the Mandel Center for Nonprofit Organizations at Case Western Reserve University. The forum's goal was to assess progress made in research on management and leadership in nonprofit organizations. After a decade of research, several basic themes are emerging as important for both continuing research and practice. The authors report on their research and its implications for professional education and practice among different types of nonprofit organizations. The research covers board structure and functions, board-staff relations, the mission of non-profits, volunteer recruitment and retention, resource development and management, management for social change, and public policy issues that affect management.

The authors of this book include scholars, educators, and practitioners. As such, the research is diverse, some of it using sophisticated methodology, some long-term field experience. Management education combines both theory and practice, and the authors provide a balance between the two. The chapters cover the broad terrain of management issues and organizational types, as well as the variety of management needs and practices that are necessary to effectively manage and lead these organizations.

Organization of the Book

This book is divided into four parts that cover some of the major areas of nonprofit management. Part One focuses on the issues of governance and organizational systems. Chapter One provides an overview of the major themes covered in this book as well as the implications for future research and design of curricula for professional degrees in nonprofit management. Chapter Two explores the effectiveness of a new tool that defines board-staff relationships and their interdependent roles and responsibilities in a variety of nonprofit institutions. Chapter Three discusses the special missions of nonprofit institutions that must be considered in management practice. Chapter Four focuses on how the sophisticated use of computers can provide managers of arts and cultural organizations with the information they need to manage more effectively and to use resources more efficiently. Chapter Five describes the kinds of organizational assessment and program evaluation that national organizations and their affiliates use most frequently.

Part Two focuses on human resource and financial management. Chapter Six reports on research about motivations of volunteers and how an understanding of these different motivations can be used to recruit, retain, and reward volunteers. Chapter Seven offers the results of a large national survey of volunteer practitioners. This survey has implications for the type of organizational support that is necessary to meet the educational needs of volunteers, as well as the kinds of courses needed to educate volunteer managers. Chapter Eight reports on a study that determined the competencies that administrators of human service agencies need, and Chapter Nine describes a study of fundraising management effectiveness in a set of higher education institutions.

The theme of managing for social change in various types of nonprofit organizations is explored in Part Three. Chapter Ten provides a case study of a small social change foundation — the Haymarket Peoples' Fund — as an example of how a foundation can set up a participatory partnership among donors and recipients to redistribute wealth and power in the larger society. Chapter Eleven traces the change in focus among international development agencies since the 1970s from relief to small business development. Finally, the impact of and change in mutual assistance organizations designed to help socialize immigrants from Indochina to United States society is explored in Chapter Twelve.

Because they serve a public purpose, charitable organizations receive tax exemptions and donors to these organizations can receive a tax deduction for their contributions. Yet, as a result of these privileges, charitable organizations are affected by various public policies that have implications and costs for managers. Part Four explores public policy issues and their current or potential effect on nonprofit organizations and their management. One of the least understood and studied concepts in nonprofit organizations is the concept of equity accumulation, or excess revenues over expenses. In Chapter Thirteen, the authors report on the equity position of several nonprofits as gleaned from 990 tax returns and address a basic question: Who owns the equity of nonprofits under state and federal law? The authors examine why nonprofits accumulate equity or excess revenues over expenses over a period of time and analyze whether such accumulation prevents the use of that money to meet current needs. Chapter Fourteen discusses several challenges to nonprofit organizations that are emerging from antitrust law. It analyzes cases involving universities and student aid policy, nonprofit hospital mergers, and United Ways with exclusive fundraising campaigns. The author questions whether nonprofit organizations should be excluded from antitrust laws, because one of their important functions is to be collaborative and not competitive. The conclusion of this book addresses the relevance of current research to practitioners and calls for a continuing effort to build better bridges between scholars and practitioners. This is necessary in order to address gaps in the knowledge base and to produce research that can more effectively respond to the needs of practitioners.

Audience

Governing, Leading, and Managing Nonprofit Organizations is designed for practitioners, scholars, and management educators. It reveals the emerging themes in research and applied research studies, offers analytical tools to inform and improve practice, and discusses the issues and organizations that should be of interest and concern to those who study nonprofit management as well as those who lead organizations. It provides an overview of the kinds of questions that scholars are addressing in their research of nonprofit organizations, as well as thoughtful discussions about research issues that are not receiving adequate attention but should be included in the ongoing research agenda. The book provides some new tools from experienced practitioners to improve management practice, board-staff relationships, and organizational assessment and evaluation. Finally, the book offers thoughtful discussion about public policy issues and challenges that are confronting leaders of nonprofit organizations and illuminates the scope and complexity of nonprofit organizations and their management issues. It reveals that the field of nonprofit management research and the education of management professionals will be multidimensional. Both research and curricula must be sensitive not only to what is common among organizations but, even more important, to what is different.

September 1992   Dennis R. Young
                                    Cleveland, Ohio

                                    Robert M. Hollister
                                    Medford, Massachusetts

                                    Virginia A. Hodgkinson
                                    Alexandria, Virginia

The Authors

Krisna Abhay is leadership and management consultant to the Indochina Resource Action Center and an entrepreneur in the suburbs of Chicago. He works to inform and enhance the leadership of the Southeast Asian–American communities through nonprofit management skills development by demonstrating that skills learned through native cultures and traditions are applicable to effective community organizing and development in the United States. Abhay came to the United States from Laos in 1974 as a Fulbright scholar. When his hopes to return home to work on social economic development were sidetracked by the communist takeover, he focused attention on the Lao community in Illinois and, on the side, studied community service management at Roosevelt University. He served as executive director at the Chicago Lao-American Community Service Center and on the Illinois governor's Asian-American Advisory Committee, the Chicago mayor's Advisory Committee on Refugee and Immigrant Affairs, the citywide advisory committee to the Legal Assistance Foundation, and the Uptown Task Force on Housing Development.

Jeffrey L. Brudney is professor of public administration in the Department of Political Science at the University of Georgia. He received his Ph.D. degree (1978) from the University of Michigan in political science. His most recent book is *Fostering Volunteer Programs in the Public Sector* (1990). In addition to publishing numerous articles on volunteers and volunteer programs, particularly as related to government, he has served as guest editor of *Nonprofit and Voluntary Sector Quarterly* and *Public Productivity and Management Review* for special issues that dealt with volunteerism. Brudney serves as chairperson of the Section on Public Administration Education of the American Society of Public Administration and chairperson of the Section on Public Administration of the American Political Science Association.

Cyril F. Chang is professor of economics at Memphis State University and adjunct professor of health care economics at the Health Science Center of the University of Tennessee, Memphis. He holds a Ph.D. degree (1979) from the University of Virginia in economics and specializes in health care economics and nonprofit organizations. He has been a consultant to a number of medical schools and other health care institutions. Chang's recent publications have appeared in such journals as *The Milbank Quarterly, Health Services Research, Journal of Policy Analysis and Management, The National Tax Journal,* and *Southern Economic Journal.*

E. Gil Clary is associate professor of psychology at the College of St. Catherine. He received his Ph.D. degree (1980) from the University of Georgia in social psychology. His interests include dispositional and motivational factors related to volunteer activity, and his research is concerned with the social climate of organizations that utilize volunteers, the meanings people attach to the concept of helpfulness, and the methods used to promote ethically informed decision making.

Margaret A. Duronio is the director of administrative services in the office of the vice president of development at the University of Pittsburgh. She received her Ph.D. degree (1985) from the University of Pittsburgh in higher education. Duronio has conducted three national studies on fundraising effectiveness and has worked as a management development consultant and a marriage and family therapist.

Margaret Harris is assistant director of the Centre for Voluntary Organisation at the London School of Economics, where she is also lecturer in social administration. She received her M.A. degree (1983) from Brunel University, England, in public and social administration. Prior to joining the Centre for Voluntary Organisation in 1981, she worked in local government, public policy research, and a local voluntary advice agency.

Virginia A. Hodgkinson is currently vice president of research at INDEPENDENT SECTOR and executive director of the National Center of Charitable Statistics. Her most recent publications include the *Nonprofit Almanac: Dimensions of the Independent Sector 1992–1993; The Nonprofit Sector in the Global Community* (1992, with K. D. McCarthy, R. D. Sumariwalla, and Associates); *Faith and Philanthropy in America* (1990, with R. Wuthnow and Associates); *The Future of the Nonprofit Sector* (1989, with R. Lyman and Associates); and *Giving and Volunteering in the United States* (1990, with M. S. Weitzman).

Robert M. Hollister is director of the Lincoln Filene Center and chair of the Department of Urban and Environmental Policy at Tufts University. In 1992 he initiated the New England Institute for Nonprofit Organizations to strengthen small- and medium-sized nonprofits through training, policy research, and organizational assistance. A specialist in citizen participation in public affairs, Hollister coordinates the Boston Foundation's Carol R. Goldberg Seminar and the Talloires Seminar on International Environmental Issues. He is coauthor of *Development Politics* (1979, with Tunney Lee) and coeditor of *Cities of the Mind* (1984, with Lloyd Rodwin), *Neighborhood Policy and Planning* (1983, with Phillip L. Clay), and *Neighborhood Health Centers* (1976, with B. Kramer and S. Bellin).

Martha W. Hughes is a research analyst at the Center for Creative Leadership. She received her B.S. degree (1987) from Guilford College in psychology. Her work has focused on leadership development in educational and nonprofit organizations as well as gender differences in managerial development.

Robert W. Hunt is professor of political science at Illinois State University. He received his Ph.D. degree (1974) from Princeton

University in politics. He has conducted research on voluntary
organizations in over a dozen Asian, African, and Latin American nations under the auspices of several Fulbright grants and
consultancies with a variety of international development agencies. He was the recipient of a grant from the Association of
American Colleges (1987–1990) to develop a model course on
the role of voluntary agencies in international development.

Thomas H. Jeavons is director of the Center of Philanthropy
and Nonprofit Leadership at Grand Valley State University.
He is the former associate director of programs for the Association of American Colleges. He is also adjunct professor of organizational theory and management at Seton Hall University.
He received his Ph.D. degree (1992) from the Union Institute
in management and cultural studies. He also earned a Graduate Certificate in Business Management (1987) from Georgetown
University. Jeavons served ten years as the denominational executive for the Religious Society of Friends (Quakers) in the
Mid-Atlantic region, and before that he was a program manager for a number of nonprofit service organizations. His current research focuses on the history, place, and management
of religious service organizations as essential contributors to and
components of the nonprofit sector. Since 1991 he has been a
research fellow with the Yale University Program on Nonprofit
Organizations' project on religious institutions.

Bruce A. Loessin is vice president for development and alumni
affairs at Case Western Reserve University. He received his
M.A. degree (1967) from the University of Wisconsin in political science. Loessin has more than twenty years' experience in
higher education fundraising practice and research.

Cynthia D. McCauley is a research scientist at the Center for
Creative Leadership. She received her Ph.D. degree (1984) from
the University of Georgia in industrial and organizational psychology. Her research activities have focused on managerial
learning in the workplace and on leadership development in
educational and nonprofit organizations. McCauley's publications include chapters in *Measures of Leadership* (1990) and *Ap-*

plying Psychology in Business: The Handbook for Managers and Human Resource Professionals (1991).

Susan A. Ostrander is associate professor of sociology and American studies at Tufts University. She received her Ph.D. degree (1976) from Case Western Reserve University in sociology. Ostrander is the author of *Women of the Upper Class* (1984) and of a number of articles and chapters in books on philanthropy and nonprofit organizations in the welfare state. She is editor of *Shifting the Debate: Public/Private Sector Relations in the Modern Welfare State* (1987, with S. Langton and J. Van Til).

Judith R. Saidel is executive director of the Center for Women in Government and research assistant professor in the Department of Public Administration and Policy at the State University of New York, Albany, where she received her Ph.D. degree (1990) in public administration. Her primary research interest is the relationship between government and nonprofit organizations, with particular emphasis on resource dependence, boards of directors in third-party government, and managing across sectors. Saidel is coauthor of *The State and the Voluntary Sector, A Report of New York State Project 2000* (1988, with S. Dawes). She has also served as a board member for a number of nonprofit organizations.

Mark Snyder is professor of psychology at the University of Minnesota, where he has been a faculty member since receiving his Ph.D. degree (1972) from Stanford University in social psychology. His research interests include theoretical and empirical issues associated with the motivational foundations of individual and social behavior. He also studies the applications of basic theory and research in personality and social psychology to addressing practical problems confronting society. Snyder is author of *Public Appearances/Private Realities: The Psychology of Self-Monitoring* (1987).

Nike F. Speltz is program associate at the New Hampshire Charitable Foundation. Formerly Director of the Arts Management Program at Case Western Reserve University, she holds an M.P.A. degree (1985) from the John F. Kennedy School of

Government, Harvard University. Speltz has been a consultant to cultural institutions and other nonprofit organizations in the United States and abroad and has contributed to publications on management in the nonprofit and public sectors.

Richard Steinberg is associate professor in the Department of Economics and the Center on Philanthropy at Indiana University/Purdue University at Indianapolis. He received his Ph.D. degree (1984) from the University of Pennsylvania in economics. His research concerns the regulation of fundraising, tax treatment of personal donations, effects of competition on nonprofit performance, and the crowding out of donations by government social service expenditures. Steinberg is co-president elect of the Association for Research on Nonprofit Organizations and Voluntary Action and has served on the editorial boards of *Evaluation Review, Nonprofit and Voluntary Sector Quarterly,* and *Abstracts of Working Papers in Economics.*

Russy D. Sumariwalla is president and CEO of United Way International. He retired in 1991 as vice president and senior fellow at the United Way Strategic Institute. Before this, he headed the Research, Development, and Program Evaluation Division of United Way of America. He received his M.A. degrees from the University of Bombay (1958) in ancient Indian culture and the University of Massachusetts (1964) in international organizations, and he received his LL.M. degree (1960) from the University of Virginia School of Law. Among his publications related to the independent sector are *UWASIS II: A Taxonomy of Social Goals and Human Services Programs* (1976) and the second, revised edition of *Accounting and Financing Reporting: A Guide for United Ways and Not-for-Profit Human Services Organizations* (1989). He is the principal author of the *National Taxonomy of Exempt Entities* and coeditor of *The Nonprofit Sector in the Global Community* (1992, with K. D. McCarthy, V. A. Hodgkinson, and Associates).

Martha E. Taylor is director of market research and program evaluation with United Way of America, where she manages public opinion research, demographic analysis, and program evaluation. Prior to this she held positions in research and program evaluation in local United Way, state government, and university settings. Taylor holds master of social work and master of public administration degrees (1984) from Ohio State University.

Dov Te'eni is assistant professor of management information systems at Case Western Reserve University. He received his Ph.D. degree (1987) from Tel Aviv University in managerial studies. Te'eni's current research interests include the design of decision support systems, the development of information systems in nonprofits, and the theory and application of human–computer interaction. He has published in *IEEE Transactions on Systems, Man and Cybernetics, Decision Sciences, Omega, International Journal of Man-Machine Studies, Behavior and Information Technology,* and other journals.

Howard P. Tuckman is distinguished professor of economics at Memphis State University. He received his Ph.D. degree (1970) from the University of Wisconsin in economics. He has held national offices in economic associations and serves on the editorial boards of three higher education journals. Tuckman is a consultant for national and local corporations, nonprofit agencies, and international, federal, state, local, and government organizations. He serves on the board of directors of several nonprofit and for-profit businesses. The author of eight books and over one hundred referred journal articles, Tuckman is cited in the *Chronicle of Higher Education,* the *New York Times,* and the *Wall Street Journal.*

Dennis R. Young is chair of the Mandel Center for Nonprofit Organizations and Mandel Professor of Nonprofit Management at Case Western Reserve University. He received his Ph.D. degree (1969) from Stanford University in engineering economic systems. From 1973 to 1987, he was professor of management and policy in the Harriman School at the State University of New York, Stony Brook. He is author and editor of numerous papers and books on public services, nonprofit organizations, and management. His recent books include *Educating Managers of Nonprofit Organizations* (1988, with M. O'Neill), *Casebook of Management for Nonprofit Organizations* (1985), and *Careers for Dreamers and Doers* (1989, with L. Cohen). Young is editor-in-chief of *Nonprofit Management and Leadership,* a journal that advances the state of knowledge about management, leadership, and governance of private nonprofit organizations.

GOVERNING, LEADING, AND MANAGING NONPROFIT
ORGANIZATIONS

Introduction

Emerging Themes in Nonprofit Leadership and Management

Dennis R. Young

Five hundred years ago, Columbus "discovered" America. Although we celebrate this event as the opening of the New World to European immigration and development, the claim of discovery is not without controversy. For one thing, Columbus was not sure what he had discovered. For another, the place he had discovered was already known to other people, whom he mislabeled as "Indians." Finally, other Europeans from the North had visited the discovered lands some five hundred years earlier.

So it has been with the nonprofit sector. In the 1970s, American universities "discovered" the nonprofit sector, when the first research program on nonprofit organizations was established at Yale University in 1977. Meanwhile, the sector was discovering itself, through the Filer Commission studies (Commission on Private Philanthropy . . . , 1975) and the formation of the national association INDEPENDENT SECTOR. Like Columbus, the discoverers of the nonprofit sector were not quite sure what they had found. Indeed, the ongoing debate about what this new "continent" in the political economy should be called — nonprofit sector? voluntary sector? independent sector?

1

third sector? — reveals this uncertainty, as well as the complexity of the discovered entity itself. Moreover, as in Columbus's case, with many different "Indian" tribes, although the entity was already known to others in part, few knew the whole. Social workers, those involved in charity and religion, health care professionals, foundation people, educators, participants in high arts and culture, advocacy and interest groups all knew that they were engaged in something that was not commercial business and was not government. But none thought about being part of a whole, larger than their own industry or field of service. This, in fact, was the key discovery of the 1970s: there was a whole sector of organizations with common characteristics, different from the other sectors (business and government), about which precious little was understood.

Other important discoveries followed. In the 1980s, the problems of management, leadership, and governance were identified as critical issues for nonprofit organizations, as the flush 1960s and 1970s, an era of growth and massive government funding, gave way to times of scarcity and competition for resources. Academics and practitioners began writing about nonprofit management and leadership issues with increasing regularity. An early, important contribution was David Mason's book *Voluntary Nonprofit Enterprise Management* (1984), which may have been the first to conceptualize generically the unique character of nonprofit management. Mason's book was an early straw in the wind, but as the decade progressed the wind grew into a virtual gale. In 1987, the Yale Program on Nonprofit Organizations published *The Nonprofit Sector: A Research Handbook* (Powell, 1987), which included several management- and leadership-related pieces. In 1988, O'Neill and Young published their edited book, *Educating Managers of Nonprofit Organizations*. The book captured the thinking of key scholars and practitioners at a watershed conference in San Francisco in 1986 addressed to the development of new programs for preparing students to work as managers in the nonprofit sector. By the end of the decade, the field of nonprofit management and leadership was furnished with many of the accoutrements of legitimacy and recognition. Dozens of universities had mounted new graduate programs in this field;

new degrees, such as the Master of Nonprofit Organizations, the Master of Nonprofit Management, and the Master of Nonprofit Administration, had been created; and dozens of books were being issued by the Foundation Center, Jossey-Bass, and other publishers. INDEPENDENT SECTOR devoted its 1990 Spring Research Forum to the theme of Nonprofit Leadership and Management, a new scholarly journal *Nonprofit Management and Leadership* began publication, and no less an eminent management scholar than Peter F. Drucker took up the cause through speaking engagements, sponsorship of a new foundation on nonprofit management innovation, published papers (1989, 1990), and a book entitled *Managing the Nonprofit Organization* (1990b).

The 1980s was a decade of discovering and conceptualizing the field of nonprofit management and leadership, but it was also a period of learning that there were many unanswered questions about this field and that precious little solid research was available to respond to these questions and to help guide practice. The 1990s promises to be a decade in which serious research in this field is undertaken in a more comprehensive and organized way than ever before. The beginnings of this movement are readily apparent. A number of university centers organized in the 1980s around the theme of nonprofit management education are now developing strong research capacities and sponsoring periodic research conferences on leadership and management issues. *Nonprofit Management and Leadership* now encourages, screens, and publishes important findings. A growing cadre of scholars from many different disciplines are now engaged in research endeavors focused on nonprofit management, leadership, and governance issues; and foundations are beginning to recognize the importance of this field with more frequent and substantial grants.

It is in this context that the present book emerges. The chapters here had their genesis in the INDEPENDENT SECTOR–United Way Strategic Institute Spring Research Forum, which was held in Cleveland in March of 1990 with the cosponsorship of the Mandel Center for Nonprofit Organizations of Case Western Reserve University. This was the first such forum devoted specifically to the theme of "leadership and management" and it signaled not only the importance that this subject had achieved but also the fact that serious research was under way. The chapters are characteristic of work in almost any research field that is in early development; they are exploratory and suggestive, and the findings are partial and preliminary, but nonetheless they are pathbreaking. It appears that, as a field, we are first beginning to understand the many nuances and distinctive features of nonprofit management and leadership, and we are only now starting to ask some of the right questions.

Key Management and Leadership Concerns

Although they are by no means comprehensive, the chapters here touch on many of the key, sometimes unique, functions and responsibilities that face nonprofit managers and leaders today. The general areas of concern are what one would expect — human resource management, finance, information management, and so on — but the emphasis is on particular dimensions that have not been well studied, or even properly identified, to date. A brief tour of these issues will set the stage for considering what kinds of insights and overall themes are beginning to emerge from the work of the contributing authors and in the field at large.

Clearly, issues of organizational governance are prominent in the minds of those concerned with the proper functioning of nonprofit organizations. The classic problem of sorting out the appropriate roles of board and staff captures the attention of both Margaret Harris and Judith R. Saidel. Margaret Harris recognizes that nonprofit organizations are complex and varied in their agendas and stages of development and may require different combinations of board-staff divisions of responsibility to suit their individual needs. She thus contributes a methodology that can be used to develop arrangements appropriate to particular circumstances. Judith R. Saidel also takes a different cut than earlier scholars of nonprofit governance. Recognizing the major role of government in financing many nonprofit organizations, she asks and helps answer the question: What is the role of the board in helping a nonprofit organization deal with its government funders? Finally, Krisna Abhay explores the issue of governance as it relates to the stage of an organization's development, showing how participation in the governance of mutual assistance organizations must broaden if they are to continue to effectively serve immigrant communities in the United States.

A second major concern here is that of *management of human resources*. A number of the authors, including E. Gil Clary and Mark Snyder, Jeffrey L. Brudney, Cynthia D. McCauley and Martha W. Hughes, Thomas H. Jeavons, Susan A. Ostrander, Robert W. Hunt, and Krisna Abhay are, in one way or another, concerned with issues of recruitment, retention, participation, motivation, guidance, or training of volunteers, paid staff, and board members. People are the key to successful operation of nonprofit organizations, and these authors explore many different dimensions of this issue and what we know and need to know about them.

The *management of financial resources* is a third area of major interest. Recognizing the pressing need for nonprofits to become more self-sufficient through their own sources of contributed and earned income, Margaret A. Duronio and Bruce A. Loessin explore the factors that contribute to effective fundraising in higher education, while Howard P. Tuckman and Cyril F. Chang investigate how nonprofit managers use accumulated financial surpluses to buffer the harsh realities of the nonprofit financial environment. Susan A. Ostrander discusses how a foundation can extend its donor base by involving donors in the work of grantees and by seeking out small as well as large donors.

A fourth significant area is the *management of information,* an aspect that seems especially underdeveloped in nonprofit organizations. Dov Te'eni and Nike F. Speltz, for example, uncover the underuse of information systems and computers in arts and cultural organizations, while Martha E. Taylor and Russy D. Sumariwalla discover the dearth of evaluation activity focused on performance outcome and participant satisfaction by affiliates and grantees of foundations, united funding organizations, and national nonprofit umbrella associations.

Managing for social change is a fifth concern. Recognizing, as Peter Drucker has become fond of saying, that nonprofits are in the business of making a difference in the lives of people, Susan A. Ostrander explores one aspect of the relationship between philanthropy and social change. In particular, she investigates how a foundation's policies and practices can be designed to support diversity and democratic decision making within the foundation and in the community at large. Robert W. Hunt discusses how voluntary organizations can effectively promote economic development in Third-World countries by involving the poor in their programs and facilitating linkages among business, government, and other elements of a "civil society." Krisna Abhay investigates the assistance mutual aid associations are giving to immigrant groups to help them adapt to American society and how these organizations must themselves change if they are to remain effective.

A sixth important interest is that of *strategic management.* Although none of the chapters here explicitly focus on strategic planning, several are concerned with the way nonprofit organizations position themselves within their economic and social environments and the methods, tools, and strategies they use to achieve their goals. Although aimed primarily at the policy level, Richard Steinberg's analysis of antitrust issues explores the factors that influence management choices of collaborative versus competitive strategies for pursuing organizational missions. Similarly, Howard P. Tuckman and Cyril F. Chang investigate how managers use accumulated equity strategically to stabilize their financial positions and achieve long-run organizational objectives. Finally, Dov Te'eni and Nike F. Speltz note with dismay how cultural nonprofits fail to exploit information technology to shape and implement their strategic decisions.

Emerging Themes

Although the chapters here are diverse in their concerns, modest in their aspirations, preliminary in their conclusions, and sparse in number compared to the size and complexity of the field as a whole, a careful reading reveals a surprising number of clear common themes worthy of continued analysis, investigation, appreciation, and general application.

Perhaps the most salient, if disturbing, theme emerging chapter after chapter is that, despite the great attention the issues of management and leadership received in the 1980s, *nonprofit organizations do not yet seem to have taken the implementation of sophisticated management and governance practices completely to heart.* For example, Saidel reports that fully a third of the boards she investigated have been "bystanders" in the process of nonprofit-government relations. And Abhay describes high tensions between traditional boards of mutual assistance associations and professional staffs who struggle to manage government funding of their programs. Te'eni and Speltz report only rudimentary use of information system technology and almost no application of information systems for strategic purposes in nonprofit arts and cultural organizations. Sumariwalla and Taylor are disappointed that evaluation techniques are rarely used by nonprofit foundations and national associations to measure the results of their programs. Brudney says that nonprofits tend not to place a high value on volunteer administration. McCauley and Hughes demonstrate that human service administrators in nonprofit organizations are under intense time pressure and plagued by uncertain or limited resources, suggesting that they can use substantially more help and support. Duronio and Loessin report that universities undervalue the need for good management in the fundraising area.

The picture is perhaps not so terribly bleak as it seems, however. The fact is that the fragments of research and inquiry reported here are part of an expanding fabric now being pieced together from many quarters to understand the issues involved in nonprofit management and leadership and to apply more sophisticated approaches in practice. The better part of wisdom here is to appreciate that more effective management and governance will not come by hitting nonprofits over the head and insisting that they adopt business methods. In fact, as the contributors here reveal, the picture is much more complex than that. Specifically, nonprofits must, by and large, develop their own management practices and must adapt these practices to widely diverse contexts within the sector itself. The apparent lack of progress, therefore, is as likely to represent caution as it is reluctance.

A second major theme that emerges here is captured by the word *variation*. In several different ways, the studies reported in this book underline how the management of nonprofit organizations must be sensitive to the differences between nonprofits and other kinds of organizations, and to the great diversity that exists within the nonprofit sector itself. Several of the contributions here highlight these differences. For example, in his discussion of shaping policies and practices with respect to interorganizational collaboration and competition, Steinberg alludes to the special governance structures of nonprofits, noting that the ordinary assumption that "monopoly is bad" does not apply as cogently to nonprofits as to profitmaking businesses. Indeed, "competition is bad" is often the rule for nonprofits. In the same vein, Tuckman and Chang note that, unlike for-profits, the generation of surpluses by nonprofits can be viewed as potentially helpful but not unequivocally good.

Other contributions here also point to these essential differences. Issues such as board-staff roles, volunteer management, fundraising, and management for social change simply do not arise much in the for-profit sector, and they are substantially different when they arise within the governmental context. In the case of human resource administrators, McCauley and Hughes find important differences in the overall challenges faced by government versus nonprofit officials. Thus, the authors here point to an overall conclusion that the field of nonprofit management and leadership as a whole, as much as it may borrow from business management and public administration, and as much as it may share with other sectors in terms of general areas of concern such as strategy, human resource management, information management, and financial management, also exhibits major differences that must be separately respected, studied, and addressed in practice.

The observation that there is variation within the nonprofit sector is equally cogent. Chapter after chapter indicate the importance of differences among nonprofit organizations and the concomitant difficulty of offering uniform prescriptions for appropriate management practice, governance structure, or public policy treatment. Harris, for example, offers her methodology of Total Activities Analysis precisely because board-staff models must be customized to fit the particular size and stage in organizational development, field of activity, and purpose of the organization at hand. Saidel's study suggests that the role of the board may be different, for instance, for an organization that is highly dependent on government funding than for an organization that is not so dependent. Jeavons suggests that religious organizations differ at least in degree from other nonprofits in that their practices must be driven more forcefully by religious values. This leads to some interesting comparisons with analyses that focus on other parts of the sector. For example, Jeavons argues that religious nonprofits should recruit only staff and volunteers who share the organization's values and should avoid an appeal to the selfish interests of donors. On the contrary, Clary and Snyder explain that effective volunteer management requires tailoring appeals to the individual motives of volunteers.

Te'eni and Speltz point to important management differences between cultural and other types of nonprofits, and, within the cultural category, between performing arts organizations and museums. Dual artistic and administrative management systems pervade these organizations, and performing and fine arts organizations focus on entirely different kinds of units (visitors and performances versus members and exhibits) in tracking their activities. Sumariwalla and Taylor find wide variation in the use of evaluation among foundations and national associations, attributable in part to differences in staff capacities and organizational purposes. McCauley and Hughes observe that the challenges facing human resource administrators in nonprofit organizations vary substantially by organizational characteristics such as age, size, and sources of funding. Thus, while there appears to be enough that is intrinsically different among nonprofits to warrant a distinct field of management study and practice, sufficient internal variation in the sector warns against simple, uniform prescriptions and models of nonprofit management intended to apply across the board. General principles may apply, but nuances of application remain important.

A third area of variation is found in the motivations, capacities, attitudes, and values of participants and contributors
to nonprofit organizations. Jeavons and Clary and Snyder recognize the differences in volunteer motivations and the importance
of recognizing these differences in the formulation of management practices and strategies. Te'eni and Speltz observe the
differences in attitudes and orientations of artistic versus administrative personnel and how these need to be accommodated
by management systems and structures. Ostrander sees the
differences in viewpoints among trustees, donors, and grantees
of nonprofit foundations and the importance of creating mechanisms for constructive interaction within and among these
groups. And Abhay acutely observes the differences in perceptions, skills, and orientations of community elders who control
old-style mutual assistance associations and the new generation
of professional and lay leaders whose support is needed if these
organizations are to continue to develop and serve their functions in the community. In all these cases, it is clear that successful nonprofit management requires ways to reconcile and
accommodate differing interests and orientations and bring them
together for coherent action toward common goals.

If variation is a common dimension with which nonprofit
management must cope, then it is not surprising that strategies
of *inclusiveness* are frequently on the minds of our authors here.
Sumariwalla and Taylor, for example, conclude that involvement of clients and other constituents is needed to determine
the best forms and uses of evaluation. Clary and Snyder argue
for multiple recruitment strategies that will appeal to a wide
range of potential volunteers. Ostrander sees the involvement
of grantees, small donors, and diverse community members as
necessary to the success of community change-oriented foundations. Hunt argues for involvement of the poor, community
and small business leaders, government officials, and others in
the successful operation of voluntary sector development organizations in less developed countries. Abhay sees the need for
broad participation and democratic governance by community
members in mutual aid organizations for immigrant groups,
and Steinberg emphasizes the merit of mutual-type nonprofits,

governed democratically by their memberships, as a protection against potential abuses of monopoly provision by nonprofits. Jeavons, on the other hand, argues that a screening of participants for religious nonprofits is necessary to avoid dissipation of the particular value base of these organizations. In all cases, however, the authors are saying that nonprofit managers and leaders must recognize and respond to the diversity of their constituents, in most cases devising policies that ensure that all important groups are involved.

The role of *values* in guiding management and governance practice and policy is another common theme that emerges from the work reported here. Frances Hesselbein, former National Executive Director of Girl Scouts of the U.S.A., is fond of saying that nonprofits must be value based and market driven. What she means is that while nonprofits must respond to their constituencies and sources of support, they must be anchored in a clear mission and set of values that constituents can understand and leaders and managers can use to guide their actions. This theme comes out most strongly in Jeavons's analysis of religious organizations, in which basic values are seen to necessarily drive all manner of human resource, financial, and planning practices in order to promote their "value-expressive" function. The theme emerges again in Clary's and Snyder's finding that the most important factor in retaining volunteers is appeal to the values these individuals are able to express through participation in the organization. Further, Duronio and Loessin find nonprofits to be skittish in applying a purely businesslike, profit-maximizing approach to fundraising, for fear of undermining the values promoted by the institution as a whole. Ostrander observes that the medium is the message in the case of foundations addressed to community change, and that both fundraising and grantmaking are best approached by viewing them explicitly as exercises in social change. Values also underlie Tuckman's and Chang's justification of equity accumulation in nonprofits, which rests on the motivations of nonprofit managers to utilize these resources for maximum social benefit. So too, Steinberg's arguments in favor of sympathetic policy treatment of such potentially objectionable nonprofit organization practices as price discrimination, cross-subsidization among programs and clientele, and restrictive united fundraising arrangements rest on the social values these practices are intended to promote, such as positive redistribution of income and more efficient solicitation of donated resources. These and other nonprofit management practices must be anchored in a clear and beneficent value base if they are to be understood and justified.

A final, and perhaps most important, theme that pervades the contributions in this book is the *need for research,* the fact that, despite the increased attention nonprofit management and leadership have received over the last decade, serious research commensurate with the need for new knowledge has barely begun. In all the work reported here, and in the extant nonprofit management literature at this point, rigorous research has been applied only to snippets and fragments of the entire subject. In the applications reported here, for example, we need to find out how general the findings are and how they apply to different segments of the nonprofit sector. We need to know, in more systematic and comprehensive fashion, what environmental and organizational variables and characteristics influence the choice of different management and governance models and public policy treatments. We need to know more precisely what happens when nonprofits fail to adapt appropriate management approaches, how pervasive the management failings of different categories of nonprofits have actually been, and what levels of investment are justified to upgrade existing management systems.

In the 1990s, the field of nonprofit management and governance is entering a new era. The subject is now recognized as a distinct, if interdisciplinary, field of study and its importance is acknowledged in practice. Institutions are now in place to study, teach, and publish about it and to educate next-generation managers and leaders. Gurus have given of their wisdom to define the field and offer sage advice to practitioners. Consultants and trainers roam the land with workshops and technical assistance packages honed through their own experiences. The complexity and nuances of the issues are gaining appreciation. But the knowledge base is thin, and what is needed is continued solid research to expand this resource and translate its findings into best practice. The interest, commitment, and capacity to carry out the required research is now in place. The next decade will witness a flowering of that activity, with concomitant benefits for the practicing community of nonprofit managers and leaders.

References

Commission on Private Philanthropy and Public Needs. *Giving in America.* Washington, D.C.: Commission on Private Philanthropy and Public Needs, 1975.

Drucker, P. F. "What Business Can Learn from Nonprofits." *Harvard Business Review,* Sept.-Oct. 1989, pp. 88–93.

Drucker, P. F. "Lessons for Successful Nonprofit Governance." *Nonprofit Management and Leadership,* Fall 1990a, pp. 7–14.

Drucker, P. F. *Managing the Nonprofit Organization.* New York: HarperCollins, 1990b.

Mason, D. E. *Voluntary Nonprofit Enterprise Management.* New York: Plenum, 1984.

O'Neill, M., and Young, D. R. *Educating Managers of Nonprofit Organizations.* New York: Praeger, 1988.

Powell, W. W. (ed.). *The Nonprofit Sector: A Research Handbook.* New Haven, Conn.: Yale University Press, 1987.

Part One

Governance and
Organizational Systems

The effectiveness of nonprofit organizations is determined to a great extent by how the organizations are organized and governed. The entire nonprofit sector has benefited greatly from the movement to couple good works and noble intentions with managerial competence. A primary dimension of change has been for nonprofit organizations to adopt and adapt the administrative methods and technologies used widely in private firms and public agencies. Just within the past decade, the role of boards of directors has received a great burst of attention. Ten years ago boards were almost entirely ignored, whereas today they are an increasing focus for administrators, providers of management assistance, and funders. In the growing movement to strengthen and to professionalize the leadership and management of nonprofits, progress is being made in relation to the different needs of the broad range of types of organizations.

In Chapter One, Margaret Harris reports on several years of experience applying the Total Activities Analysis (TAA), a practical analytical tool for clarifying the functions of boards. Key characteristics of TAA are that it is nonprescriptive, facilitates collaborative problem solving, and recognizes the dynamic nature of board-staff relations.

Chapter Two by Judith R. Saidel discusses the role of boards of directors in mediating the relationship between nonprofit organizations and government agencies. This topic is especially timely due to the increasing interdependence of the two sectors as governments increasingly contract for services from nonprofits. Based on a survey of eighty nonprofit executive directors, Saidel offers a typology of board roles: facilitator, maintainer, buffer (protecting nonprofits "from the danger of vendorism or the surrendering of autonomy to the requirements of government contracts"), and bystander.

Thomas H. Jeavons in Chapter Three builds a powerful argument that the management of religious organizations is, or should be, different from the management of other nonprofit organizations. Starting with the premise: "What distinguishes religious organizations is their values-expressive character, their concern to 'give witness' to certain truths or tenets of faith," Jeavons discusses how this basic difference influences how religious organizations perform three types of management functions: finances and fundraising, human resources, and planning.

Chapter Four, by Dov Te'eni and Nike F. Speltz, analyzes the use and management of information systems in ten Cleveland nonprofit cultural organizations. They ask, "How is information created and consumed, for what purposes is it collected, in what functional areas is it employed, and how useful has the information been to the overall management of the organization?" The authors demonstrate that the groups' use of information systems is limited to operational purposes, none use them as a strategic planning tool, and none allocate much funding or staff time to their development.

In Chapter Five, Martha E. Taylor and Russy D. Sumariwalla report on a major survey of national nonprofits' practices with respect to program evaluation. They document that the most common types of evaluation are measurements of the volume of program delivery and compliance; least common are assessment of participant satisfaction and of program outcomes. Nonprofit executives cited two main obstacles to evaluating program outcomes: lack of financial support and lack of qualified staff.

1.

Clarifying
the Board Role:
A Total Activities Approach

Margaret Harris

What is the job of a voluntary board? Nonprofit sector journals in the United Kingdom frequently carry articles on the difficulties of clarifying the board role. Empirical studies confirm that both staff and board members find the implementation of the board role an intractable problem (Gerard, 1983; Mellor, 1985; Platt and others, 1985). Setting boundaries between boards and staff with respect to work and responsibilities is especially difficult (Handy, 1981; Harris, 1989a; Leat, Smolka, and Unell, 1981).

The experience of practitioners and researchers in the United Kingdom reflects the North American literature. Hartogs and Weber (1974, p. xxv) studied presidents, executives, and board members and found "a large number of key problems." Discrepancies have been widely noted between official statements about board functions and what happens in practice (Fink, 1989; Middleton, 1987). Other common findings have been that staff tend to dominate boards (Gouldner, 1969; Kramer, 1981; Senor, 1963) and that boards abdicate responsibility to staff (Connors, 1980; Gouldner, 1969). Generally, research has found "uncertainty and confusion" about what board members are "*really* expected to do" (Herman, 1989, p. 4).

What help, then, is available for those struggling to implement the board role? Numerous handbooks, pamphlets, and articles prescribing board functions and behavior have been produced in both the United Kingdom and the United States. Yet it seems that, despite all the advice, nonprofit practitioners — paid staff, volunteers, and board members themselves — still experience major difficulties in clarifying what should be expected of boards.

In this chapter, I will describe a new response to the problem of defining the job of voluntary boards: Total Activities Analysis. TAA builds on research experience — my own and that of others in the United Kingdom and the United States — to provide a practical organizational tool. It has been continuously tested and modified in research workshops run by the Centre for Voluntary Organisation of the London School of Economics over an eight-year period. Board members and staff of more than 100 nonprofit agencies — of varying sizes and operating in the fields of social welfare, health, arts, and the environment — have applied TAA to their own work situations. Comments and suggestions from workshop participants have enabled us to further refine the technique. So the ideas presented here have been subjected to the rigorous test of "usefulness to practitioners." TAA reflects "usable theory"; that is, it comprises "ideas that can actually be utilized in organizational design and change" (Billis, 1984, p. 1). TAA differs in two main respects from the usual handbook approach to clarifying the board role. It is not prescriptive. Also, it does not view the role of the board in isolation; it considers it in relation to other roles within the agency.

Boards and Staff: Interdependent Roles

Recent studies of the work of boards in the United Kingdom and the United States indicate that, in practice, the role of a voluntary board in an agency tends to be interlinked and interdependent with the roles of members of staff (Harris, 1989a; Hartogs, 1989; Heimovics and Herman, 1990; Kramer, 1985). Platt and his colleagues (1985, p. 30) found that the extent to which boards were able to play "a real role in decision-making"

depended on what staff were "prepared to allow." Similarly, a
study of local boards in a national advice agency in the United
Kingdom found "a self-fulfilling and self-reinforcing" pattern of
relationships between boards and staff (Harris, 1987, p. 12).
Staff withheld information from boards, who were then unable
to participate fully in decisions or exercise control over staff.
An example of role interdependence of another kind was found
by Herman and Tulipana in their study of seven U.S. nonprofit
agencies (1985). They identified "dominant coalitions" compris-
ing both board *and* staff members (p. 57).

Evidence of interdependence does not necessarily imply
equality or stability in the relationship between boards and staff.
Recent commentators have questioned prescriptions of the board-
staff relationship as a "team" or "partnership" (Herman, 1989,
p. 2). Kramer (1985, p. 29) argues that since there tends to be
"unequal distribution of power" between staff and board, the
"shared partnership" view of the relationship should be replaced
by "a contingency model," which involves "collaboration, difference and discensus." Other writers have also emphasized the
organizational tension and dynamism inherent in the relationship (Conrad and Glenn, 1983). On the basis of a literature
review, Middleton (1987) says that the relationship is "a dynamic
interaction; to state that it is a partnership implies a resolution
of the tension rather than a complex shifting of power" (p. 150).

In light of these findings, the starting question about the
job of the board becomes more complex. It would be mislead-
ing to conduct an analysis of the board role in isolation from
a consideration of other roles. The challenge for those who wish
to help the nonprofit sector, then, is to clarify the role of boards
in relation to other organizational roles, especially those of paid
staff. TAA, described in the following sections, attempts to meet
this challenge.

Identifying the Functions of Nonprofit Agencies

In searching for a response to the problem of clarifying the board
role, our aim was to provide a practical analytical tool that could
be applied to organizational problems in the nonprofit sector.

At the same time, we wanted to take into account research findings and theories about the relationship in practice between boards and staff.

A starting point was provided by earlier research on the work and organization of governmental social welfare departments in England and Wales (social services departments) carried out by a university-based team, Social Services Organization Research Unit (SSORU, 1974; Billis, Bromley, Hey, and Rowbottom, 1980). Their studies suggested that many questions about work were related to fundamental issues about departmental "functions" — assumptions about "the general and continuing aims, goals, or objects, which are to be served" (SSORU, 1974, p. 36). It was possible to "tease out" such functions by asking about a social services department: "What is it in business for?" (SSORU, 1974, p. 35). This could then be used as a basis for tackling organizational problems raised by practitioners.

Working with staff and board members of nonprofit agencies, we developed an approach to clarifying the board role derived from the social services departments experience. Instead of focusing directly on the job of the board, or even on the board-staff relationship, we started from a different perspective. We asked participants to look at their nonprofit agency as a whole and to "brainstorm" around the question: "What activities have to be done by this agency as it tries to achieve its goals?" From this, we developed a list of agency functions or activities as perceived by project participants.

Usually participants distinguished one or more key operational functions. These were closely linked to the prime purpose of the agency; for example, delivering a particular service, raising funds, pressing for changes in the law, monitoring consumer satisfaction, or maintaining contacts with others working in the same field. Then a number of activities, such as clerical, accounting, and personnel work, would support the main operational functions.

In research workshops attended by practitioners in more than 100 nonprofit agencies with at least one paid staff member, this exercise was repeated many times. Gradually we were able to develop a list of ten broad nonprofit agency functions, a distillation of the accumulated experience of workshop participants.

1. Providing services (direct provision and/or advocacy work)
2. Designing and developing services and structures (including setting policies and priorities, planning, and monitoring)
3. Developing and maintaining an understanding of need and demand (for example, in housing, health, human services, or the arts)
4. Maintaining good public relations (including publicity and keeping links with key people, groups, and agencies in the field)
5. Fundraising (from a range of sources and using a variety of arrangements, including donations, grants, and contracts)
6. Finance work (including collection and disbursement of cash, accounting, budgeting, and budgetary control)
7. Staffing and training (including recruitment, induction, and staff welfare work)
8. Managerial and coordinative work (including selection and induction of staff, prescription and coordination of work, and appraisal)
9. Logistical work (including providing premises and equipment, materials, and other supporting services)
10. Clerical and secretarial work (including recording and communication of decisions, actions, and events)

Before moving on to describe the next stage of our approach to clarifying the board role, some comments are needed about this list and the analysis of nonprofit agency functions presented here. First, the list is not the product of a single research study. It has been constructed and developed over an eight-year period from a process of repeated testing and modification. Second, it is derived not from "official" statements but from practitioners' perceptions of the activities that actually take place in their agencies. Finally, unlike the lists provided in handbooks and some academic articles, it is not prescriptive. It aims to provide an initial framework for describing and understanding existing situations and for tackling organizational problems.

Analysis of Board Functions in Practice

The analysis of functions exercise described in the previous section has now been widely tested with a range of nonprofit agencies. It can be used as it is, or individual nonprofits can develop their own list of functions using our list as a "prompt." Either way, the list of functions stands as a tool for organizational analysis in its own right (Stage 1 in Figure 1.1). However, it can also be a stepping stone to the next stage in a process of clarifying the role of an agency's board, as I shall illustrate in this section of the chapter.

Figure 1.1. The Stages of Total Activities Analysis.

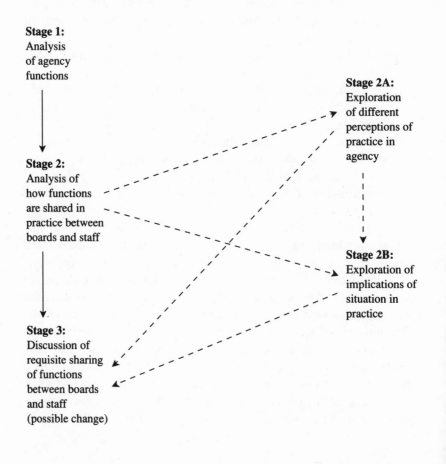

Stage 1:
Analysis
of agency
functions

Stage 2A:
Exploration
of different
perceptions of
practice in
agency

Stage 2:
Analysis of
how functions
are shared in
practice between
boards and staff

Stage 2B:
Exploration of
implications of
situation in
practice

Stage 3:
Discussion of
requisite sharing
of functions
between boards
and staff
(possible change)

In projects and workshops with senior staff and members of voluntary boards, we take a list of nonprofit agency functions, either our constructed list as described above or a version developed by practitioners for their own agencies. We then invite individual participants to ask themselves a series of questions about the situation in practice in their agencies (Stage 2 in Figure 1.1). In keeping with the research findings on board-staff interdependence discussed earlier, the questions do not focus exclusively on what board members do, but they assume that in practice functions are often shared in some way between board members and staff. For each function, participants ask themselves:

- Is this function being carried out currently in the agency?
- If so, is it being done by staff, by board members, or by a combination of the two?
- If the function is being shared between board and staff members, what is the relative weight or strength of the contribution of each one?

   Further questions are asked.

- What are the criteria by which the apportionment of activities has been made between staff and board?
- Over all, is one party generally more heavily engaged in the agency's work than the other?

Once participants in the TAA have considered these questions individually, the results can be compared.

   In some agencies, the most important outcome of TAA is the realization that individual board and staff members hold very different perceptions of who is doing what. Discussions often also reveal a variety of ideas about who *should be* doing what. Differences arise especially with regard to perceptions of strength of involvement in a particular function by board or staff. For example, some participants may think that an agency's board is heavily involved in fundraising, whereas others within the same agency may see the same board as having a weak or min-

imal involvement in that activity. Often the very discovery of
these discrepancies explains problems in the board-staff relationship and the difficulties of clarifying the board role. Participants can go on to look at the reasons for their differing expectations (Stage 2A in Figure 1.1).

In one agency, TAA revealed that staff and board members
agreed that the board had a weak involvement in management
activities. However, discussion of the TAA results also indicated
that staff were resentful that the board was "failing" to manage
them, whereas board members did not see this as part of their
role. TAA provided a framework within which these different
understandings of responsibilities could be discussed openly.

In another agency, the staff regarded service provision
as their distinctive prerogative, and they saw no role for the
board in this activity. Board members, on the other hand, put
less emphasis on the professionalism of staff and expected to be
actively involved themselves in work with clients. They regarded
staff as "there to do what we tell them."

In addition to describing perceptions of the way in which
specific activities are shared in an agency, TAA provides an overview of the *balance* of activities between boards and staff. So,
if they wish, participants can develop a series of further questions about the practical implications for the agency, after looking
at the sum of individuals' TAAs (Stage 2B in Figure 1.1). For
example, a membership-based agency providing information
and day care for children with learning difficulties wondered
about the long-term implications of the fact that staff seemed
to be far more heavily involved in public relations work than
board members. Whose views about the needs of the children
were being given to the public? What was the image the agency
was presenting to potential beneficiaries?

Another agency was interested to discover that staff and
board members were *both* widely perceived to be playing a strong
role in personnel and managerial work. They decided to explore
further the reasons why this situation had arisen. What was the
impact, for example, of the agency's history and traditions? They
also went on to question whether the situation was an appropriate
or effective deployment of resources within the agency.

A nonprofit agency whose original presenting problem was uncertainty about the job of the board decided after conducting Total Activities Analysis that the more important issues related to the agency as a whole, rather than to the allocation of tasks between individuals and groups. TAA can thus also reveal that a function that all participants previously agreed was vital for the agency has in practice slipped through a gap between the roles of the staff and the board. In an agency delivering a welfare service to physically disabled people, for example, whereas staff and board members together had service provision and supporting administration in hand, another function essential for long-term agency survival — monitoring and development — was always left out. It emerged from the TAA that, in practice, neither staff nor board members felt responsible for that function.

Thus TAA can reveal a wide range of perceptions about existing situations in nonprofit agencies (Stage 2A in Figure 1.1). It can also provide a basis for exploration of the implications of the current distribution of agency activities (Stage 2B in Figure 1.1). For many nonprofit agencies, this is a sufficient response to issues surrounding the role of the board. The intraagency analysis and collaboration entailed in conducting a TAA provide new insights into the nature of the board role in theory and practice and a basis for a working relationship between board and staff in the future.

Other agencies wish to move to a further stage of analysis and explore explicitly the possibilities for change (Stage 3 in Figure 1.1). In that case, a start can be made on tackling questions about what is "requisite," about how activities might be shared between staff and boards "if things were differently and better arranged" (Rowbottom, 1977, p. 43). In exploring the possibilities, agencies consider a range of factors: not only official statements found in constitutions and public relations materials but also expectations that they will be efficient and effective; demands for internal and external accountability; preferences and skills of members of staff and boards; the history and culture of the agency; and the nature of the work to be done.

　　　　Having looked at the three stages of Total Activities Analysis, I turn to a broader discussion of our experiences in developing and using TAA with nonprofit agencies.

A Practical Tool

Our research experience suggests that both paid staff and board members find TAA a useful analytic tool for tackling organizational problems surrounding the role of boards in nonprofit agencies. It provides a framework for analysis of existing organizational arrangements, as well as opportunities to explore organizational change. The usefulness of TAA reflects a number of features.

　　　　First, it avoids prescription. As discussed at the beginning of this chapter, research indicates that gaps exist in nonprofit agencies between official statements about the role of boards and organizational reality. Many staff and board members are aware of these gaps and, indeed, feel defensive about their failure to conform to set standards. In such circumstances, training or handbooks that provide further prescriptive statements are unwelcome — an approach that focuses initially on the situation *in practice* is less threatening. Not only does TAA carry no judgmental implications but it also places positive value on practitioners' own perceptions.

　　　　Second, it acknowledges that individuals and groups within nonprofit agencies vary in their perceptions of organizational reality and requisite structures (Heimovics and Herman, 1990; Middleton, 1987; Widmer, 1991). And it does not suggest that any one perception is more correct than another. In fact, uncovering varying perceptions about the way in which activities are shared between boards and staff is an integral part of TAA. Thus it opens the way for a collaborative approach to tackling organizational problems (Rowbottom, 1977), an approach in keeping with the operating style of many nonprofit agencies where there is often a wish to avoid conflict (Harris, 1987; Middleton, 1987). There can be distrust of exercises or actions that emphasize differences within the board itself, or between the board and paid staff (Harris, 1989b). TAA offers a means whereby boards and staff can work together in a nonconfrontational manner toward "a shared set of role expectations with which they are relatively comfortable" (McLaughlin, 1986, p. 220).

A third useful feature of TAA is that it takes account of the tension and dynamism inherent in the board-staff relationship. In practice, the roles of board and staff vary according to the history, size, and purposes of a nonprofit agency and its stage of organizational development (Fink, 1989; Murray and Bradshaw-Camball, 1990; Zald, 1969). Relative roles tend to be renegotiated at frequent intervals (Harris, 1987; Kramer, 1985; Middleton, 1987). TAA is a tool to which nonprofit agency practitioners can return as necessary for reanalysis of the board role as the organizational characteristics and environment of their agency change. It does not offer definitive answers or solutions. It acknowledges the "processes of conflict and accommodation" which underlie apparently "rational" organizational forms (Morgan, 1990, p. 64), and it provides a framework within which ideas about requisite structures can be reexamined.

Finally, by employing the concept of board-staff interdependence, TAA sanctions working arrangements that exist in practice in many nonprofit agencies but are generally unacknowledged. Advice that urges clarification of the board role generally focuses attention on the job of boards in isolation from consideration of other agency roles (Conrad and Glenn, 1983, and Leduc and Block, 1985, are exceptions). This is not helpful for the person whose nonprofit sector experience indicates the "interactive" nature of the board role in relation to staff (Hartogs, 1989, p. xxiii). At the same time, general exhortations to share responsibilities or to work as partners are not sufficiently explicit to provide a practical guide for board members and staff. TAA, on the other hand, provides a framework reflecting practitioners' own experience of interdependence. It also offers a tool for discussing how tasks can be allocated and shared between boards and staff.

Conclusions

Our experience suggests that, as a practical tool, TAA has much to offer the nonprofit sector. It provides explanations for organizational difficulties, a framework within which possible responses can be explored, and pointers toward organizational change. Numerous nonprofit agencies in the United Kingdom have applied TAA to both the local and national levels of their organization. They have found that TAA both recognizes and responds to the distinctive need within nonprofits for periodic renegotiation of the board-staff relationship.

The application of TAA in a number of nonprofit agencies over a period of years also suggests some implications for research and theory development. It confirms, for example, the relevance to practice of contingency theories of the board that have emerged from earlier research studies. The nonprofit board role is not susceptible to analysis or implementation in isolation from other organizational roles. It is more appropriately conceptualized as interlinked and interdependent with other organizational roles. Moreover, the application of TAA has demonstrated that the degree of interdependence varies according to the organizational function under consideration.

Experience using TAA also suggests that it would be appropriate for future researchers to reconsider the applicability of the partnership concept. As noted earlier, scholars have questioned the idea of the board-staff relationship as a team or partnership, thinking that it does not adequately reflect the tensions and inequalities of power inherent in the relationship (Herman, 1989; Kramer, 1985; Middleton, 1987). We have numerous examples, however, from projects and workshops of staff and board members taking a shared responsibility approach to organizational problems when they are provided with the TAA working framework. This raises doubts about previous writers' suggestions that the board-staff relationship in nonprofits is inherently unbalanced and tense, doomed to dominance by one or the other party—usually the staff. A research study using a collaborative, participative methodology might well reveal that the tensions and inequalities between board and staff noted by earlier researchers mask an underlying drive toward a cooperative approach to nonprofit sector leadership—a drive that can come to fruition within the context of an appropriate framework such as TAA.

Several possibilities for the further development of TAA have been suggested to us by practitioners and scholars, ranging from additions to the list of organizational functions to the possibility of adapting TAA for application to the paid staff-volunteer staff relationship. Our work in this area is continuing. In the meantime, TAA has already opened a number of new paths for nonprofit organizations and researchers to explore.

References

Billis, D. *Welfare Bureaucracies: Their Design and Change in Response to Social Problems.* London: Gower, 1984.

Billis, D., Bromley, G., Hey, A., and Rowbottom, R. *Organising Social Services Departments.* London: Heinemann, 1980.

Connors, T. "The Boards of Directors." In T. Connors (ed.), *The Non-Profit Organization Handbook.* New York: McGraw-Hill, 1980.

Conrad, W., and Glenn, W. *The Effective Voluntary Board of Directors.* Athens, Ohio: Swallow Press, 1983.

Fink, J. "Community Agency Boards of Directors: Viability and Vestigiality, Substance and Symbol." In R. D. Herman and J. Van Til (eds.), *Nonprofit Boards of Directors, Analyses and Applications.* New Brunswick, N.J.: Transaction, 1989.

Gerard, D. *Charities in Britain: Conservatism or Change?* London: Bedford Square Press, 1983.

Gouldner, A. "The Secrets of Organizations." In R. Kramer and H. Specht (eds.), *Readings in Community Organization Practice.* Englewood Cliffs, N.J.: Prentice-Hall, 1969.

Handy, C. *Improving Effectiveness in Voluntary Organizations.* London: Bedford Square Press, 1981.

Harris, M. *Management Committees: Roles and Tasks.* Working Paper no. 4, Centre for Voluntary Organisation. London: London School of Economics, 1987.

Harris, M. "The Governing Body Role: Problems and Perceptions in Implementation." *Nonprofit and Voluntary Sector Quarterly,* 1989a, *18*(4), 317–323.

Harris, M. *Management Committees in Practice: A Study in Local Voluntary Leadership.* Working Paper no. 7, Centre for Voluntary Organisation. London: London School of Economics, 1989b.

Hartogs, N. *Volunteer and Professional Leadership.* Alexandria, Va.: Sales Service, 1989.

Hartogs, N., and Weber, J. *Boards of Directors.* Dobbs Ferry, N.Y.: Oceana, 1974.

Heimovics, R. D., and Herman, R. D. "Responsibility for Critical Events in Nonprofit Organizations." *Nonprofit and Voluntary Sector Quarterly,* 1990, *19*(1), 59–72.

Herman, R. D. "Board Functions and Board-Staff Relations in Nonprofit Organizations: An Introduction." In R. D. Herman and J. Van Til (eds.), *Nonprofit Boards of Directors, Analyses and Applications.* New Brunswick, N.J.: Transaction, 1989.

Herman, R. D., and Tulipana, F. P. "Board Staff Relations and Perceived Effectiveness in Nonprofit Organizations." *Journal of Voluntary Action Research,* 1985, *14*(4), 48–59.

Kramer, R. M. *Voluntary Agencies in the Welfare State.* Berkeley: University of California Press, 1981.

Kramer, R. "Towards a Contingency Model of Board-Executive Relations." *Administration in Social Work,* 1985, *19*(3), 15–33.

Leat, D., Smolka, G., and Unell, J. *Voluntary and Statutory Collaboration: Rhetoric or Reality?* London: Bedford Square Press, 1981.

Leduc, R., and Block, S. "Conjoint Directorship—Clarifying Management Roles Between the Board of Directors and the Executive Director." *Journal of Voluntary Action Research,* 1985, *14*(4), 67–76.

McLaughlin, C. *The Management of Nonprofit Organizations.* New Work: Wiley, 1986.

Mellor, H. *The Role of Voluntary Organisations in Social Welfare.* London: Croom Helm, 1985.

Middleton, M. "Nonprofit Boards of Directors: Beyond the Governance Function." In W. W. Powell (ed.), *The Nonprofit Sector: A Research Handbook.* New Haven, Conn.: Yale University Press, 1987.

Morgan, G. *Organizations in Society.* London: Macmillan, 1990.

Murray, V., and Bradshaw-Camball, P. "Voluntary Sector Boards: Patterns of Governance." In *Towards the 21st Century:*

Challenges for the Voluntary Sector. Proceedings of the 1990 Conference of the Association of Voluntary Action Scholars, London School of Economics, 1990.

Platt, S., and others. *Control or Charade?* (Housing Association Research Team) Portsmouth, England: Portsmouth Polytechnic, 1985.

Rowbottom, R. *Social Analysis: A Collaborative Method of Gaining Usable Scientific Knowledge of Social Institutions.* London: Heinemann, 1977.

Senor, J. M. "Another Look at the Executive-Board Relationship." *Social Work,* 1963, *8*(2), 19–25.

SSORU (Social Services Organization Research Unit). *Social Services Departments: Developing Patterns of Work and Organization.* London: Heinemann, 1974.

Widmer, C. "Board Members' Perceptions of their Roles and Responsibilities." In *Collaboration: The Vital Link Across Practice, Research and Disciplines.* Proceedings of the Association of Researchers in Nonprofit Organizations and Voluntary Action (ARNOVA), Chicago, 1991.

Zald, M. "The Power and Functions of Boards of Directors: A Theoretical Synthesis." *American Journal of Sociology,* 1969, *75,* 97–111.

2.

The Board Role
in Relation to Government:
Alternative Models

Judith R. Saidel

In the last several decades, researchers have begun to examine empirically what many practitioners have experienced for some time: the substantial interdependence between the public and nonprofit sectors. The reliance of government and nonprofit organizations on each other for critical resources positions their relationship at the center of the modern welfare state. The shrinking capacity of public bureaucracies, increasing demand for services, and continuing trend toward decentralized program delivery underscore its importance.

The recognition of this evolutionary development has prompted a variety of warnings. Some people caution that the diffused authority and structural complexity inherent in the blurred boundaries between sectors are major impediments in a democracy. These obstacles seriously hamper the ability of both legislators and public managers to hold nonprofits with government contracts accountable and the ability of the public to understand the system of service delivery (Sharkansky, 1975; Seidman and Gilmour, 1986; Kettl, 1988).

I would like to thank the editors, Sharon L. Harlan, and the anonymous reviewers for their helpful comments.

Others decry the undermining by government contracting of important values historically associated with nonprofits, such as independence, variety, responsiveness to particular individual and community needs, and progressive reform. Lipsky and Smith, for instance, question "whether nonprofit organizations operate according to standards derived from the community of interest from which they arise, or whether they are operated according to standards imposed by law and the values of public agencies" (1989–1990, p. 646). Wolch argues that "the transformation of the voluntary sector into a shadow state apparatus could ultimately shackle its potential to create progressive social change" (1990, p. 646). Similar fears have also been expressed about the impact of expanding commercial activities by nonprofits (Estes, Alford, and Binney, 1987; Salamon, 1989).

Given this significant shift over time in the pattern of public services, critical questions for nonprofits have not received much research attention. What roles do boards of directors play in the relationship of interdependence between the public and nonprofit sectors? Are they players in "third-party government," the system in which government relies on nongovernmental entities to implement public programs (Salamon, 1987), or are they bystanders? What factors contribute to board participation or nonparticipation?

If boards are more ceremonial than substantive, they are not acting as instruments of democracy and vehicles for meaningful citizen participation in community organizations. A related possibility is that boards of directors may be involved in the relationship between nonprofits and government without exerting any influence to mitigate the potentially negative effects of government contracts. On the other hand, if boards are fulfilling certain buffer functions in intersectoral activities, they may be a crucial factor in the balance of mutual dependence between government and nonprofit organizations.

This chapter proposes a typology of roles played by boards of directors in the interactions between the public and nonprofit sectors. The typology is drawn from open-ended qualitative data collected in an extensive empirical investigation of the resource relationship between public agencies at the state level and nonprofits with state government grants or contracts. Responses from eighty nonprofit executive directors about the involvement of their boards in the relationship with government are examined to develop this new framework.

Important questions flow from this typology of board roles. Under what conditions are different roles more likely to be performed? What explains board participation or nonparticipation in the interdependence between the public and nonprofit sectors? A review of the literature on the general functioning of boards of directors yields a set of factors that may influence the nature of board involvement in this particular context. These factors are briefly described along with related comments from the current study's interviewees. Statistical results from this study's database about the relationship among several of these factors and board roles are presented. The chapter concludes with implications of the findings for the government/nonprofit relationship, for nonprofit leaders, and for future research.

Research Methodology

The study on which the results reported here are based focused on New York state executive branch agencies and public benefit nonprofits, classified as 501(c)(3) in the Internal Revenue Code, that contract with state government for the delivery of public services. Research interviews, conducted by the author, took place from October through December, 1989. The statewide sample included eighty nonprofit organizations in four service areas: arts, culture, and humanities; general health; mental retardation and development disabilities; and human services. These service areas are four of the twenty-four primary service types from the National Taxonomy of Exempt Entities, developed by the National Center for Charitable Statistics, a program of INDEPENDENT SECTOR, Washington, D.C. The selection of these service areas built on previous research with the largest number of respondents from an original statewide random sample of 300 nonprofits with state contracts in 1985 (Dawes and Saidel, 1988). Although they were not chosen on theoretical grounds, they are representative of at least a large part of the voluntary sector. Nonprofit study participants included twenty executive administrators from each of the service areas. Of the eighty respondents, fourteen were top-level managers other than the executive director. All respondents participated in two-part, on-site interviews, including a self-administered survey completed immediately and an interview with demographic and open-ended questions.

Survey items, elements of multi-item Likert-type scales, were designed to assess the dependence of public agencies and nonprofits on each other for resources. The conceptual anchors of each scale were (1) independence and (6) dependence. Response categories were strongly disagree, generally disagree, disagree a little, agree a little, generally agree, and strongly agree. Three scales measured the dependence of state agencies on nonprofit organizations for resources: (1) the importance of the resource, (2) the availability of alternative resources, and (3) the ability to pressure for provision of the resource. State agency dependence on nonprofits was operationalized as the average of the three scale scores. Three parallel scales measured the same dimensions for resource dependence in the other direction, and nonprofit dependence on state agencies was operationalized in the same way. Resources that flow from state agencies to nonprofits were revenues; information; political support and legitimacy, in the sense of external validation (Galaskiewicz, 1985); and access to the nonlegislative policy process (Rourke, 1984). Nonprofit organizations supplied their service delivery capacity, information, political support, and legitimacy to state agencies. There were no board-related items on the survey.

The interview schedule consisted of six open-ended questions about government/nonprofit interdependence and five informational questions. The sixth open-ended question was "What role *do* nonprofit boards of directors play with respect to the relationship of resource interdependence between state agencies and nonprofits?" After a pretest of the interview schedule, this question replaced "What *is* the role of nonprofit boards of directors?" to avoid eliciting socially desirable responses. Answers to the reworded question are the basis of the following typology.

Data were also collected from seventy-three public managers in the four primary state agencies with whom the nonprofits contract. The principal findings of this study are summarized below, and more detailed results are presented in Saidel, 1991.

Background

Although a number of studies have examined the general functioning of nonprofit boards of directors and their relations with executive staff (Middleton, 1987; Herman and Van Til, 1989), few have focused specifically on board activities related to government/nonprofit interactions. Hartogs and Weber (1974) asked 115 executive directors of organizations with over 25 percent of their budget from government about the impact of public funds on board member participation. A majority responded that the level of participation had not changed.

In a multinational study of nonprofits in the personal social services, Kramer (1981) found that boards of directors in both England and the United States were considered to be key factors in intersectoral relations. "Agencies in the United States and in England that received over half of their income from governmental bodies regarded board members as an important asset because of their influence in the highly politicized process of allocating public funds" (p. 123). In addition to board influence in the political arena, British and American political cultures that encourage citizen participation also bolstered board member involvement.

In contrast to these studies, more recent investigations suggest that boards are, in fact, bystanders in the contracting process between government and nonprofits (Fink, 1989; Gronbjerg, 1990; Bernstein, 1991). Two intensive sets of case studies document this view. In an ethnographic analysis of eighteen human service nonprofits in New York City, Bernstein found that "[m]any managers seem to view the Board as irrelevant in terms of the major political issues regarding contracted services" (1991, p. 187).

Gronbjerg's case studies of six human service agencies in Chicago indicated that "reliance on centralized and institutional funding sources (such as public funding) appears to be related to more centralized control by the Executive Director and a more peripheral or adjunct role for agency boards" (1990, p. 49). This view was reinforced by the general finding of Herman and Heimovics (1990) that nonprofit executives, not boards of directors, are at the center of responsibility for organizational consequences.

As explained above, data about board involvement in the government-nonprofit relationship were collected as part of a larger study of reciprocal resource dependence between state agencies and nonprofit organizations. Perhaps the single most striking finding of that study was the symmetry in the distribution of resource dependence between sectors. All four service areas were characterized by aggregate resource flows upon which agencies and nonprofits were equally dependent. Whether nonprofits were producing cultural events, delivering health care, or providing social services, public and nonprofit administrators assessed the overall distribution of dependence at the same level, about 60 percent of the theoretical maximum (Saidel, 1991).

Substantial mutual resource dependence between government and nonprofit organizations is the context within which the issue of board participation gains particular importance. In theory, a board of directors can help maximize resources available from government to fulfill the nonprofit's mission and, at the same time, shield the nonprofit from the influence of government-set priorities that may undermine or divert the mission. The exploratory interview question—"What role do boards of directors play with respect to the relationship of resource interdependence between state agencies and nonprofits?"—was designed to surface a set of actual board behaviors that could subsequently be examined in a larger random sample of nonprofits providing government-funded services.

After role types were identified, two raters independently analyzed each response and assigned the appropriate role or roles. Without consultation, there was agreement on forty-five of the seventy usable responses and partial agreement on fifteen additional cases (inter-rater reliability = .86). Interestingly, only nine responses indicated multiple roles. In these cases, the primary role emphasized in the response was coded. In the following section, a typology of board roles is elaborated and frequencies are presented for this data set. The statistics presented here are suggestive of possible trends and should be considered with the limits of a single-state study and nonrandom sample in mind.

Typology of Board Roles

Analysis of responses revealed that about one-third of the study's eighty nonprofit executives described their board members as bystanders in the government/nonprofit relationship. "Very little [role]," said one executive. "Most of the interface is at the staff or line level between state agency staff and nonprofit staff." An arts manager responded, "Unfortunately very small. The primary interdependence and dialogue is between the management of our institution and the state agency." In the arts and mental retardation service areas, more boards were bystanders than any other role.

In contrast to the board-as-bystander description, however, many more responses suggested substantive board participation in the interdependent relationship between sectors. Four role categories that capture board activities are facilitator, maintainer, buffer, and bystander (see Figure 2.1).

Figure 2.1. Board Roles in the Government-Nonprofit Relationship.

I.   *Facilitator*
        Legitimator
        Procurer
        Approver

II. *Maintainer*
        Protector
        Defender

III. *Buffer*
        Alternative resource generator
        Values guardian

IV. *Bystander*

Board as Facilitator

Boards of directors perform a number of different functions that facilitate interdependence between government and voluntary organizations. Nonprofit executives described a long-recognized role of board members as *legitimators*. Individual board members validate the worthiness of a nonprofit organization in the eyes of important constituencies, including funders from all sectors, consumers of nonprofit services, and the community of volunteers. In a study of the grants economy in one midwestern community, Galaskiewicz (1985) explored legitimacy in this sense, identifying the legitimizing function of corporate contributions and government grants or contracts in the eyes of other corporate donors. Perrow (1963) and Pfeffer and Salancik (1978) also identified legitimacy in this way, emphasizing its value as leverage for other financial contributions.

As widely documented, government is a critical source of revenues for many nonprofits (Hodgkinson and Weitzman, 1989; Abramson and Salamon, 1986). The New York state study cited earlier reported 55 percent as the median annual percent of revenues from all government sources (Dawes and Saidel, 1988). In the research analyzed here, the median percent of revenues for all nonprofits from state government sources was 36 percent. As reported in Table 2.1, there was wide variation across the four service areas.

The ability of board members to enhance the legitimacy of a nonprofit in the eyes of public funders is a valuable role indeed. As one manager noted, "In the process of getting acknowledged by the [Arts] Council, being a bona fide arts organization, it made an enormous difference that we had a quality board. . . ." A mental retardation executive director remarked that the change in board membership from parents to more business-oriented, financially knowledgeable individuals provided more credibility in the nonprofit's presentation to the state.

As legitimators, board member involvement is indirect, in that socioeconomic status, other demographic characteristics, or particular knowledge are the elements that determine board

Table 2.1. Median Annual Nonprofit Revenues and
Percent of Revenues from State Government Sources in 1988.

	Arts N = 20	Health* N = 20	MR/DD N = 20	Human Service N = 20
Median revenues	500,000	2,500,000	5,800,000	1,700,000
Median percent	9	33	75	26
Percent ranges	0–46**	8–97	30–100	0–90**

*The health nonprofits include four medical center hospitals, five community health centers, and eleven community-based health organizations.

**Four of the eighty nonprofits had no state revenues in 1988. The original random sample was drawn from nonprofits with state contracts in 1985.

contribution to legitimacy. More active participation in the interactions between public agencies and third-sector organizations may occur in the facilitator roles of *procurer* and *approver*.

Occasionally board members serve important procurement functions when they participate in grant preparation and press for support of grant applications in meetings with government funders. According to a human services executive, "Every not-for-profit tries to construct a board of directors that would have some political clout. You try to use the board in relation to any funding proposal you might have, to do some lobbying."

More frequently, however, the board reviews, approves, and receives reports about contracts with public agencies. As one executive said, "They have to agree on entering into contracts with the state. They get updated reports. There are monthly meetings at which we discuss the problems we have with state agencies." This may amount to rubber-stamping agreements negotiated by staff or it may involve more critical probing of the contract and its implications.

Another way in which individual board members facilitate interdependence between sectors may occur if they formerly worked in government. A human service manager noted that, in this instance, board members "have friends in government and investment in government. They would encourage nonprofits to take on more and greater contracts, to have closer relationships with government."

Slightly more than one-quarter of the executive directors in this study described activities of board members that promoted interactions between their organization and a state agency from whom revenues were derived. In the health and human service subsectors, facilitator was the most dominant role among board members (see Table 2.2).

Table 2.2. Cross-Tabulation of Board Role
and Primary Service Type: N-70*.

	Arts	Health	MR/DD	Human Service	Total
Facilitator	3	9	3	8	23
Maintainer	5	0	2	3	10
Buffer	2	3	5	1	11
Bystander	9	4	7	6	26
Total	19	16	17	18	70

*10 responses were either missing or not usable.

Note: Pearson chi-square is 17.730, p = .1. Because more than one-fifth of the cells contain less than five cases, this significance test is suspect.

Board as Maintainer

In addition to fostering the relationship between sectors, boards of directors often work hard to maintain that interdependence. Two primary maintenance roles are *protector* of the tangible benefits nonprofits derive from government and *defender* of government agency interests against threats from other public policy actors, such as the governor, division of the budget, or the legislature.

In a classic study of bureaucratic politics, Rourke (1984) argued that attentive publics, receiving benefits from public bureaucracies, are often engaged in efforts to maintain those benefits. The protector and defender roles are consistent with this analysis. "They're part of the troops to call out for support, part of broad-based support on policy issues, funding, advocacy," said one executive.

The defender role, involving lobbying on behalf of public agencies to fend off adverse budgetary or other policy actions, was captured in this description of board participation by an arts executive: "Primarily in the lobbying effort. The not-for-profit world is increasingly vigilant about protecting the agency and attempting to influence legislators."

About 13 percent of the respondents mentioned elements of the maintainer role. When combined with the 29 percent of boards who facilitate the interconnection between government and the voluntary sector, a picture emerges of about two-fifths of nonprofit boards engaged in fostering and sustaining the interdependence between sectors.

Board as Buffer

Buffering an organization from the external environment is a boundary-spanning role of boards described by about 14 percent of executive directors and noted in previous studies (Price, 1963–1964; Middleton, 1987). As described here, the buffering function protects nonprofits from the danger of vendorism or the surrendering of autonomy to the requirements of government contracts (Kramer, 1985). Respondents suggested two major elements: *generator* of alternative nonstate resources and *guardian* of values, mission, and self-set priorities. Both behaviors demonstrate that boards can be a countervailing influence in the government/voluntary sector relationship.

Generating alternative resources, especially revenues, preserves some autonomy for nonprofits and thereby contributes to balance in the resource relationship between sectors. This is an element of independence universally acknowledged in the power-dependence and resource-dependence literatures. Cook's (1977) explanation is representative. "To the extent that alternative sources are available to an organization in an exchange network, dependence is less" (p. 66). (See also Levine and White, 1961; Emerson, 1962; Blau, 1964; Thompson, 1967; Jacobs, 1974; Pfeffer and Salancik, 1978; Brudney, 1978; Provan, Beyer, and Kruytbosch, 1980; Provan and Skinner, 1989).

Several managers in this study pointed to board effects to raise funds for projects and services in which government had no interest. One manager reported: "Their overview of general budgeting puts them in a direct active relationship with resource funding. They can see what's needed and what's not. They can determine areas of reasonable support from state agencies so they can divert their attention elsewhere." Generating revenues from private sources can also supplement public funding in that private dollars can make up for shortfalls and cover cash flow problems caused by delayed contract approval and government reimbursement. (This illustrates, however, more a facilitative than a buffer function.)

The executive director of a mental retardation nonprofit described the guardian role of boards of directors in this way: "The role they play is setting priorities for community services— what we need to provide. I in turn go back to the state agency and ask for funding to provide it." Here the board acts as a buffer against the force of state priority setting by weighing local community need as the organization's first responsibility. A health administrator focused on the board's role as guardian of organizational mission. "Boards of Directors certainly look at policy that state agencies come out with and assess whether those things fit in with the mission of the overall agency."

Factors Affecting Board Involvement

The preliminary identification of board roles in the government/ voluntary sector relationship prompts additional researchable questions. What factors contribute to board involvement or noninvolvement in the interactions between sectors? Under what conditions are boards more likely to play these roles? The literature on the general functioning of boards of directors suggests some interrelated variables that should be part of an effort to answer these complicated questions. Data and responses from the present study, relevant to factors affecting board involvement, are included in the following overview of these variables.

Resource Dependence

The linkage activities of boards of directors with resource providers in the organizational environment have received some
research attention (Pfeffer, 1973; Pfeffer and Salancik, 1978).
Data from the current study, reported in Table 2.3, suggest that
there may be an important connection between the role of boards

Table 2.3. Analysis of Variance by Role for
Revenue Dependence and Overall Resource Dependence.

	Facilitator N = 23 *Mean*	Maintainer N = 10 *Mean*	Buffer N = 11 *Mean*	Bystander N = 26 *Mean*	F-Ratio
Revenue dependence (percentage from NYS)	32	29	67	46	3.04*
Overall resource dependence (scale: 1 = independent; 6 = dependent)	3.5	3.9	3.7	3.7	1.74

*p < .05

in third-party government and the degree of dependence on public resources. There are significant differences (p < .05) in the
average percent of revenues across role categories. The twenty-
six boards described as bystanders served organizations with
almost half their revenues from state government. At the same
time, however, a smaller group of nonprofits with 67 percent
state government revenues, the highest proportion of public
funding, had boards who were buffering the powerful effects of
state government contracts. The evidence from this exploratory
study, suggestive of an important link between resource dependence and board function, points to the need for further exploration of this connection.

Size and Stage of Organizational Development

Zald and Middleton included size and stage in organizational development in theoretical syntheses of board power and functions. Closely related is the degree of organizational complexity, including structural, technical, and fiscal dimensions (Zald, 1969; Middleton, 1987; see also Stone, 1989). Several nonprofit respondents also mentioned size, distinguishing board involvement in policymaking and operations. "With contracts, the size of the organization grows. Therefore, the board moves more to policy instead of operational detail." Whether this increases or decreases board participation in third-party government is an empirical question as yet unanswered.

Professionalism

Closely linked to size and phase of organizational life cycle in explaining board involvement is the degree of professionalization within the nonprofit. Although there are different analyses of exactly how this pervasive force affects board participation, there is general agreement that it results in a diminished board role (Zald, 1969; Kramer, 1981; Middleton, 1987; Dawes and Saidel, 1988). One nonprofit manager articulated this development clearly. "As the state moves its dependence to nonprofits to provide service, we're developing a nonprofit network of professionals who deal with the complexity of putting together program financing. We're seeing more and more professionals."

Board-Executive Relations

Board involvement in the interactions between government and nonprofits is both a function of and a contributor to board relations with staff, especially the executive director. A number of nonprofit administrators indicated that the board role in third-party government depends on the attitude and actions of the executive staff. One nonprofit administrator commented, "The administration is the variable who accounts for the difference—

the ability of the chief administrator and other agency administrators to understand the system at large, the give-and-take in the system and then explain it to the board and enable the board to live it along with the administration."

At the same time, the ability of influential or knowledgeable board members to lobby policymakers effectively on behalf of nonprofit interests may increase the power of board members in their relations with staff. This is an example of access and ability to influence external resources that Zald (1969) identified as a source of board power. Although he applied this observation to private contributions, it seems relevant to public funds as well.

The distribution of power between board members and executive staff as a function of their relative influence in government contracting is a subject for empirical investigation. One distinction suggested by the respondents in this study is that nonprofit managers handle the ongoing operational aspects of contracting and both board members and managers participate in the intermittent politics of contracting.

Interorganizational Coalitions

The presence of interorganizational associations and coalitions may indirectly reduce the role of individual organizational boards. For instance, Bernstein (1991) found that coalitions between agencies, as opposed to individual boards, were the key political force in contracting. In describing the board role as nominal, one manager in the present study supported this perspective. "There are whole organizations formed," he said, "to lobby the state on mental health, such as the Mental Health Coalition."

Individual-Level Characteristics

Individual-level characteristics should also be included as factors influencing the role of the board of directors in relations between sectors. Middleton (1987) pointed to socioeconomic status differences between board members and executive directors as important. Another significant characteristic may be whether board members are also clientele of the nonprofit organization and public funding agency. Parents of service recipients or consumers themselves may wield unique political influence that contributes to their involvement in government/voluntary sector interactions.

Conclusions

The larger study of which these data were a part documented a relationship of substantial and symmetrical resource interdependence between public agencies and nonprofit organizations with government contracts. As facilitators and maintainers of nonprofit involvement with government, some boards of directors foster and sustain this interdependence between sectors and share policymaking responsibilities with executive staff. They are participants in third-party government, encouraging the entry of nonprofits into contracting relationships with public agencies and defending the tangible benefits of that relationship once it is established.

Board involvement in a resource relationship so central to the continued and expanded availability of nonprofit services is an important contribution to the financial well-being of organizations for which board members have fiduciary responsibility. That responsibility also extends to safeguarding the mission of the organization. The buffer roles of the board of directors as guardian of organizational values and generator of alternative nonstate resources contribute to nonprofit autonomy and, therefore, help maintain balance in the government/nonprofit relationship. This balancing function, now being performed by some boards under certain circumstances, is particularly important in the current period of increasing nonprofit vulnerability to governmental budget crises. However, the small proportion of boards in this study who act to buffer the negative impacts of government-derived revenues offers preliminary evidence that the balance of dependence between the public and nonprofit sectors is precariously tipped toward the power of government.

At the same time, the board role as bystander, reported by about one-third of this study's respondents, reinforces the warnings of researchers cited earlier. If boards are nonplayers in a primary resource relationship of nonprofit organizations and in a central pattern of public service delivery, they are not acting as substantive instruments of citizen participation and control.

Responses from executive directors in four service areas in New York state suggest that in a critical set of resource-related interactions bystanders is the most dominant role among board members. Of those boards who do participate in third-party government, many act to facilitate and maintain the reciprocal dependence between sectors. Fewer are buffering the force of government-set priorities that conflict with or undermine the values and mission of the nonprofit organizations for which they are responsible.

As nonprofit leaders recruit board members, they should identify individuals with the capacity to perform important roles in third-party government. In time set aside for board development, managers and board members should assess the balance of dependence between sectors and its implications for the nonprofit's values, mission, and program priorities.

Further research is necessary to determine the generalizability of these patterns and to analyze the conditions under which different board roles are more likely to be performed. Evidence from a larger sample that includes executive staff and board members will shed additional light on this critical element in the relationship of interdependence between government and nonprofit organizations.

References

Abramson, A. J., and Salamon, L. M. *The Nonprofit Sector and the New Federal Budget*. Washington, D.C.: Urban Institute, 1986.

Bernstein, S. R. *Managing Contracted Services in the Nonprofit Agency*. Philadelphia: Temple University Press, 1991.

Blau, P. M. *Exchange and Power in Social Life*. New York: Wiley, 1964.

Brudney, J. L. "An Exchange Approach to Intraorganizational

Power." Unpublished dissertation, University of Michigan, 1978.

Cook, K. S. "Exchange and Power in Networks of Interorganizational Relations." *The Sociological Quarterly,* 1977, *18,* 62–82.

Dawes, S. S., and Saidel, J. R. *The State and the Voluntary Sector, a Report of New York State Project 2000.* New York: Foundation Center, 1988.

Emerson, R. H. "Power-Dependence Relations." *American Sociological Review,* 1962, *27,* 31–41.

Estes, C. L., Alford, R. A., and Binney, E. A. "The Restructuring of the Nonprofit Sector." Unpublished manuscript, University of California, San Francisco, 1987.

Fink, J. "Community Agency Boards of Directors: Viability and Vestigiality, Substance and Symbol." In R. D. Herman and J. Van Til (eds.), *Nonprofit Boards of Directors, Analyses and Applications.* New Brunswick, N.J.: Transaction, 1989.

Galaskiewicz, J. *Social Organization in an Urban Grants Economy.* Orlando, Fla.: Academic Press, 1985.

Gronbjerg, K. A. "Managing Nonprofit Funding Relations: Case Studies of Six Human Service Organizations." Working Paper no. 156, Yale University Program on Nonprofit Organizations, 1990.

Hartogs, N., and Weber, J. *Boards of Directors.* Dobbs Ferry, N.Y.: Oceana, 1974.

Heimovics, R. D., and Herman, R. D. "The Salient Management Skills: A Conceptual Framework for a Curriculum for Managers in Nonprofit Organizations." *American Review of Public Administration,* 1989, *19*(4), 294–312.

Herman, R. D., and Heimovics, R. D. "Characteristics and Expectations of Effective Nonprofit Chief Executives." Proceedings of the Conference of the Association of Voluntary Action Scholars, London, 1990.

Herman, R. D., and Van Til, J. (eds.). *Nonprofit Boards of Directors, Analyses and Applications.* New Brunswick, N.J.: Transaction, 1989.

Hodgkinson, V. A., and Weitzman, M. S. *Dimensions of the Independent Sector.* (3rd ed.) Washington, D.C.: INDEPENDENT SECTOR, 1989.

Jacobs, D. "Dependency and Vulnerability: An Exchange Approach to the Control of Organizations." *Administrative Science Quarterly,* 1974, *19,* 45–59.

Kettl, D. F. *Government by Proxy: (Mis?)Managing Federal Programs.* Washington, D.C.: Congressional Quarterly Press, 1988.

Kramer, R. M. *Voluntary Agencies in the Welfare State.* Berkeley: University of California Press, 1981.

Kramer, R. M. "The Voluntary Agency in a Mixed Economy: Dilemma of Entrepreneurialism and Vendorism." *Journal of Applied Behavioral Science,* 1985, *21,* 377–391.

Levine, S., and White, P. E. "Exchange as a Conceptual Framework for the Study of Interorganizational Relationships." *Administrative Science Quarterly,* 1961, *5,* 583–601.

Lipsky, M., and Smith, S. R. "Nonprofit Organizations, Government, and the Welfare State." *Political Science Quarterly,* 1989–1990, *104,* 625–648.

Middleton, M. "Nonprofit Boards of Directors, Beyond the Governance Function." In W. W. Powell (ed.), *The Nonprofit Sector: A Research Handbook.* New Haven, Conn.: Yale University Press, 1987.

Perrow, C. "Goals and Power Structures, a Historical Case Study." In E. Freidson (ed.), *The Hospital in Modern Society.* New York: Free Press, 1963.

Pfeffer, J. "Size, Composition, and Function of Hospital Boards of Directors: A Study of Organization-Environment Linkage." *Administrative Science Quarterly,* 1973, *18,* 349–364.

Pfeffer, J., and Salancik, G. R. *The External Control of Organizations, a Resource Dependence Perspective.* New York: HarperCollins, 1978.

Price, J. L. "The Impact of Governing Boards on Organizational Effectiveness and Morale." *Administrative Science Quarterly,* 1963–1964, *8,* 361–378.

Provan, K. G. "Board Power and Organizational Effectiveness Among Human Service Agencies." *Academy of Management Journal,* 1980, *23,* 221–236.

Provan, K. G., Beyer, J. M., and Kruytbosch, C. "Environmental Linkages and Power in Resource-Dependence Relations Between Organizations." *Administrative Science Quarterly,* 1980, *25,* 200–225.

Provan, K. G., and Skinner, S. J. "Interorganizational Dependence and Control as Predictors of Opportunism in Dealer-Supplier Relations." *Academy of Management Journal*, 1989, *32*, 202–212.

Rourke, F. E. *Bureaucracy, Politics, and Public Policy.* (3rd ed.) Boston: Little, Brown, 1984.

Saidel, J. R. "Dimensions of Interdependence: The State and Voluntary Sector Relationship." *Nonprofit and Voluntary Sector Quarterly*, 1989, *18*(4), 335–347.

Saidel, J. R. "Resource Interdependence: The Relationship Between State Agencies and Nonprofit Organizations." *Public Administration Review*, 1991, *51*(6), 543–553.

Salamon, L. M. "Partners in Public Service: The Scope and Theory of Government-Nonprofit Relations." In W. W. Powell (ed.)., *The Nonprofit Sector: A Research Handbook.* New Haven, Conn.: Yale University Press, 1987.

Salamon, L. M. "The Changing Partnership Between the Voluntary Sector and the Welfare State." In V. A. Hodgkinson, R. W. Lyman, and Associates (eds.), *The Future of the Nonprofit Sector: Challenges, Changes, and Policy Considerations.* San Francisco: Jossey-Bass, 1989.

Seidman, H., and Gilmour, R. *Politics, Position and Power.* (4th ed.) New York: Oxford University Press, 1986.

Sharkansky, I. *Whither the State? Politics and Public Enterprise in Three Countries.* Chatham, N.J.: Chatham House, 1975.

Stone, M. M. "Planning as Strategy in Nonprofit Organizations: An Exploratory Study." *Nonprofit and Voluntary Sector Quarterly*, 1989, *18*(4), 297–315.

Thompson, J. D. *Organizations in Action.* New York: McGraw-Hill, 1967.

Wolch, J. R. *The Shadow State: Government and Voluntary Sector in Transition.* New York: Foundation Center, 1990.

Zald, M. N. "The Power and Functions of Boards of Directors: A Theoretical Synthesis." *American Journal of Sociology*, 1969, *75*, 97–111.

3.

The Role of Values: Management in Religious Organizations

Thomas H. Jeavons

The Apostle Paul identifies "administration" as one of the ministries in the Church for which one is equipped by a gift of the Spirit (1 Cor.12:28). Very early in the life of the Church, its leaders recognized the need to choose specific persons with the appropriate talents to handle the management of the practical needs of the faith community and its service work (Acts 6). Today the Church and other religious groups have spawned and operate a whole host of organizations to provide needed social services and offer a variety of ministries of practical caring to the world. The size and complexity of these organizations often require considerable sophistication in their management.

As in other areas of the nonprofit sector, there has been an increasing interest in and understanding of the concepts and approaches of modern management among many religious organizations, and this is to be welcomed. This is clearly not true of all, perhaps not even of the majority of these organizations, but there is progress. On the other hand, some of us now have concerns that in striving for "more effective performance"—and the definition of "effectiveness" is a key issue here—religious groups may adopt concepts of and approaches to management developed in for-profit contexts without giving adequate thought to the differences in organizational missions, characters, and cultures between the for-profit realm and the religious one. It is obviously important that religious organizations be as efficient and careful as possible in the use of their resources to serve their constituencies; but when efforts to increase efficiency threaten in any way to compromise the basic religious values or character of these organizations, the cost of efficiency is too high.

One observer has noted, "The American genius for commercializing everything is perhaps our least admirable quality. Religious holidays, rituals of birth and death, sport, art, family vacations, college reunions, pets, patriotism — all are promoted and marketed as if they were culturally and spiritually indistinguishable from chewing gum or cheeseburgers" (Payton, 1990). As these observations about the often inappropriate use of for-profit marketing techniques in nonprofit, voluntary, and familial realms are true, so there is the potential for serious problems when there is an adoption of other alien management techniques and activities in the nonprofit and religious realms.

The question to be raised and addressed in this chapter is: "Is there anything distinctive about religious organizations that makes the management of such organizations an endeavor essentially — or, at least, significantly — different from the management of other enterprises?" I will argue here that in most cases the answer to this question is (or should be), "Yes." I will define and make the case for the significance of a distinctive facet in the character of organizations that are more than nominally religious, and I will show how this characteristic changes the context for the management of such organizations in a crucial way.

This chapter will go on to suggest briefly some of the implications of this distinctive context for management in religious organizations in specific areas of management practice — for example, finances, human resources, and planning. These areas and practices of management need particular, thoughtful attention in religious organizations that wish to be truly effective.

Finally, I will close with suggestions of some subjects that need further research to improve our understanding of how religious organizations can best be managed given their unique character and function in our society.

Nonprofit and Religious
Organizations: What Is Different?

Since the publication of Peter Drucker's seminal work *The Practice of Management* in 1954, an extraordinary body of literature has appeared on the field of "management" and its many subfields: finance, planning, human resources, marketing, and so on. Recently, particularly over the last ten or fifteen years, we have also seen the emergence of a body of literature on "nonprofit management," which is by no means extensive but is growing and includes many useful pieces.

Beginning with the publication of books that were collections of articles (Borst and Montana, 1977; Zaltman, 1979) and continuing with the development of more unitary and complete texts on nonprofit management (Schulman and Setterberg, 1985; Hay, 1990), this literature is largely directed toward advising managers of nonprofit organizations about how they can improve the performance of their organizations. The first thing that strikes one in reading many of these pieces, however, is how little difference there is between the advice offered to nonprofit managers and the counsel offered in other management texts to for-profit managers.

There is, of course, a need to focus some attention on functions that are unique to nonprofits—for example, fundraising or the management of volunteers—or to deal with the fact that nonprofits perform some management tasks with different tools—for example, fund-accounting versus standard accounting techniques. The principles suggested, however, to nonprofit managers about how to make their organizations more effective often seem virtually identical to those suggested to for-profit managers.[1] Indeed, this tendency is perhaps most dramatically, if somewhat ironically, emphasized in a recent piece by Peter Drucker on what for-profit organizations might learn from well-run nonprofits (Drucker, 1990a). The essence of this lesson is to stay attentive to and act more consistently out of a strong and clearly focused sense of mission. A good lesson, indeed; yet surely this is not very different from the lesson the corporations' executives were supposed to have learned in business schools, where some professor must have emphasized the old adage about the importance of businesses "sticking to their knitting" (Peters and Waterman, 1982).

How then does this literature explain the difference between nonprofit and for-profit organizations? Most of these books, especially the earlier ones, distinguish nonprofits from for-profits primarily, if not solely, in economic terms. Gerald Zaltman (1979) tells us that "a nonprofit organization is one whose major goal is not the maximization of monetary gains" (p. 5). More recently, Robert Hay (1990) says, "A nonprofit organization is one that is formed to provide services for its clientele, with profit being a minor objective" (p. 3).

Michael O'Neill and Dennis Young provide us with a more sophisticated and helpful distinction when they say: "One way to understand the difference between nonprofits and organizations in other sectors is to realize that the particular activities that business and government organizations undertake are *instrumental* to achieving their overall objectives. For non-profits, the particular service or the given constituency or the articulated cause is of *primary* concern, not subservient to an overriding financial or political bottom line" (1988, p. 4). O'Neill and Young's distinction, while still referencing the contrast of economic interests, begins to make the point that it is the complexity and ambiguity of mission, purpose, and activity — and of the relationships among these elements of organizational life and structure — that changes the context of management for nonprofit organizations.

Peter Drucker, in his latest contribution to this discussion (Drucker, 1990b), takes this line of distinction even further in contending that the business of nonprofits should be conceived of neither in terms of making money nor in providing service as an end in itself but rather in effecting change. "Business supplies, either goods or services. Government controls."

But the "product" of a nonprofit, claims Drucker, "is a changed human being. The nonprofit institutions are human-change agents" (1990b, p. xiv).

One might well, I believe rightly, take issue with that statement as a generalization. Even a cursory examination of the range of nonprofit organizations and their activities tells us Drucker's claim cannot be held to be true about all nonprofits, perhaps not even about most. Still, it is undoubtedly true of some. And perhaps it is most true of those kinds of nonprofits that the public most readily identifies with nonprofit endeavors — for example, social service agencies, many advocacy groups, private educational institutions, and others. And while the general public may not often think of religious bodies as nonprofit organizations, that is what many are; and Drucker's description certainly fits most of them.

Drucker's comments point to another, perhaps more useful way to distinguish nonprofit organizations, or at least a class of them: by examining their initial and essential purposes. We can begin this examination by asking a fundamental question: "If the work of business revolves around wealth, and the work of government revolves around power; then what does the work of private, nonprofit organizations revolve around?" I want to contend here that the answer to this question for many of these organizations is "values."[2]

The work of the voluntary sector at its origins — which, we should recall, were explicitly religious — was essentially "values-expressive." (Please note that in speaking of "values" in this context I mean something entirely different from what management consultants — like Peters and Waterman — mean when they insist "excellent companies" are "value-driven".)[3]

Drucker may be half right. The work that many nonprofits do, serving people in an expression of the organizations' values, is intended to change people's lives in specific, practical ways. But it is often hoped that, being exposed to the values that undergird and inform the work of the organization, the people served will adopt these values as their own and so be changed in yet another way. It is a mistake to assume that the first focus of these organizations and those who work in them is always on the practical change the work evokes. It may be as much or more—and appropriately, given the organizations' missions— on the rightness and clarity of the value statement the work offers, or on the establishment of loving relationships among the servers and those served that bear witness to certain ideals of care and community (Hall, 1990). What is more, the hoped- for changes may be as much transformations—for instance, in spiritual growth—of those serving as transformations in the lives of those served.

This is especially true for religious organizations where service is undertaken as a form of witness. Here, in terms of ultimate goals, "making the witness" may be as important as providing the service. And, in terms of ultimate justifications, the rationale for the service undertaken may not finally be rooted in the world's needs but rather in individuals' or the group's "call- ing." That is to say, what is done in the service of others is un- dertaken as an expression of the agents' deepest ideals, a com- mitment to and understanding of what is ultimately important in human existence and the divine order.

What distinguishes some nonprofits, then, and all orga- nizations that are more than just nominally religious, is their values-expressive character, their concern to "give witness" to cer- tain truths or tenets of faith. Additionally, this distinction takes on special weight for religious organizations, where the values are not merely political or social but rather "ultimate" (in the ontological sense). When this unique facet of their place and purpose is understood, it fundamentally changes the context of management for them.

If this claim is accepted, the question that follows is "*How* does it alter the tasks of management?" We turn now to answer- ing that question—first in framing one of the basic questions to be asked about all management and then in considering some specific functions.

Defining Effectiveness for Values-Expressive Organizations

The ways in which the values-expressive character of religious organizations creates a fundamental change in the context for their management may be seen first when we try to answer the

question that is basic to evaluating the appropriateness and usefulness of any approach to management in any specific organization. That is, "What constitutes 'effectiveness' for this organization?"[4] How does one define or evaluate the effectiveness of
an organization that is as much concerned with the witness it
makes as the particular service it provides?

Often these two aspects of the organization's mission may
not be easily separated. That religious body, be it a local con-
gregation or a service organization, which says it is responding
to Jesus' call to "feed the hungry, clothe the naked, welcome
the stranger, or care for the sick" (Matt. 25:35–36), or to the
Prophets' exhortations to care for "the poor, the widow, and the
stranger," but which cannot perform those tasks with some
efficacy, will not effectively witness to the power and pertinence
of these religious teachings.[5] On the other hand, many groups
are engaged in such tasks, and some may be more efficient than
religious groups in providing specific services; but they may well
not be witnessing persuasively to God's special love for "the poor
and the needy," for those "who have no helper" (Ps. 72) in the
way they provide this service.

It may have been — and may still be — true that religious
organizations have too often not been concerned enough about
effectiveness and efficiency, about whether they were — or are —
"doing the right things" or "doing things right" in relation to their
specific intentions for meeting practical needs in the world. Too
often these organizations use their religious character as an excuse for not considering these issues seriously and not taking
on the hard planning and evaluation efforts that can help them
make God's love real in service more useful and more powerful
as both service and witness.

It is not uncommon to hear people in these organizations
say, for instance, "This is God's work, we cannot measure its
significance." In one sense that is true, but it is no excuse to
fail to evaluate whether one is achieving some practical and measurable goals for good stewardship in the work one is doing.
I have heard these kinds of comments less frequently in recent
years, however, and see greater recognition among staff and
boards of these groups that being faithful "stewards," in the re-

ligious sense, means concerning themselves with matters of efficiency. It means asking some businesslike questions about the work they do and the ways they do it.

However, there are very real risks when it is not understood that the work of religious organizations cannot be businesslike in many senses, and thus questions of effectiveness and efficiency need to be understood in different ways. Indeed, evidence suggests that when the primary focus of service groups is efficiency, it is easy for them to undermine the dignity of the recipients of their aid and convey a lack of concern for the whole person by the manner in which the service is provided. If that is the case for a religious group whose intentions are to demonstrate God's love for all people, then that organization must be considered *ineffective* — given its two-fold mission — regardless of how efficient it might be in service delivery.

This distinction in what constitutes effectiveness in this realm may be helpfully illuminated by an examination of the historic division and tension in the American philanthropic tradition between religiously based charitable endeavors and those emerging from and shaped by the tenets of "scientific" philanthropy.[6]

As noted before, the independent or voluntary sector as a whole has its roots in (indeed, I would argue, it owes its existence to) religion and religious groups. Many specific institutions — schools, hospitals, service agencies, and others — were begun by religious groups. In addition, scholars have made a strong case for the idea that the "social space" in our culture that allows these independent and voluntary organizations to exist was carved out by developments within the religious sphere, and then between the religious and political spheres (Adams, 1976; Stackhouse, 1990). They further argue that it was precisely because they claimed to be giving expression to values of ultimate importance that these religious groups succeeded in establishing this social space for their independent existence.

The essence of this argument is that religious groups — often sects and advocates of marginalized faiths rebelling against established and state religions — established the right of voluntary association for themselves, and that right came to be transferred to other charitable and values-expressive organizations.

"In the name of God, they claimed the right to be, to organize, to care for the neighbor, and to set forth their views publicly. . . . What religious communities fought for was eventually institutionalized: The right of people to form intentional religious associations outside established religion was more and more tolerated, acknowledged, celebrated, and subsequently expanded to include non-religious charitable and ethical organizations." Stackhouse continues, "These chapters in church history . . . are what has made modern, Western societies more or less safe not only for religious pluralism, but for the host of organizations and causes represented in the independent sector today" (1990, pp. 25–26).

This is the historical dynamic that was essential to allowing the establishment of an independent sector early in the formation of the American political economy. That sector was largely populated by religious and "quasi-religious" organizations who justified their existence in terms of these claims of their right to undertake certain kinds of work, often service work, as an expression of fundamental religious and moral convictions and commitments. Thus, for much of the first century and a half of this nation's existence, most of the social service provision and delivery was done by churches and other religious groups as an expression of their commitment to the biblical admonition to "love thy neighbor" (Lev. 19:18; Luke 10:27).

Beginning in the middle 1800s, however, we see the development of another approach to and rationale for undertaking such work. This approach, known as "scientific" philanthropy, dominated American philanthropic practice by the end of the century. It may have been given its most succinct and powerful statement in Andrew Carnegie's essay, "Wealth" (Carnegie, [1889] 1983). Commenting on the values undergirding this perspective, Peter Dobkin Hall (1990) notes, "Though employing a rhetoric of benevolence, 'scientific' philanthropy's desire to put charity on a businesslike basis was anything but humanitarian. [It was] far more concerned with efficiency and 'race progress' than with alleviating suffering" (pp. 46–47).

This movement and way of thinking about the work of charity and philanthropy was so pervasive and persuasive that even many of those working in religiously based organizations soon came to adopt these views. Other religious people saw the clash between the values of this perspective and the values of the Judeo-Christian tradition more clearly. They rejected scientific philanthropy, "believing that Christian charity involves far more than the economical provision of services. As, if not more, important was the creation of a community of feeling, a set of human bonds, which are in themselves perhaps far more valuable than the service" (Hall, 1990, p. 52).

In many ways one can see scientific philanthropy as embodying the values we might expect someone like Carnegie to bring from a business background. The point to recognize here is that, as this approach to philanthropy became dominant, it transformed the criteria by which people judged the effectiveness of charity and service and the nonprofit organizations that provided these. Concerns for fidelity to biblical ideals of compassion and alleviation of suffering (or even long-range improvement) in individuals' lives became secondary to considerations of efficiency in the use of resources for the purposes of promoting the "progress" of "the race" or "the nation" — as defined by an intellectual and industrial elite. There is a striking parallel between that situation and the one religious organizations face today.

For example, many of today's Christian service agencies began simply as expressions of the sense of "calling" of an individual or group of individuals to make visible the "good news" of the Gospel in feeding the hungry, caring for those in need, or helping those who are oppressed (Luke 4:12). As they have grown, many have acquired professional staff and boards dominated by successful business people who may be inclined to guide and evaluate their performance in businesslike terms. However, although it is important that these groups be well managed to be competent in service provision and efficient in their use of resources, that is not an adequate definition of "effectiveness" in their sphere of operations. Equally important, if much harder to measure, is the matter of whether they do what they do in such a way as to make visible, meaningful, and attractive to others the "good news" of the Christian faith. Any judgment of effectiveness for these groups must include a measure of how well they integrate providing a service with making a witness.

It is certainly true that preaching about the love of God to hungry people without attempting to alleviate their hunger is offering a hollow, if not hypocritical, witness to that love. It is also true that the ways in which one attempts to alleviate people's hunger — and the kind of relationship one establishes with them in the process — may or may not move toward affirming the dignity of those people as children of God or conveying to them the reality of God's love for them. Managers of religious service enterprises who fail to keep these issues in mind, who let the concerns for effectiveness as an economist would define it — meaning efficiency — overshadow the concern for making God's love visible in that work, will soon find themselves running enterprises that may offer service but offer little or no testimony to the principles and tenets that inspired that service.

If space allowed I could offer a number of illustrations of these points from my current studies of Christian service organizations.[7] I think immediately, for instance, about one that has adopted a personnel structure and policies that promote and reward competition within its staff as a way of promoting higher performance by individuals. In the economic sense it may be getting greater production out of individuals on staff — or it may not; I could not get a measure of this. What is certain, however, is that this organization's staff "burns out" and turns over fairly rapidly, and the sense of community in the organization has been eroded. They have thus gained a reputation as a place that does not provide a supportive, caring — which is to say Christian — working environment. Their intention "to glorify God" in their work (which is explicit in their mission statement) thus goes partly unfulfilled; and they are likely to have increasing difficulty getting people who are both highly skilled professionals and deeply committed Christians to work there, which will further diminish the witness of the organization.

The implications of such changes in organizational character, which stem from and lead to less fidelity to the fundamental religious (or moral or social) values these organizations are created to foster are broader than might first seem evident. They may have detrimental effects on more than the specific organization involved.

As the essentially religious character of an enterprise erodes when definitions (and evaluations) of effectiveness are incomplete or skewed in the ways I have mentioned, the organization is more likely to move into other patterns incongruous with its religious roots. For instance, fundraising techniques that run counter to religious tenets, but are acceptable in the secular world, are sometimes adopted. If these techniques discredit one such organization, through guilt by association other religious agencies may be unfairly discredited as well. When even a few religious groups "do business as business does business," and so are seen as more calculating and self-interested than compassionate and altruistic, the trustworthiness and eventually the effectiveness in philanthropic service of all religious groups may be threatened.[8]

In summary, then, it is crucial that those responsible for the management of religious organizations understand and keep in mind their unusual character as values-expressive agencies. It is essential that these people think about and evaluate their effectiveness in such a way as to include, always, attention to how the manner in which they operate makes a statement about the values their organizations represent.

If an organization does define its goals and think about effectiveness, what does this mean for specific management tasks? With this question in mind, let's look at three areas of particular prominence for nonprofit and religious organizations: fundraising, human resources, and planning.

How Religious Management Is Different

Fundraising

One of the obvious ways that most religious organizations are unlike for-profit groups, and clearly like other nonprofit groups, is that they are dependent on fundraising—in various forms—for their economic support. Here again, however, the distinctive character of religious organizations must be understood, or else wholesale and unreflective borrowing of techniques from secular nonprofits may lead religious groups into trouble. The potential for difficulties arises, as our examination of the larger context leads us to expect, in relation to the message both the manner of raising funds and the sources of those funds may create. In addition, the more distinctive the witness a religious group wishes to make, the more problems dependence on funds from people outside the tradition may cause.

In the first instance, as religious groups are supposed to be committed to nurturing altruistic values among their members and others, they will have to be very cautious about many of the trends and techniques of modern fundraising. Increasingly such techniques are built on marketing ideas that assume all human interactions are "exchanges" (in the economists' sense of the term), and only appeals made to people's self-interest are likely to be very successful.[9] But appeals to self-interest reinforce self-interested attitudes and behaviors, not altruistic ones; and at the core of many religious traditions — certainly of the Christian tradition — is the understanding that one of the essential fruits of faith is capacity and willingness to act in ways that put others first (Matt. 5:38–42).

Nurturing and deepening people's altruistic instincts is one of the essential works of religion. It is one of the clearest expectations most Americans hold of churches and religious organizations.[10] When religious groups try to raise funds by appealing to people's self-interest rather than appealing to the ideals and principles their faith community espouses, they undermine that work. In contrast, when religious groups appeal to potential donors by demonstrating how the finest ideals of their religious tradition are given practical expression in the groups' work, they may reinforce the donors' commitment to those ideals. Moreover, by publicly affirming those ideals in their manner of fundraising, the fundraising activities themselves extend the witness the groups are trying to make.

Virtually all of the great religious traditions of the world hold truth and love (*agape, caritas*), as central and primary values. Many of the approaches to fundraising management being recommended to nonprofit organizations today ignore or even run counter to these values. In fact, many contravene the idea of appeals on an altruistic basis. Religious organizations cannot in good faith employ such approaches, regardless of their short-term efficacy in bringing in money. Religious fundraising that does not focus on reflecting the expression of the primary values of its own spiritual tradition betrays the cause—or, at least, one of the causes—it is supposed to serve.[11]

In a related concern, the more distinctive the character of the witness the organization is trying to make, the more important it may be that its funds come from members of the religious tradition it represents. Religious groups, like other non-profits, need to concern themselves with "dirty money" and the message they send when they accept funds from morally suspect donors. Beyond this, though, there is another point, which is more subtle. When organizations solicit and accept funds from donors who do not share their values, because "that's where the money is," they run the risk of growing dependent on those donors. Then it is hard to avoid having those donors influence the organizations' missions and operations in ways that may be incongruous with the organizations' principles.

Again, my studies of Christian service organizations suggest this is a powerful dynamic. The example of two such organizations, which were started primarily to provide an avenue of service to the members of the small denominations that founded them, comes immediately to mind. For one, the small denomination it represents has been known—and favorably regarded—for a number of fairly distinctive aspects in its Christian witness and its approaches to service. These distinctive spiritual characteristics were originally very clearly reflected in the work of this organization, but (most would agree) have become less and less so in recent years. Indeed, this has been the cause of considerable friction between the organization and the denomination.

There are probably many reasons for this change. One has to wonder, though, if the fact that 70 to 80 percent of its funds now come from people who do not belong to the founding denomination is not a significant factor. This likelihood suggests itself even more powerfully when this first organization is compared with the second, one that is very similar in size, history, and character but has consciously chosen to remain financially dependent on the members of its denomination for resources. The service of the second group, which is one of the most highly respected of all Christian service agencies, continues to reflect the unique spiritual character and commitments of the denomination it represents.

Religious groups, like all others, need to remember that there is some truth to the old saying that "he who pays the piper calls the tune"; or in more modern language of organizational theorists, "resource dependency" can cause "goal displacement" and create real problems for the autonomy of any organization if it is dependent on the wrong sources. If this is true, and some forms of resource dependency are unavoidable, then religious organizations should consider carefully whom they wish to be dependent on.

Human Resources

In the matter of managing human resources, many religious organizations face a task with two different components — as do many other nonprofits. They must often concern themselves with the recruitment, retention, and supervision of volunteers as well as professional staff. Let us consider the case of volunteers first.

Many of the same observations that were just made about fundraising apply to recruitment. A great deal of literature is now available, much of it very useful, to help us understand how to get volunteers to give their time and energy. There is ample empirical evidence that "different types of individuals have different motives for becoming volunteers" (Anderson and Moore, 1978). We also now have very helpful analyses of the types of motivations (Clary and Snyder, forthcoming) that cause people to volunteer and are likely to keep them involved. So, when all is said and done, we know we have many choices about how to interest persons in contributing their time (as well as their money) to the work of these organizations, but these choices have important implications and may or may not be in keeping with the organizations' missions and the witness they wish to make.

Here too appeals can be made to self-interest or to more altruistic and idealistic motives, and the prior comments, that appeals to self-interest reinforce self-interested behavior and attitudes, apply with equal force. If one of the important functions of religion is to nurture a broader, more generous sense of human community, to nurture the roots of altruism, then appeals by religious organizations directed primarily to self-interest are inappropriate.

This is not to say we cannot learn from the kinds of studies just cited, and try to structure volunteers' jobs, and support systems provided for them, to make their service also an opportunity for learning and development and self-actualization in ways that they desire. Jesus said that in losing our lives (for others) we will find them (Mark 8:35). Religious values are not antithetical to self-fulfillment, only to self-centeredness. If religious organizations can appeal to volunteers first in terms of the volunteers' potential interests in service, rather than their aspirations for career advancement or self-aggrandizement, these organizations can make this expression of values clear. Leaders of religious groups need to consider the possibility that if some people are not moved by such appeals, they may not be the kind of people who should be serving in or on behalf of those groups.

This raises the crucial matter of selection of personnel, both staff and volunteers. Charles Perrow makes the point that the selection of people to participate in organizations according to their values and previous socialization may provide a valuable alternative to "bureaucratic" controls in shaping the life and work of the organization (Perrow, 1986, pp. 129–130). In other words: "If you really want to keep your organization focused on making a witness as well as providing a service, recruit and retain people who believe in the importance of that witness and the values that undergird it."

My recent examinations of Christian service agencies have powerfully affirmed the truth of this observation. Of those organizations I have studied, three of the four ranked by their peers as "most effective" make the depth and clarity of the applicants' faith commitments a primary consideration for selecting staff; whereas two organizations not so ranked by their peers, that I have examined for comparative purposes, pay little or no attention to the faith commitments of applicants.

A number of religious agencies, for example, those doing community and economic development, have become involved in fairly technical work. There is then a pressure and a temptation to hire or recruit people more for their technical expertise than their commitment to these organizations' larger mission and core values. But that undermines the religious, values-expressive character of the organization and dampens its witness. Several clear examples of this dynamic have appeared in my examination of such agencies. If the work undertaken is so specialized that it narrows the choices of personnel in such a way as to make this problem unavoidable, it should be a signal to the organization's leaders that the commitment to this particular kind of work needs to be reconsidered.

Finally, whoever is hired or recruited as a volunteer or for staff needs to be treated in accordance with the highest ideals for personal relationships in the religious tradition represented. This does not mean there cannot be supervision and oversight, the exercise of organizational authority, or implementation of essential elements of personnel management. Such things are essential if the organization takes seriously the obligation to help each volunteer or employee fully develop his or her God-given potential. It does mean, however, that all aspects of human resources management must be undertaken with a genuine, moral commitment to respecting the dignity of each participant. In religious organizations especially, that commitment would extend to a concern for the participants' personal and spiritual, as well as professional, development. Whether the managers of such organizations attend to these things will be reflected in others' experience of the organizations' effectiveness, as well as in the quality of the employees or volunteers and their work. A religious organization that treats its members or employees poorly will soon be seen as hypocritical, at best.

Planning

Only one facet of planning in religious organizations may be truly distinctive, but it is, I think, a crucial one: adjusting our view and use of planning to embrace a spiritual or theological insight that is central to many religious traditions.

In addressing this, we should begin by noting the changing attitude toward, or perspective on, planning in much progressive management literature. This literature (for example, Peters, 1987; Vaill, 1989) raises important questions about the limited usefulness of planning in the conventional sense in all kinds of organizations — business and governmental as well as nonprofit. Vaill (1989) says, "Planning is the specification of a sequence of events or action steps that will move a system from where it is at present to some intended new state, usually called the planning objective. . . . But the logic of a sequence of events depends on the surrounding context . . . [and] if the context changes, the sequence may no longer make sense" (p. 89). Vaill's point, which is similar to Peters's, is that in a world where dramatic and continuing change rather than stability is the norm, all forms of planning based on assumptions of linear logic will be of limited value. Indeed, Peters believes "strategic planning, as we conventionally conceive of it, has become irrelevant, or worse, damaging" (1987, p. 615).

In at least some religious organizations, however, managers need to focus their attention inward as well as outward to pick up the signals that change is needed. An undeniable reality of the spiritual life and the nature of individuals' and groups' "callings" is that they too may change.[12] The managers of religious organizations may undertake planning (as Vaill describes this), but they should do so with the recognition that the desirability of the "intended new state" they seek for their organization may have to be reevaluated — even as they progress toward it — not only because of changes in their environment but also because of changes in their organizations' callings.

Simply put, this is to say that approaches to planning — "strategic" or otherwise — based *solely* on logic will prove incompatible with organizations that aim to be spiritually guided in fulfilling their mission. Here again, I know religious organizations that refuse to engage in any sort of planning — including planning that could be very useful — because they see it as incompatible with being "open to the immediate guidance of the Spirit," and that claim just does not hold up to serious scrutiny. Still, once it has engaged in planning, the religious organization that fails to employ prayer as well as analysis, that does not look at its spiritual resources as well as its technical capacities and environment, in trying to determine its opportunities, goals, and strategies will not long be effective in offering the witness of service.

Questions Deserving More Attention

Although some research is being done in regard to nonprofit organizations and management on virtually all the subjects I have mentioned, almost none of it focuses on religious organizations. Indeed, it is amazing how often this portion of the independent sector is completely ignored in research on nonprofits, volunteers, and philanthropy. Persons involved in such research must recognize and include religion and religious organizations in their considerations.

My own current research focuses on Christian service organizations, and coming to those organizations with the perspective of a student of organizational theory and behavior, as well as theology, this has raised a whole new set of questions. For instance, I saw many problems in those organizations stemming from the fact that they have adopted organizational structures and models deriving from industry and government (largely bureaucratic), which are mostly incompatible with the biblical (Christian) vision of how people should live and work together, especially in expression of their faith.

That raises a number of interesting questions. What might a Christian, scriptural model of organization look like? How could such a model draw upon the idea and insights currently available in organizational theory? Would the creation of such a model require entirely new ways of thinking about organizations?

Other, more general questions also arise about religious organizations, including ones concerning the relationships between theological tenets and organizational structures or management practices. How, for instance, does appropriate management practice vary according to the type of beliefs or values a group wishes to promote? Are different types of religious groups, or different denominations, inclined to put together organizations in different ways? What are the patterns; how do these express those groups' values?

To answer all the above questions, it would be helpful to have a set of comprehensive studies of religious organizations that have been successful in integrating service and witness. What seem to be the key dynamics in their success? Do they operate differently from other organizations, and if so, how? I hope the fruits of my current work will offer a beginning for such studies.

Finally, in relation to the particular topics I have raised in this chapter, a number of areas emerge as important and intriguing.

Motivations for Giving and Volunteering

Although much of the work being done in this area now may be useful to managers of religious organizations, more research that focuses specifically on the ways in which religious commitments and experiences foster altruistic behavior, and on the differences in patterns and practices of giving among different religious groups, would be both interesting and helpful. Obviously, this has vital implications for fundraising management.

Human Resources Management

Much of what is often termed "progressive management" has included ways of looking at and treating employees that are more congruent with religious values of respect for individuals' dignity and potential, and less hierarchical patterns of organizational (community) structure. This has not generally come from a moral commitment, however, but largely because it serves to make organizations more economically productive. Recognizing that previous studies provide no conclusive findings on the relationships between worker satisfaction and productivity, it would still be extremely interesting to see some research on whether it makes a difference to workers whether management's good treatment of them is rooted in a genuine, ethical commitment to the workers' welfare or in economic self-interest. Along the same lines, it would be fascinating to see if persons working for altruistic organizations are, or perceive themselves as, better or more poorly treated than persons working in for-profit settings.

Planning

It would be immensely useful to have some research on how religious organizations use planning, and whether their approaches are shaped in some identifiable way by their theological tenets. If so, how? How do we see this played out in different religious bodies and traditions? What kinds of planning are really helpful in the context of religious management?

Conclusions

The general lack of attention to and understanding of the place and functions of religion and religious organizations in the nonprofit sector is most unfortunate. I am convinced that other nonprofits could learn a great deal from religious groups who are conscious of the distinctive values-expressive character of their organizations. It is also certain that many religious groups can learn something about effective management from secular nonprofits and for-profit businesses.

In this last respect, though, it is crucial that persons with a working understanding of both theological and managerial perspectives get involved in thinking about the management of religious organizations in their distinctive spiritual as well as practical witness-bearing missions.

For religious organizations, the proverbial "bottom line" is "faithfulness." The question is not just whether they provide a particular service and do so well; it is also whether they do so in such a way as to make the love of God and their own vision of faith clear and visible to others. Only when they do this can we surely say they are effective in their mission.

Notes

1. To question this is not to say that good management does not have much in common in both for-profit and nonprofit environments; but it is to wonder, when so little distinction is made, whether these authors are taking seriously the possibility of real differences between for-profit and nonprofit organizations and their environments.

2. The occasion for this dialogue was the Indiana University Center on Philanthropy's Symposium on Taking Fund Raising Seriously, held in June of 1990.

3. When Peters and Waterman (*In Search of Excellence,* 1982) emphasize that well-managed companies are "value driven," they are not talking about moral, ethical, or spiritual values. They are talking about what are essentially "production values," like quality or high performance. And all the values they recommend should drive a company (see p. 285) are *not* "ends" to be achieved but means to improving the economic performance of the company. This brings us back to O'Neill and Young's point (1988, p. 3) about how nonprofits differ — that is, the values that drive nonprofits are "primary concerns, they are moral, ethical, or spiritual values, and not merely instrumental to the achievement of other ends."

4. For one of the most useful brief discussions in print on questions of how to define and evaluate "organizational effectiveness," see Chapter Thirteen of W. Richard Scott's book, *Organizations: Rational, Natural, and Open Systems,* 1987.

5. In addition, they need to be concerned with their fidelity to other aspects of Jesus' teaching, such as his admonitions to be good stewards, if they are using funds in a wasteful manner that others have given for these purposes.

6. For an excellent discussion of the development and emergence of the scientific philanthropy movement and its relationship to religiously based charitable work, see two pieces by Peter Dobkin Hall: "A Bridge Founded Upon Justice and Built of Human Hearts: Reflections on Religion, Science, and the Development of American Philanthropy," in the *Working Papers for the Independent Sector Spring Research Forum, 1989* and "The History of Religious Philanthropy in America," in *Faith and Philanthropy in America,* Wuthnow and Hodgkinson (eds.), 1990.

7. The observations that follow about these agencies derive from a study of the management of Christian service organizations presently in progress. Over the last year I have conducted a survey where forty U.S.-based, Christian, international relief and development agencies were asked to

rank their peers regarding which were the "most effective" in *both* providing service *and* making a witness to their own faith tradition. I then spent most of a week at each of those organizations rated as "most effective," as well as at two that were not so rated, observing their operations, interviewing their staff, and examining records and documents to see how they were managed, especially in relation to the functions of planning, fundraising, personnel management, and work with their executive leadership and board.

8. Opinion polls have consistently shown religion to be the most trusted institutional element of American society, but this approval rating has been declining in recent years. It has obviously not been helped by the PTL and Swaggart scandals, which clearly have had a "guilt by association" effect on other honest religious groups. We would only note here that it was unclear how much these scandals affected the public's trust in other fundraising groups, but they certainly had a negative effect on other television ministries.

9. These assumptions, which are incongruous with much of the constellation of values and assumptions on which the philanthropic tradition is built, are as evident in the literature about "nonprofit marketing" as about marketing more generally. For an example, look at *Strategic Marketing for Nonprofit Organizations* (3rd ed.), Kotler and Andreasen, 1987.

10. For an interesting discussion of the role of the church in inculcating people with the values the public assumes are crucial to the maintenance of a democratic society, see Chapter Four of *The Restructuring of American Religion,* Robert Wuthnow, 1988.

11. For a much more complete treatment of the history of religious fundraising, and of these questions about the relationships of approaches to theological values and the witness religious groups wish to make, see my earlier work "Giving, Getting, Grace, and Greed: An Historical and Moral Analysis of Religious Fund Raising," in *Taking Fund Raising Seriously,* 1991.

12. It is probably important to note here my own affiliation with a religious community that stresses the importance of "continuing revelation." Such traditions, which encompass much of the Judeo-Christian tradition, hold that not all the truth that God has to teach us has been revealed in Scripture or in the life and teachings of a Messiah, Prophets, of holy men and women who came before. Rather, they assume that much of what we need to learn about what God hopes for the world and what we must do to bring those hopes to fruition are revealed to us in the unfolding of life around us. These assumptions clearly undergird the perspective offered here.

References

Adams, J. L. *Voluntary Associations: Socio-Cultural Analysis and Theological Interpretation*. Chicago: Exploration Press, 1976.

Anderson, J. C., and Moore, L. "The Motivation to Volunteer." *Journal of Voluntary Action Research*, 1978, *7*, 120–129.

Borst, D., and Montana, P. J. *Managing Nonprofit Organizations*. New York: AMACOM, 1977.

Carnegie, A. "The Gospel of Wealth." In B. O'Connell (ed.), *America's Voluntary Spirit*. New York: Foundation Center, 1983. (Originally published 1889.)

Clary, E. G., and Snyder, M. "A Functional Analysis of Volunteerism." In M. Clark (ed.), *Review of Personality and Social Psychology*. Newbury Park, Calif.: Sage, forthcoming.

Drucker, P. F. *The Practice of Management*. New York: HarperCollins, 1954.

Drucker, P. F. "Profiting from the Nonprofits." *Business Week*, Mar. 26, 1990a, pp. 66–70.

Drucker, P. F. *Managing the Nonprofit Organization*. New York: HarperCollins, 1990b.

Hall, P. D. "A Bridge Founded upon Justice and Built of Human Hearts: Reflections on Religion, Science, and the Development of American Philanthropy." *Working Papers for the Independent Sector Spring Research Forum, 1989,* INDEPENDENT SECTOR, 1989.

Hall, P. D. "The History of Religious Philanthropy in America." In R. Wuthnow, V. A. Hodgkinson, and Associates, *Faith and Philanthropy in America: Exploring the Role of Religion in America's Nonprofit Sector.* San Francisco: Jossey-Bass, 1990.

Hay, R. D. *Strategic Management for Nonprofit Organizations.* New York: Quorum Books, 1990.

The Holy Bible (New International Version). Grand Rapids, Mich.: Zondervan, 1979.

Jeavons, T. H. "Giving, Getting, Grace and Greed: An Historical and Moral Analysis of Religious Fund Raising." In D. Burlingame and L. Hulse (eds.), *Taking Fund Raising Seriously.* San Francisco: Jossey-Bass, 1991.

Kotler, P., and Andreasen, A. *Strategic Marketing for Nonprofit Organizations.* (3rd ed.) Englewood Cliffs, N.J.: Prentice-Hall, 1987.

O'Neill, M., and Young, D. (eds.). *Educating Managers of Nonprofit Organizations.* New York: Praeger, 1988.

Payton, R. "Philanthropic Virtue, Philanthropic Virtue." Unpublished paper, Indiana University Center on Philanthropy, 1990.

Perrow, C. *Complex Organizations: A Critical Essay.* (3rd ed.) New York: Random House, 1986.

Peters, T. J. *Thriving on Chaos.* New York: HarperCollins, 1987.

Peters, T. J., and Waterman, R. *In Search of Excellence.* New York: Warner Books, 1982.

Schulman, K., and Setterberg, F. *Beyond Profit.* New York: HarperCollins, 1985.

Scott, W. R. *Organizations: Rational, Natural, and Open Systems.* Englewood Cliffs, N.J.: Prentice-Hall, 1987.

Stackhouse, M. L. "Religion and the Social Space for Voluntary Institutions." In R. Wuthnow, V. A. Hodgkinson, and Associates, *Faith and Philanthropy in America: Exploring the Role of Religion in America's Nonprofit Sector.* San Francisco: Jossey-Bass, 1990.

Vaill, P. B. *Managing as a Performing Art: New Ideas for a World of Chaotic Change.* San Francisco: Jossey-Bass, 1989.

Wuthnow, R. *The Restructuring of American Religion.* Princeton, N.J.: Princeton University Press, 1989.

Zaltman, G. (ed.). *Management Principles for Nonprofit Agencies and Organizations.* New York: AMACOM, 1979.

4.

Management Information Systems in Cultural Institutions

Dov Te'eni
Nike F. Speltz

As reliance on computers and management information systems has increased throughout the nonprofit sector, museums, performing arts organizations, galleries, and other cultural institutions have increased their use of computer-based, automated systems in their operations. Even a small historical society run by volunteers uses a personal computer to catalogue its collection and generate financial information, while a large performing arts complex depends on an extensive computer system for box office management, scheduling information, and development lists. In this context, it becomes important to ask the following questions: How effectively do cultural organizations use computer equipment and information systems? What are the limitations to effective use of information systems by nonprofit cultural organizations? Are these limitations functional, systemic, or environmental, and how might they be overcome? To date, these issues have largely been ignored by researchers or examined in a limited fashion.

This chapter examines the use and management of information systems in ten nonprofit cultural organizations in

Cleveland, Ohio. Working with these organizations, we asked how information is created and consumed, for what purpose it is collected, in what functional areas it is employed, and how useful the information has been to the overall management of the organization. We looked at how information systems are developed, operated, and managed within the organization and what resources are allocated to their use and management.

Previous research on these topics is limited. The studies that have been done on information systems (IS) in cultural institutions suggest that, in general, cultural institutions do a poor job of using and managing information technology (Doty, 1990; Pick, 1990a, 1990b), especially when compared to profit-seeking organizations. The main points of these studies are summarized here.

- Expenditure on IS in museums (including pay) is 1.5 percent of annual budget, which is lower than in profit seeking organizations (PSO).
- Museums are generally micro based, not networked.
- Primary applications are accounting and finance, contributions, collections, and word processing. Some additional educational applications exist.
- Two-thirds of the applications are purchased; some are modified in house; there is very little in-house programming.
- Only 50 percent have full-time IS staff, who are paid 9 percent less than in PSO and in education.
- Relative to PSO, there is no formal, structured planning around information systems.
- Museums had some applications, such as research, educational use, and exhibition design, devoted to the artistic functions.

In a paper that examines previous studies on collection management at museums, Doty (1990) offers some insights into why museums fail to use computers effectively. He describes several characteristics of the museum environment that directly affect IS use and management. Museums are often divided by department factionalism, making cooperation around new projects such as IS design or implementation difficult. They may also be conservative in their approach to change and new technology. These barriers may be unwittingly reinforced by an apparent communication gap between the museum's artistic, cultural, or scholarly staff and the IS managers and technicians, whether they are on-staff or brought in from the outside as consultants. Moreover, they may be compounded by philosophical objections to automation expressed by museum staff trained in a humanistic or esthetic tradition. Furthermore, the lack of general long-range or strategic planning in many museums seriously inhibits the effective use of IS systems. Finally, the ambiguous, inconsistent, and sometimes conflicting terminology for describing artifacts in many museums creates logistical problems for even basic inventory functions. The complexity of documenting each object and its individual history for multiple purposes in changing situations makes an apparently straightforward task much more complicated.

In this chapter, we follow Doty's explanation of the general state of IS computerization for museum collections, but we take a more systematic view of the role of information in organizations and look at other cultural institutions. Specifically, we examine issues that can be tracked to the micro level of creating and using information, as well as more general issues of technology management.

Our study begins by describing the characteristics of ten organizations in Cleveland and follows by examining these characteristics from two perspectives: the perspective of the organization's functional areas and the perspective of the data objects. Put together, the two form a new framework for looking at the organization's use of IS, which we then use to understand how the more general characteristics of cultural organizations affect IS use and management. Finally, we point to further directions for studying the impact of certain characteristics of cultural institutions on their use of IS. Our findings suggest that cultural institutions rarely make effective use of IS when there are high marginal costs for gathering data, even though marginal benefits may be high and their long-term impact significant.

Major Findings

During the summer of 1990, a team of three researchers analyzed the use and management of IS in ten local organizations in Cleveland, Ohio. The ten organizations represent a range of size (as indicated by annual budget and number of employees) and type (they include museums and performing arts). Both museums and performing arts ranged from small local organizations to large, internationally renowned institutions. Data sources included interviews with management, IS personnel and users, reviews of publications about the organizations, and IS documentation such as sample inputs/outputs and file descriptions.

In a general way, the organizations had similar organizational charts, as shown in Figure 4.1. The diagrams portray a typical division as two subsystems: the artistic and the administrative. There are major differences between performing arts

Figure 4.1. Organizational Structures of Performing Arts Institutions and Museums.

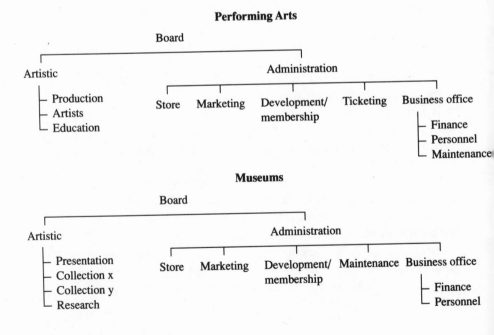

and museums in the organization of the artistic function, but there are also some differences in the organization of the administrative function, particularly with regard to admissions (ticketing).

Table 4.1 presents a profile of each organization type, as well as a list of the application areas for IS.

In nonprofit cultural institutions, it is usually believed that the administrative function exists to support the artistic, esthetic, or education mission and that IS is part of this administrative support to the larger mission. Thus the major applications of IS cluster around the administrative departments, such as box office, accounting, or development, and few, if any, attempts are made to use IS functionally in the artistic areas, such as casting, rehearsal scheduling, preservation, or display of objects. Our study of organizations in Cleveland confirmed this pattern.

Within the administrative function, the applications of IS were operational rather than strategic. Computerized IS replaced previously manual operations, such as ticketing and bookkeeping, that tend to be highly structured and performed by clerical staff. We did not find IS used effectively to support decision-making processes such as setting ticket prices, evaluating purchases, or planning logistics.

In the artistic area, we found an attempt to maintain information on performances, such as lists of musicians and their instruments, that might help in planning future performances. In one performing arts organization, most of the artistic managers had newly acquired stand-alone computers, which were used primarily for word processing, including structured reports about production and performances. Yet there was generally little computerized data processing. Moreover, there was no attempt to use information technology as part of the artistic performance or display, such as computerized displays positioned next to original objects, on-line catalogues of collections, or computer-based multimedia presentations. In fact, none of the institutions used information technology that interacted directly with their audiences.

More important from a management point of view, hardly any of the top managers viewed IS as a strategic tool in the sense

Table 4.1. Organizations.

Number of employees	125	250	175	80	70	75	80	25	10	10
Age of firm (years)	15	75	70	75	15	75	74	13	5	22
Total expenses ($ million)	9.0	18.0	4.5	2.5	5.0	5.5	21.0	2.8	.5	.6
EDP expenses Annual ($ thousand)	20	100	20	.5	65	35	220	10	0.5	0.4
Investment	50–75	100–150	50–75	125	150	250	350–400	25–50	10–15	26
Application areas	financial accounting fundraising payroll	desktop publishing financial accounting fundraising LIS	collections management desktop publishing exhibit display financial accounting fundraising LIS	financial accounting fundraising LIS	box office fundraising	box office financial accounting	box office fundraising	financial accounting fundraising	financial accounting fundraising visitor schools	members financial accounting
Years of computer use	0.5	5	8	5	8	7	4	4	3	3
Decentralized/ centralized EDP	decentralized	decentralized	decentralized	decentralized	centralized	centralized	centralized	decentralized	decentralized	decentralized

that an airline may view its computerized reservation system as a strategic weapon. One manager did articulate the strategic value of IS in providing more information about patrons, information that could be used to better serve audience members in choosing performances and to raise contributed income more effectively. But in general, managers of cultural institutions, both large and small, view IS as an operational tool rather than a strategic resource.

Related to the lack of strategic use of IS is the issue of systems integration. In integrated systems, data are automatically transferred from one application to another, consolidated from several applications, or otherwise used effectively across functions and management areas. Integration can occur vertically, between organizational levels of an operation such as middle management and top management, or horizontally, across the organization's functional areas.

Vertical integration is usually found in medium to large hierarchical organizations in which there are formal procedures for internal reporting that form a basis for computerized data integration. This integration is usually effected by automatically constructing managerial IS that rely on transactions occurring at the operational level. In our study of arts organizations, we found very little vertical integration, although their centralized IS could easily provide vertical reporting. In spite of this possibility, only one performing arts organization received weekly computer-generated reports from the administrative subsystems.

Horizontal integration is usually found when middle management wants to use IS to help make decisions that rely on information from different functional areas, such as making pricing decisions based on production and marketing data. We found no horizontal integration in the ten organizations.

In addition to the vertical and horizontal integration that is now commonplace in the business world, integration of IS across business companies is becoming increasingly common. With this kind of integration, organizations can gain competitive advantages by facilitating automatic transactions between the partners, as in automatic ordering from suppliers. We did not find any such integration in cultural institutions, although there are situations where such integration could be beneficial.

The organization of the IS function in nonprofit cultural institutions varied. Some had centralized computing facilities, using mid-range computers, while some were completely decentralized, using stand-alone desktop PCs. A particular problem in the small organizations was the lack of standardized equipment. In some instances, the organization had several types of stand-alone equipment that could be linked together only through a local area network hooking up several types of basically incompatible equipment. The lack of uniform equipment stems from low initial expenditures and a tendency to rely on donations or other methods of acquiring equipment that appear to reduce the investment in hardware. However, the lack of standard and up-to-date equipment not only created a barrier to systems integration but also led to serious maintenance problems and ultimately higher costs.

Similar problems exist in the choice and use of software. Any development of IS in the cultural organizations was usually done with application generators (fourth-generation languages), such as Lotus and dBase in the decentralized systems. In the larger centralized organizations, applications were tailored (particularly report generation) to specific needs, using generic software. In a number of instances, these homemade or off-the-shelf solutions were inadequate, increasing staff dissatisfaction with IS and reinforcing personal skepticism about the use of technology in cultural organizations.

The impact of staff attitude is a topic that arose forcefully in our discussions with the IS personnel in the cultural institutions, who find it difficult to communicate with artistic managers about IS issues. IS personnel are typically "self-made" IS experts with an interest or background in the arts rather than graduates of professional schools or academically trained IS managers, and they repeatedly describe their difficulties in developing IS. Communication with both superiors and peers seems to break down on matters such as formal analysis of technology-related opportunities and in long-range planning for IS needs. The IS personnel attribute these difficulties to different orientations and thinking styles, but the factors that affect this problem may be more complex than these differences.

Significantly, none of the organizations studied had a long-range plan showing how IS should be developed or how it should relate to the business plan over a period of time. The lack of such planning, and the ensuing tendency to build IS hardware and software in an ad hoc manner, reinforce our earlier point about the absence of IS as an element in top management's strategic thinking.

Analysis of Findings

This section develops a biperspective framework for analyzing our findings. We characterize the use of information by looking at information processing from two viewpoints: the systems orientation and the data object orientation. The systems orientation follows directly from the functional organization of work, but it makes explicit the requirement that a system has one or more measures of performance and that its components coproduce the system's measure of performance. The object orientation follows a more concrete way of thinking about information, and yet it is a dramatic departure from the traditional way of analyzing cultural institutions.

Figure 4.1, which depicts a characteristic organizational chart in the performing arts and in a museum is also a good approximation of the systemic description of the organization. Both systems are partitioned into two subsystems: the artistic and the administrative. Each subsystem can be further divided into a lower level of subsystems. The number of personnel in these systems varies, but most are small, with no more than one or two dozen employees. What is most striking about this division is the different terminology, in particular the different measures of success, that are used in the two subsystems.

In talking about horizontal integration, we mentioned the lack of systems integration between departments. As there is hardly any structured computerization of the artistic functions in cultural organizations (beyond text files), we could not expect systems integration between artistic and administrative functions. Even where there are islands of computerization in the artistic function, as in the curatorial department of a museum or the casting unit of a theater, there appears to be low formal interdependence between those areas and the administrative function. Certainly, when compared to interdepartmental communication in a profit-seeking organization, there is relatively little coordination or communication to warrant such a system.

With regard to systems integration between subsystems within the administrative function, the low level of integration seems to be, at least partly, caused by the available technology. Some packages developed for cultural organizations support several functions, such as marketing and fundraising, and provide integration mainly through data sharing. In institutions where each administrative subsystem is supported with different commercial packages, there was practically no attempt to integrate them. While the issue of technology restraints will be discussed later, it should be noted that managers of cultural organizations did not even mention this lack of integration as a major problem. Any needed integration was done manually, which was possible because management generally concentrated on analyzing relatively few objects — performances or exhibitions — that would require detailed data from multiple subsystems.

Looking at cultural institutions from a data object perspective describes how data are created, maintained, and used. The broad categories discussed are the major data objects with which computer and data users in cultural institutions interact. Typically these areas are patron or audience data, exhibits, and performances. For now, the description excludes other objects such as personnel or financial information. This description helps underscore the differences among types of cultural organizations, the role of box office applications, and some of our macro-level interpretations. Note, however, that this approach neglects general packages such as word processors that are not associated with specific data objects but may have an impact on the IS workload.

Figure 4.2 depicts two major objects for each type of organization. Museums have patrons and exhibits; performing arts have patrons and performances. The detailed descriptions are given below. Overall, Figure 4.2 shows similar structures between organizational type. Patrons can be classified into donors and visitors, although for museums, only members are designated.

Figure 4.2. Major Objects in Cultural Organizations.

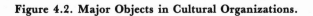

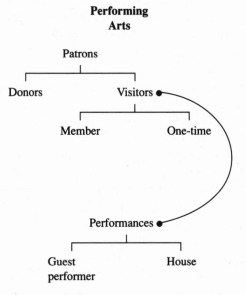

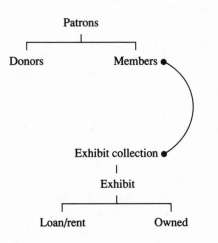

Exhibits and performances represent the major "product" of museums and performing arts. In museums it is meaningful to represent the individual exhibits as well as collections of exhibits, which can be transitory or permanent, and in the performing arts it is meaningful to talk of performances, which are always transitory in nature. Figure 4.2 also shows some links between objects, as detailed below.

In performing arts, the bulk of data on audience, as opposed to donors, are produced through the box office application and are then used for communicating with individual audience members to sell other performances or track payment. These data are important for associating audience attendance with specific performances, information that is later used to target marketing efforts and to plan future performance seasons.

In a process that is usually a separate function and often undertaken with completely different technology, the names and history of donors, individual patrons who have contributed or may be willing to contribute funds to the organization beyond the cost of tickets, are created and maintained within the organization's development department. The creation of donor lists and history is an internally driven process, with data files designed to be used in various membership or fundraising campaigns and activities. Donor data are not usually available to other departments in an organization, although data on visitors and audiences are often used to identify possible donors, thus forming a link between the two "siblings" under patrons. In most organizations, patron data summarized in various forms (box office activity, contributed income status) for reports to top management assist the activities and performances of the finance, marketing, and development departments. This type of reporting is usually the extent of vertical integration in cultural organizations.

As previously noted, museums and performing arts organizations are similar in the structure and use of their data objects but differ substantially in the objects that are created and maintained. Although many museums now have an admissions charge, there is usually no box office for advance sales and so visitors' names are not captured electronically when they purchase admission tickets. Membership and donor lists are created at the initiative of development personnel, either behind the scenes or voluntarily at the entrance when visitors are asked to sign a guest book. Donor data for museums are further complicated by the fact that contributions may take the form of objects and artifacts for the museum collection, in which case there can also be a link between donor data and collection or exhibit information.

In performing arts organizations, performances of opera, ballet, orchestral music, or theater may be house performances produced by the organization or guest performances using local facilities. Data are collected on production factors (hours spent, special problems, equipment used) and actual shows (seats sold, real timing of scenes) used by the artistic personnel before and during the run of a performance. In the organizations we interviewed, this information was not generally computerized or if it was, it was stored as text in free form, making it practically impossible to manipulate automatically.

The link between performance and patron is usually made in the form of an indication of which performance or series of performances a patron has selected, made at the box office at the time of ticket purchase. No performing arts organization reported storing information on visitors' evaluations after a performance, which would require a dedicated mechanism for data input.

The main function of IS in the artistic or curatorial area of most museums is to maintain records on collections and exhibits, which have a history that must be recorded as well as other information, such as conservation actions, market value, and descriptive information. Loaned and rented exhibits have contracts with rental terms and information on the physical condition of each object, as well as insurance, shipping, and storage information. Data on museum objects must fully document each individual item as well as the objects' existence in an exhibit or permanent collection. Here, too, information is kept as free-form text on a computer but not usually integrated into more advanced record-keeping or decision-making systems.

As with performing arts organizations, the other main use of computers in museums is to collect and maintain donor information, a function that is also usually performed with free-standing equipment and generic software. There was no report

of visitors' evaluation collected on the computer, although attendance figures for particular time periods and events are gathered
at most museums.

Conclusions

This chapter developed a biperspective framework for defining
informational needs of cultural institutions and applied this
framework to the analysis of findings from ten local institutions.
The most important observation from our analysis using the
object orientation is that where data are easily available to nonprofit cultural organizations they are used effectively. That is,
tasks like documentation of collections, ticket and subscription
sales, development and membership lists, and in-house financial and activity reporting have been converted to computer-
based systems with a reasonable degree of success in most organizations. In our study, we could not find instances of successful IS that required the organization to conceive a long-range
plan and create a dedicated mechanism for gathering data before using them. Furthermore, preliminary inquiries suggest that
the ten organizations studied in Cleveland are not exceptional
in this way but truly represent the normal range of cultural institutions across the country.

Although a number of factors may account for this limited
use of IS and computer technology in nonprofit cultural institutions, two stand out in our study. The first is a consistent lack
of strategic or long-range planning around IS and technology,
whether as part of comprehensive long-range planning or as a
distinct area of management. As has been noted, IS are never
really viewed as more than an add-on tool for basic operations
and a distant resource for accomplishing the artistic mission of
the institution. The second, related factor is the inability of even
the largest cultural institutions to commit a substantial amount
of funding or staff time to the development of IS either on an
annual or long-range basis. As long as the IS functions at these
institutions are underfunded and understaffed, their potential
will never be understood or explored.

In a similar way, the state of the industry, both hardware
and software, has had an impact on the use of IS in cultural

institutions. Software products are available to museums and performing arts organizations, but they have tended to be expensive and cumbersome. Although the products in some instances are becoming more highly developed, the limited demand within an already small market has made development a risky business for most software companies. Clearly, cultural organizations do not have the ability to create their own systems and so must rely on what have been, from their point of view, unreliable and costly suppliers. Although this situation is slowly changing, product diffusion probably will continue to be haphazard and frustrating to both consumer and supplier. Furthermore, the market has been ineffective in addressing the specific needs of cultural organizations, particularly in collections management and other areas where ambiguous terminology and other variables present logistical problems.

Using the systems perspective, the most striking finding is the lack of horizontal integration; here the difficulty is integrating measures of performance in the artistic and administrative subsystems. In the smaller institutions, such efforts are also hampered by the incompatible technology (Rainey, Backoff, and Levine, 1976; Fottler, 1981). Interestingly, the object perspective complemented this observation by uncovering some of the potential links between objects that traditionally fall into separate subsystems and emphasizing the need for integration. The lack of vertical integration is due primarily to the small size and somewhat informal nature of the management structure (Solomon, 1986) and may also explain why we did not find decision support systems beyond rather simplistic use of spreadsheets.

Implications for the Future

Our purpose is to use the biperspective framework as a foundation for studying and developing IS for cultural institutions. This foundation can be used on a practical level to determine the requirements of information technology and on an academic level to direct future research. There are many topics for further exploration, but perhaps the most significant for academically based researchers relate to the overarching questions of IS and strategic planning. IS management in organizations is faced with chronically short resources that inhibit long-term planning for IS and intensify the costs of creating and using new information. Research that is directed at understanding the variables for success or failure, that anticipates likely problems and suggests ways of addressing them, and that creates a vision of information technology would be important in overcoming these obstacles.

In our effort to look at IS use in cultural institutions from two dimensions, we have undoubtedly created simplifications and glossed over important questions. For example, our analysis defines informational needs without being specific about future technology, a critical area that must be addressed if there is to be any real progress in the management of IS by cultural organizations. Furthermore, our study focuses on the micro level as exemplified by ten organizations, but a macro-level analysis that examines industrywide needs is an obvious next step. Finally, it is critically important to continue working with the managers and staff of the cultural institutions themselves, as we have begun to do in Cleveland, to understand more completely the limitations and opportunities within the particular environment of museum, theater, or cultural center that will shape the use of information systems and technology.

References

Doty, P. "Automating the Documentation of Museum Collection." *Museum Management and Curatorship,* 1990, *9,* 73–83.

Fottler, M. "Is Management Really Generic?" *Academy of Management Review,* 1981, *6*(1), 1–12.

Pick, J. "The 1989 National Art Museum Computer Survey." *Spectra,* 1990a, *17*(2), 1–7.

Pick, J. "Computer Staffing, Planning and Control in Art Museums: Findings from a National Survey." *Archives and Museums Informatics,* Summer 1990b, *4*(2), 1–14.

Rainey, H., Backoff, R., and Levine, C. "Comparing Public and Private Organizations." *Developments in Research,* 1976, Mar.-Apr.

Solomon, E. "Private and Public Sector Managers: An Empirical Investigation of Job Characteristics and Organizational Climate." *Journal of Applied Psychology,* 1986, *71*(2), 247–259.

5.

Evaluating Nonprofit Effectiveness: Overcoming the Barriers

Martha E. Taylor
Russy D. Sumariwalla

It is becoming increasingly clear that much of our investment in such areas as education, health, poverty, jobs, housing, urban development, transportation and the like is not returning adequate dividends in terms of results. Without for a moment lessening our commitment to provide for these pressing human needs, one of Congress' major, though oft-delayed, challenges must be to reassess our multitude of social programs, concentrate (indeed, expand) resources on programs that work where the needs are greatest, and reduce or eliminate the remainder. We no longer have the time nor the money to fritter away on nonessentials which won't produce the needed visible impact on problems.

       —Florence P. Dwyer

Two decades after it was made, Representative Dwyer's plea takes on an even greater sense of urgency. Today there is a new interest in finding ways to demonstrate results of programs designed to enhance the human condition. The purpose of this chapter is not to present a treatise on evaluation. Rather, it begins by providing a summary of existing knowledge of evaluation in the nonprofit sector and then goes on to present findings and recommendations from a survey of nonprofit managers.

Background

The quest for effectiveness-assessment approaches can be traced back to antiquity. Egon G. Guba and Yvonna S. Lincoln (1981) take us back to 2200 B.C. when the emperor of China is said to have instituted proficiency requirements for his public officials. The subject of evaluation — effectiveness assessment, success measurement — has occupied the attention of lawmakers, funders, business leaders, and social thinkers during most of this century, but more intensely during the last three decades. Library shelves are full of material on evaluation. At the most basic level, people want to know if their "investment" has produced results or benefits. What good did it do? What difference did it make?

At United Way of America, the quest for evaluation tools can be traced back to the early 1970s, when the "House of Accountability" was launched. In fact, effectiveness-assessment tools were widely advertised as the "roof" on "the House," implying the completion of a series of tools for the use of local United Ways and other human service organizations. Other elements of the "House of Accountability" consisted of service identification, definition, and classification; accounting and budgeting guides; campaign and allocation analyses; and needs assessment.

Early efforts at United Way of America to develop effectiveness-assessment tools focused primarily on measuring efficiency rather than effectiveness. Agency evaluation meant an assessment of the agency's operations, its managerial performance, and its input measures as opposed to outcome measures. In the United Way of America Services Identification System (UWASIS)

(1976), each of the 587 program definitions identified and suggested "program products." This UWASIS taxonomy described programs within the framework of fundamental goals in the field of human services. But in most cases the products were input or output measures: number of days of day care provided, number of children adopted, number of hours of counseling provided, and so on.

A number of local United Ways developed good manuals for agency evaluation. Several major national organizations also distributed such manuals to their affiliates. Some of these were called Self-Assessment Guides. But again, these manuals evaluated agency operations and not program effectiveness, which remained elusive to most. In the absence of practical, cost-effective program evaluation tools, greater reliance was placed on fiscal accountability and managerial effectiveness.

Now, however, there seems to be a resurgence of interest in program evaluation—locally, nationally, and even internationally. Increasing competition for tax as well as contributed dollars and scarce resources prompt donors and funders to ask once again: What good did the donation produce? What difference did the foundation grant or United Way allocation make in the lives of those affected by the service funded? The government spends billions of dollars annually on social programs to help individuals and families. Particularly in the political arena, therefore, there is a great urgency and frustration with regard to evaluating these programs' success (or lack of success). Taxpayers have a right to know whether their taxes are helping to improve the condition of the neediest among us.

This chapter is a modest effort, first, at learning what exists, and next, at suggesting some directions. The remainder covers two areas: the next section presents a brief discussion of evaluation concepts; the remaining sections present a summary of findings based on what we learned from our survey.

What Is Evaluation?

"We defined the concept of evaluation as: an activity to arrive systemically at objective, optimal evidence with regard to the degree to which a given action (or inaction) has or has not achieved its predefined (or hypothesized) objectives (or consequences), as also, to reach conclusions as to the nature and extent of the unintended consequences which may have resulted from such action" (United Way of America, 1972). In short, evaluation means finding out whether a given effort has or has not produced the results it was supposed to, and how well or how badly.

Specific uses of program evaluation include

- Selection of programs for funding among competing programs
- Continued funding of existing programs
- Defunding of obsolete or ineffective programs
- Improvement of program practices and procedures and increased effectiveness
- Replication of successful programs elsewhere
- Testing and validating of program approach and theory

A number of reasons come to mind when one questions why so many evaluation efforts have failed or why there is reluctance to conduct or commission program evaluation in the first place.

Particularly with respect to human service programs, a major obstacle to evaluation is what is to be evaluated: human behavior and changes in this behavior. The number and type of variables add to the complexity of assessment, as controlling for variables can pose a major problem. This arena is less susceptible to purely scientific or quantitative inquiry. A second obstacle is the sensitive issue of confidentiality, which has often been held up to kill evaluation efforts before they can even get started. A third obstacle deals with the fact that many effects of human service programs take a long time to show results; that is, only a longitudinal study can ascertain conclusively whether the effort was successful or a waste. A fourth issue deals with the question of agency capacity. Regardless of funder demands, a program evaluation cannot be conducted without the full cooperation and participation of the service provider. Finally, there is the issue of cost: program evaluation is expensive, and a high-quality effort is even more expensive. Only a few well-endowed groups can afford the cost of longitudinal evaluation studies. These and other obstacles make program evaluation efforts difficult at best.

Evaluation literature is replete with types, models, and various approaches. It is not within the scope of this chapter to discuss them even briefly. Suffice it to note that approaches grounded in hard sciences and complex quantitative formulations have not proved successful in evaluating human health and development endeavors. We lean toward a less formal approach. Characterized in literature as "responsive evaluation," which focuses on the interests and concerns of stakeholders, it produces information that audiences want and need for direct application and decision making. In a sense this approach incorporates elements of various evaluation models. The responsive evaluation approach trades off some measurement precision in order to increase the usefulness of the findings to persons in and around the program. It relates to different value perspectives present in reporting the success and failure of the program. R. E. Stake (1979), the originator of the responsive evaluation model, describes it as follows.

> To do a responsive evaluation, the evaluator conceives of a plan of observations and negotiations. He arranges for various persons to observe the program, and with their help prepares brief narratives, portrayals, product displays, graphs, etc. He finds out what is of value to his audiences, and gathers expressions of worth from various individuals whose points of view differ. Of course, he checks the quality of his records: he gets program personnel to react to the accuracy of his portrayals; authority figures to react to the importance of various findings; and audience members to react to the relevance of his findings. He does much of this informally—iterating and keeping a record of action and reaction. He chooses media accessible to his audiences to in-

crease the likelihood and fidelity of communication.
He might prepare a final written report, he might
not—depending on what he and his clients have
agreed upon [p. 14].

A basic question is: How does one arrive at truth? Episte-
mologists from around the world have failed to resolve this question. A number of paradigms are discussed in the literature;
the two most widely used are scientific and naturalistic. Traditionally, sciences apply the scientific method, and the naturalistic
paradigm is more useful and applicable to social-behavioral
investigations.

E. R. House (1976, p. 37) describes naturalistic evaluation methodology as "that evaluation which attempts to arrive
at naturalistic generalizations [sic] on the part of the audience;
which is aimed at nontechnical audiences like teachers or the
public at large; which uses ordinary language; which is based
on informal everyday reasoning; and which makes extensive
use of arguments which attempt to establish the structure of
reality."

Sometimes less rigorous evaluation approaches may yield
equally satisfactory results as the more scientific ones. In some
instances, we must satisfy ourselves with input measures as sur-
rogates for output and even outcome measures.

Finally, client satisfaction (or satisfaction of those related
to the client, such as the client's family, friends, neighbors, and
so on) can be a key indicator of program effectiveness in the
absence of other hard evidence or as a supplement to other evidence of program effects.

Evaluation of human health and development efforts is
a difficult and costly undertaking. Past experience indicates
the need for caution, patience, and low expectations. However, the potential risk of failure should not deter us from
launching an essential and worthwhile effort. In the following
sections, we describe what we learned about the current status
of program evaluation as practiced by major national philanthropic organizations.

Survey Methodology

Description of the Sample and Respondents

In November of 1990 surveys regarding activities in evaluation were sent to 186 organizations (see Exhibit 5.1). This purposive sample was drawn by United Way of America staff. Organizations in the sample were intentionally selected for their representation of a larger group of nonprofit organizations, either as a funder or as the national representative of a group of organizations (such as Girl Scouts of the U.S.A.). The sample consisted of the following organizations:

25 largest foundations, according to grant amount
25 largest community foundations, according to grant amount
25 largest United Ways, according to amount raised
37 largest national social service agencies
20 largest national health agencies
54 additional national organizations with membership in the INDEPENDENT SECTOR, representing educational, environmental, health, social service, and arts and cultural organizations.

Ninety-one organizations responded, for a response rate of 48.9 percent. Respondents were divided among types of organizations as follows:

Foundations	26 percent
United Ways	22 percent
Social service	19 percent
Health	16 percent
Education	9 percent
Other	9 percent

Respondents from arts and culture and environmental organizations were coded as Other, due to the low number of respondents in these groups alone.

Exhibit 5.1. Survey on Evaluation
in Nonprofit Organizations.

In completing this survey we ask you to think about the organizations that you represent or support. For national headquarters, associations or membership organizations, this would include your members or affiliates. For foundations or United Ways, this would include the organizations that receive funding from you.

1. Listed below are some specific types of evaluation activity. Please rate the extent to which this activity is carried out by your members, affiliates or grantees. The scale beneath each item reflects the proportion of your members/affiliates/grantees that conduct such evaluation.

		All	Most	Some	Few	None
A.	Assessment of management practices (such as board govern-ance, human resource management, organizational planning).	5	4	3	2	1
B.	Compliance with program delivery standards (such as licensing or accreditation standards).	5	4	3	2	1
C.	Measurement of volume of program delivery (such as hours of service, number of participants).	5	4	3	2	1
D.	Tracking of individual program participant characteristics (such as age, race, gender, etc.).	5	4	3	2	1
E.	Measurement of participant satisfaction.	5	4	3	2	1
F.	Assessment of program outcomes or results (such as participant, client or target area improvement).	5	4	3	2	1

2. In the following section, please indicate if your organization provides assistance to your members, affiliates or grantees in these areas. Then indicate what type of assistance you provide by checking the boxes below.

A. Management Practices ___ We provide no assistance in the area

___ We provide the following:

- ☐ consultation by our staff
- ☐ consultation by paid consultants
- ☐ on-site assessment
- ☐ training/workshops
- ☐ handbooks/manuals/videos
- ☐ software
- ☐ other_____

B. Compliance with Standards ___ We provide no assistance in the area

___ We provide the following:

- ☐ consultation by our staff
- ☐ consultation by paid consultants
- ☐ on-site assessment
- ☐ training/workshops
- ☐ handbooks/manuals/videos
- ☐ software
- ☐ other_____

C. Volume of Delivery ___ We provide no assistance in the area

___ We provide the following:

- ☐ consultation by our staff
- ☐ consultation by paid consultants
- ☐ on-site assessment
- ☐ training/workshops
- ☐ handbooks/manuals/videos
- ☐ software
- ☐ other_____

D. Participant Characteristics ___ We provide no assistance in the area

___ We provide the following:

- ☐ consultation by our staff
- ☐ consultation by paid consultants
- ☐ on-site assessment
- ☐ training/workshops
- ☐ handbooks/manuals/videos
- ☐ software
- ☐ other_____

E. Participant Satisfaction ___ We provide no assistance in the area

___ We provide the following:

- ☐ consultation by our staff
- ☐ consultation by paid consultants
- ☐ on-site assessment
- ☐ training/workshops
- ☐ handbooks/manuals/videos
- ☐ software
- ☐ other_____

F. Program Outcome/ Results ___ We provide no assistance in the area

___ We provide the following:

- ☐ consultation by our staff
- ☐ consultation by paid consultants
- ☐ on-site assessment
- ☐ training/workshops
- ☐ handbooks/manuals/videos
- ☐ software
- ☐ other_____

Exhibit 5.1. Survey on Evaluation
in Nonprofit Organizations, Cont'd.

3. Please indicate any additional types of evaluation activities, from number 2 above, in which you PLAN to provide assistance over the next two years:

_____

4. How many staff people do you have that work in the area of evaluation?_____

5. How many of these are dedicated to this area full-time?_____

6. If your affiliates, members or grantees provide you with information resulting from any of these types of evaluations, please list the type of evaluation (from number 2 above):

_____

_____

7. Thinking now specifically of EVALUATING THE OUTCOMES OR RESULTS OF PROGRAMS, what two things from the list below do you believe are the greatest barriers to conducting this type of evaluation in the nonprofit sector? (Please check TWO of the items below.)

☐ Lack of staff with skills in program evaluation.
☐ Lack of technology in the field of program evaluation, such as methods, instruments and reliable measures.
☐ Insufficient financial resources to support such activities.
☐ Program evaluation is given a low priority by nonprofit managers.
☐ Concern about punitive use of information by funders.
☐ Nature of many nonprofit programs makes meaningful evaluation of program outcomes/results impossible.
☐ Client confidentiality issue.
☐ Other_____

8. Which two of the following do you think would be most successful in increasing the utilization of evaluation of program outcomes/results in the nonprofit sector? (Please check TWO of the items below.)

☐ Access to an organization that provided expertise and consultation in evaluating program outcomes/results.
☐ A national clearinghouse on program evaluation for information sharing among nonprofits.
☐ Increased willingness of funders to support program evaluation.
☐ Additional research to create reliable measures and instruments.
☐ Tools such as handbooks, workbooks, software.
☐ More formal education in academic programs.
☐ Training program for staff of nonprofit organizations.
☐ Dedication of a set percentage of agency revenues toward evaluation.
☐ Other _____

9. Name of Respondent_____ 10. Title_____

11. Organization_____ 12. Telephone Number_____

13. If your organization has any workbooks, instruments, reports or reference materials on evaluation that you are willing to share, please enclose a copy or an order form.

14. Please share any additional thoughts, concerns or suggestions you have on improving evaluation in nonprofit organizations.

_____

_____

_____

_____

Methods of Data Collection and Analysis

The survey asked respondents to rate the extent to which their
grantees or members/affiliates conducted various types of evaluation activity and to indicate the type of assistance provided by
the funder or national organization for each type of evaluation.
In addition, respondents were asked to provide some opinions
specifically related to assessment of program outcomes/results.
In this section, respondents indicated the greatest barriers and
the strategies they thought would best increase utilization of this
type of evaluation. Respondents were also asked to provide any
materials, such as manuals, workbooks, or reports, that they
used in evaluation.

    In addition to a quantitative analysis of the results, con-
tent analysis of the comments and of evaluation materials supplied by respondents was conducted. There were telephone interviews with those respondents who indicated that *all* of their
grantees/members conducted evaluation of outcomes or results.
The focus of these interviews was to gather more details about
the nature of data collected and methodologies. Additionally,
telephone interviews were conducted with those respondents who
provided materials that included tools or instructions for conducting evaluation of outcomes or results. The focus was to determine how the tools were used and how effective they had been
in increasing such evaluation among grantees/members.

Survey Findings

Types of Evaluation Conducted by Grantees/Members

The focus of evaluation activity in the nonprofit sector is on measuring the volume of program delivery and compliance with standards. The lowest areas of activity are assessment of program
outcomes/results and participant satisfaction. United Ways tend
to report assessment of volume of program delivery and participant characteristics more than other types of organizations and
to report assessment of program outcomes/results less. The focus of national educational organizations seems to be largely

on compliance with standards. They report this occurring more often than other organization types, and this is the only area in which they are not less likely than all others to provide assistance.

Respondents were asked to rate whether all, most, some, few, or none of their grantees/members conducted six various types of evaluation. Several organizations were not able to reliably state the extent to which their members/grantees conducted these types of evaluation. Of the ninety-one respondents, eighty-two answered this section.

Table 5.1 outlines the responses for each type of evaluation.

Table 5.1. Frequency of Each Type of Evaluation.

	All	*Most*	*Some*	*Few*	*None*
Volume of program delivery	39%	27%	20%	2%	0%
Compliance with standards	34%	26%	26%	22%	0%
Participant characteristics	22%	27%	23%	16%	1%
Management practices	18%	38%	26%	7%	3%
Program outcome/results	13%	19%	27%	29%	0%
Participant satisfaction	4%	14%	43%	26%	1%

The most common type of evaluation reported was measurement of volume of program delivery, with 39 percent reporting that all conducted such evaluation. Sixty-six percent responded either all or most. United Ways were more likely than other types to report measurement of volume of program delivery, with 70 percent reporting that all of their grantees conduct such evaluation. Social service organizations were also higher than the remaining types, with 47 percent reporting that all members conducted such evaluation.

The second most common type was compliance with program delivery standards, with 34 percent reporting that all conducted such evaluation. Sixty percent responded either all or most. Social service organizations were more likely than other types to report compliance with program delivery standards as a frequent type of evaluation. Of these organizations, 59 percent reported that this occurred among all of their members.

Educational organizations were also higher on this item than the remaining types, with 50 percent reporting that all of their members conducted such evaluation.

The third most common evaluation type was tracking of characteristics of program participants, with 22 percent reporting that all conducted this. Forty-nine percent reported all or most. United Ways were significantly more likely than other types to report this, with 50 percent reporting that all grantees conducted this.

Fourth was assessment of management practices, with 18 percent responding that all conducted this. However, 56 percent reported that all or most conducted such evaluation; more than the item above. All types of organizations were equally likely to select this type.

One of the key areas of interest of this study is the assessment of program outcomes/results, which ranked fifth. United Ways reported the lowest incidence, with 15 percent reporting that all or some of their grantees conducted this type of evaluation.

The least frequent type of evaluation was assessment of participant satisfaction.

Assistance Provided by
Funders and National Organizations

The focus of assistance provided by funders and national organizations is on management assessment and program outcomes/results. It is interesting that these are not the most commonly carried out activities, indicating that our assistance is directed toward growth and change rather than status quo. These two areas are arguably the most difficult and require some expertise in management and evaluation practices, which nonprofit organizations may be less likely to have internally. National social service organizations report the greatest amount of assistance available to members in assessing management practices, compliance with standards, volume of program delivery, and participant satisfaction.

Table 5.2 presents the percentage of all organizations reporting that they provide assistance with each type of evaluation.

Table 5.2. Percentage of Funders and
National Organizations Providing Assistance.

Management practices	88
Program outcomes/results	81
Volume of program delivery	73
Participant characteristics	69
Compliance with standards	66
Participant satisfaction	62

Educational organizations are less likely than others to provide assistance in all areas, with the exception of compliance with standards, where they are equally as likely as other types to provide assistance. Otherwise, the following differences among types of organizations are observed.

- Assistance with management practices: health and social services are more likely to provide assistance (93 percent and 94 percent respectively). Foundations are less likely, with 65 percent.
- Volume of program delivery: social service organizations are most likely to provide assistance, with 94 percent reporting this, and United Ways are more likely, with 85 percent.
- Participant characteristics: foundations are less likely to provide assistance (48 percent).
- Compliance with standards: social service organizations are most likely (94 percent) and health organizations are more likely than others to provide assistance in this area (86 percent).
- Participant satisfaction: social service organizations are also more likely to provide assistance in assessing participant satisfaction (82 percent).

Types of Assistance Provided

The types of assistance most widely available now are consultation by funder or national organization staff and training/workshops. Within each type of evaluation, the most frequent type of assistance provided is consultation by our staff. The only type of evaluation with a close second is assessment of management practices. In addition to 80 percent reporting that they provided staff consultation in this area, 76 percent reported providing training/workshops.

Other common types of assistance are

- Handbooks for management practices
- On-site assessment, training, and handbooks for compliance with standards
- On-site assessment and training for program outcomes/ results

Across all types of evaluation, the least offered form of assistance is software. Second to last is consultation by paid consultants in all categories except program outcomes/results, where it is more common.

Plans for Providing Assistance in the Future

Thirty-four of the respondents (37 percent) have plans to expand their assistance in evaluation over the next two years.

Staff Resources Dedicated to Evaluation

Responding organizations reported that on average they have 6.5 staff with at least some degree of responsibility in evaluation, although they are not necessarily dedicated to this full time. Across all respondent organizations, this ranges from 0 staff to 55 staff. However, the average number of staff dedicated to evaluation full time is only 1.4. This ranges from 0 to 11 full-time evaluation positions across all respondents.

Foundations and United Ways reported much fewer staff in evaluation than national social service and health organizations. This is probably because the funders rely on staff of these types of organizations to conduct evaluation and, additionally, foundations rely on outside consultants for larger evaluations. (See Table 5.3.)

Table 5.3. Average Total and Full-Time Staff
Working in Evaluation by Type of Organization.

	Total	Dedicated Full Time
Education	5.8	1.5
Foundations	3.0	.7
Health	11.5	2.8
Social service	10.5	1.8
United Ways	3.8	.8
Other	7.6	2.0

Health and social service organizations reported the highest staff support for evaluation, with health organizations reporting an average of 11.5 total and 2.8 dedicated full time and social service organizations reporting an average of 10.5 total and 1.8 dedicated full time. Foundations reported the lowest staff support, with an average of 3 total and .67 dedicated full time. United Ways are not far above, with an average of 3.8 total and .79 dedicated full time.

Types of Information Provided to Funders and National Organizations

Fifty-nine respondents (67 percent) reported that their grantees/members provided them with some type of evaluation results. The most frequent was program outcomes/results, with 28.7 percent. This essentially means that almost all of those funders and national organizations whose grantees/members collect these data ask that it be reported to them. Second most frequent were volume of service delivery and participant characteristics, each mentioned by 30 percent of the respondents.

Perceived Barriers to Evaluating Program Outcomes/Results

The two greatest barriers to conducting assessment of program outcomes/results are perceived to be lack of funding and lack of skills among staff of nonprofit organizations. Foundations are less likely to see funding as a barrier to conducting assessment of program outcomes/results, but they are not more likely to report this type of evaluation occurring among grantees. They identified the greatest barrier to this as lack of staff skills.

Respondents were asked to indicate these two greatest barriers to evaluating the outcomes or results of programs, with results as shown in Table 5.4.

**Table 5.4. Barriers to Assessing
Outcomes/Results: Percentage Selecting Each.**

Insufficient financial resources	54
Lack of skilled staff	41
lack of technology and tools	33
Low priority/punitive use	30
Meaningful evaluation impossible	14
Client confidentiality issues	3

Insufficient financial resources ranked first among all types of organizations, with the exception of foundations, who ranked it third with 35 percent, behind lack of staff skills and low priority/punitive use.

The next most frequently selected item was lack of staff with skills in program evaluation. Foundations were most likely to select this, with 61 percent. United Ways and other organizations ranked this more highly than other types, with 45 and 50 percent, respectively.

Ranked third was lack of technology in field of program evaluation. United Ways and Social Service organizations ranked this more highly than others, with 60 and 47 percent, respectively.

The fourth item was a combination of two concepts. Due to a production error, two response categories were accidentally combined on the survey, so it is difficult to know which of these two concepts participants were reacting to. However, the statement read "program evaluation is given a low priority by managers/concern about punitive use of information by funders." Thirty percent selected this item. This was more likely to be selected by foundations, with 43 percent selecting it.

The idea that meaningful evaluation of program outcomes/ results is impossible received little support. An exception to this was among health organizations, who ranked this as the second barrier with 43 percent. The idea that client confidentiality would be jeopardized received the least support.

Strategies to Increase Evaluation of Outcomes/Results

The two most useful strategies to increase assessment of program outcomes/results are increased willingness of funders to support it and training for staff. Access to an organization with expertise and better measures and tools were close to training as choices three and four. Health organizations are much more likely to identify research to create better measures and instruments as a strategy to increase assessment of program outcomes/results, ranking it second to funding. They are much less likely to view additional training as a useful strategy.

Respondents were asked to indicate the two strategies that they thought would most increase the utilization of this type of evaluation among nonprofit organizations. Table 5.5 presents the percentage selecting each item.

Table 5.5. Strategies to Increase Evaluation of
Program Outcomes/Results: Percentage Selecting Each.

Increased support by funders	51
Training for staff	29
Additional research on measures/instruments	24
Access to organization with expertise	22
Dedication of percent of agency revenues	17
National clearinghouse	14
Handbooks/workbooks/software	13
Formal academic education	1

There was a great deal of consistency across the different types of organizations in their response to this question. All respondents, except those in education, rated increased support by funders as the first strategy. Only 13 percent of educational organizations selected this.

Training for staff of nonprofits ranked as the second strategy for all but health organizations, of whom only 7 percent selected this. Foundations were more likely than other types to select this, however, with 48 percent.

Ranked in the third position was additional research to create measures and tools. The percentage selecting this was similar across all types of organizations, with the exception of health organizations, which were more likely to select this, with 57 percent compared to 24 percent overall.

Ranked fourth was access to an organization with expertise. Social service and other organizations were more likely to select both dedication of a percent of revenue and creation of a national clearinghouse, with 25 percent of each group selecting each of these items.

Comments on Evaluation

There was consensus across respondents that evaluation is beneficial and necessary, especially in the case of evaluation of program outcomes/results. Thirty-one respondents (35 percent) provided some comment on the conduct of evaluation in nonprofits. Twelve of these statements reflected the need to identify valid models and accurate measures for program evaluation. Of these, seven focused on the difficulty of creating such models and measures. Nine reflected views that program evaluation was beneficial and important, six reflected concerns regarding the high cost of conducting evaluation, and four emphasized that training was critical to the utilization of program evaluation.

Those Reporting That All Grantees/ Members Assess Outcomes/Results

Those who have developed a systematic process of assessment of program outcomes/results have gone through a staged process, bringing grantees/members through the following evolution.

Appreciation
Understanding
Ability to define objectives
Ability to design evaluation measures
Data collection
Discussion of results

Each of these stages was achieved as a team, with consultation and training available at each step.

Interviews were conducted with eleven of those respondents who indicated that all of their grantees/members conducted assessment of program outcomes/results. Of these eleven, seven had actually institutionalized this type of evaluation. The others had an institutionalized evaluation program that was regularly carried out, but it focused more on compliance with standards or reporting volume of activity than on assessing results. The seven that routinely conducted assessment of outcome/results did so through a variety of mechanisms. Indeed, the mechanisms even varied within organizations where different types of programs with different levels and sources of funding were evaluated through different means.

Of the seven, five were funders (foundations or United Ways) and two were national organizations. One of the national organizations also provided programmatic funding to local chapters. In general, grants of significant dollar amounts and large scope in terms of duration and potential impact are evaluated by outside consultants. Smaller grants, or funding for ongoing program activities, are generally evaluated by the provider organizations themselves, with input into the design from the funders and review of the results by funders and providers together.

One common feature across these seven organizations was the existence of a formal training program for providers regarding the design and conduct of evaluation, with accompanying workbooks or manuals. Each organization developed this training independently, although many built on existing materials. Where examples of training materials were provided, the references cited from evaluation literature were remarkably similar.

Staffing of the evaluation function also varied, with one organization having ten staff members dedicated to the area full time and others having none. One commonality, however, was that all of the organizations had staff in other areas with dual responsibility for evaluation. In most cases these were the staff involved in the funding process; in the case of the national organization, it was in the chapter accreditation process.

Respondents from these seven organizations were asked for advice that they might give others desiring to implement a similar approach. Suggestions mentioned by at least two of the seven respondents were as follows:

- Build a common understanding among staff, volunteers, and providers about the purpose and nature of evaluation.
- Be willing to commit the requisite staff and time to the development and conduct of the process.
- Involve all players in the development of the process from the beginning.
- Be flexible in the design of individual evaluations.
- Allow programs time to fully evolve before conducting evaluation.

Review of Materials

Many organizations provided materials that they used in evaluation, the majority of which focused on accreditation or self-evaluation criteria. Some of these included outcome assessment as a criterion, although most did not. (Numbers and percentages are not being used in this section because not all of those with materials submitted them with their survey, so we do not have a complete sample.)

Four organizations, other than the seven mentioned in the above section, had materials that included both provisions for outcome assessment and instructional materials and instruments. Three of these were funders and one was a national organization. Three of them were interviewed to discuss the extent to which these tools were used and the subsequent effect on the actual conduct of evaluation.

At this stage, the respondents stated that the instructions in conducting evaluation were well used to develop sound program outcome objectives and evaluation plans, but that this was the end result for most grantee/member organizations. Thus, the benefit of the materials was to improve organizational focus and strategic planning, not necessarily to conduct evaluation. This was felt to be part of an evolutionary process, however, that would lead ultimately to actual evaluation. All of the materials were accompanied by a training/workshop program.

Recommendations for Evaluation

This chapter has discussed the development of program evaluation as it now exists in the nonprofit sector and has also summarized the findings of our survey of nonprofit managers about program evaluation. From these studies, we are able to offer the following recommendations for the future development of program evaluation in the nonprofit sector.

1. If funders wish for evaluation to occur, particularly the assessment of program outcomes/results, they must be willing to allow grantees to use funds for this purpose, especially because funders evidently do not have dedicated staff in their *own* organizations to conduct evaluation. Funding of evaluation should be viewed as a necessary investment in program improvement.
2. Provider organizations and their boards must see assessment of outcomes/results as necessary and integral to their business, not as fluff to be added with extra money.
3. A new paradigm of program evaluation, separate from that of rigorous evaluation research models, needs to be developed for nonprofit organizations. The consistent focus on cost of evaluation among respondents demonstrates that outcome evaluation is regarded as something complex and costly. We know that evaluation requires dedication of financial and staff resources, but it cannot be seen as something so prohibitively expensive and sophisticated that it is beyond reach. There are many quasi-experimental and qualitative evaluation methods that can be routinely and realistically applied in nonprofit agencies. The development of these models should be furthered, rather than continuing a focus on pure evaluation research.

4. Additional training in program outcome evaluation is needed
    for staff of funders and providers. This training is not de-
    sired in an academic setting, again reinforcing the notion
    of a new paradigm of applicable evaluation models. Addi-
    tional research to develop sound measures and instruments,
    and access to an outside organization with expertise in the
    area, will complement and increase application of skills
    taught in training workshops.

5. Nonprofit organizations must work in concert to develop
    this training and the resources to support program outcome
    evaluation. Currently, duplicate effort is occurring as var-
    ious national groups independently develop their own ma-
    terials, and no clear national resource or training program
    is meeting the need. A forum should be created where ex-
    isting materials can be shared and opportunities for col-
    laborative efforts identified and implemented.

6. Funders and national organizations should also work to-
    gether to design outcome measures and instruments to be
    used by member organizations nationwide so that the fun-
    der expectations and available techniques will be compatible.

7. Funders must work with their grantees to develop program
    evaluation strategies that make sense and can be imple-
    mented by providers. The approach to this must be im-
    plemented incrementally with training and mutual partic-
    ipation at each stage.

8. More attention should be given to the assessment of par-
    ticipant satisfaction. This provides a very basic measure
    of the recipients' perception of the quality and benefit of
    services and can generally be collected using simple, inex-
    pensive, easy-to-interpret methods. Until program outcome
    data become more widely available, this type of evaluation
    can serve as a reasonable proxy.

References

Alkin, M. C., and Fitz-Gibbon, C. T. "Methods and Theories
of Evaluating Programs." *Journal of Research and Development
in Education,* 1975, *8,* 2–15.

Attneave, F. "How Do You Know?" *American Psychologist,* 1974, *29,* 493–499.

Babchuk, N. "The Role of the Researcher as Participant Observer and Participant-as-Observer in the Field Situation." *Human Organization,* 1962, *21,* 225–228.

Becker, H. S. "Problems of Inference and Proof in Participant Observation." *American Sociological Review,* 1968, *58,* 652–660.

Bogdan, R., and Taylor, S. J. *Introduction to Qualitative Research Methods.* New York: Wiley, 1975.

Braskamp, L. A., and Brown, R. D. (eds.). *Utilization of Evaluative Information.* New Directions for Program Evaluation, no. 5. San Francisco: Jossey-Bass, 1980.

Cook, T. D., and Reichardt, C. I. (eds.). *Qualitative and Quantitative Methods in Evaluation Research.* Newbury Park, Calif.: Sage, 1979.

Dwyer, F. P. *Report to the People,* 12th district of New Jersey, Jan. 22, 1970.

Filstead, W. J. (ed.). *Qualitative Methodology: Firsthand Involvement with the Social World.* Chicago: Markham, 1978.

Guba, E. G. "Problems in Utilizing the Results of Evaluation." *Journal of Research and Development in Education,* 1975, *8,* 42–54.

Guba, E. G., and Lincoln, Y. S. *Effective Evaluation: Improving the Usefulness of Evaluation Results Through Responsive and Naturalistic Approaches.* San Francisco: Jossey-Bass, 1981.

House, E. R. *The Logic of Evaluative Argument.* Los Angeles: Center for the Study of Evaluation, University of California, 1976.

House, E. R. *Evaluating with Validity.* Newbury Park, Calif.: Sage, 1980.

MacMurray, V. D., and others. *Citizen Evaluation of Mental Health Services: An Action Approach to Accountability.* New York: Human Sciences Press, 1976.

Murphy, J. T. *Getting the Facts: A Fieldwork Guide for Evaluators and Policy Analysts.* Santa Monica, Calif.: Goodyear, 1980.

Patton, M. Q. *Utilization-Focused Evaluation.* Newbury Park, Calif.: Sage, 1978.

Patton, M. Q. *Qualitative Evaluation Methods.* Newbury Park, Calif.: Sage, 1980.

Perloff, R. (ed.). *Evaluator Interventions: Pros and Cons.* Newbury Park, Calif.: Sage, 1979.

Rossi, P. H., Freeman, H. E., and Wright, S. R. *Evaluation: A Systematic Approach.* Newbury Park, Calif.: Sage, 1979.

Rossi, P. H., and Wright, S. R. "Evaluation Research: An Assessment of Theory, Practice, and Politics." *Evaluation Quarterly,* 1977, *1,* 5–52.

Rutman, L. (ed.). *Evaluation Research Methods: A Basic Guide.* Newbury Park, Calif.: Sage, 1977.

Stake, R. E. "Validating Representations: The Evaluator's Responsibility." In R. Perloff (ed.), *Evaluator Interventions: Pros and Cons.* Newbury Park, Calif.: Sage, 1979.

Suchman, E. A. *Evaluative Research: Principles and Practice in Public Service and Social Action Programs.* New York: Russell Sage Foundation, 1967.

Tripodi, T., Fellin, P., and Epstein, I. *Social Program Evaluation: Guidelines for Health, Education, and Welfare Administrators.* Itasca, Ill.: Peacock, 1975.

United Way of America. *"PPBS" Approach to Budgeting Human Service Programs for United Ways.* Alexandria, Va.: United Way of America, 1972.

United Way of America Services Identification System. *A Taxonomy of Social Goals and Human Service Programs.* (2nd ed.) Alexandria, Va.: United Way of America, 1976.

Willis, G. (ed.). *Qualitative Evaluation.* Berkeley, Calif.: McCutchan, 1978.

Part Two

Managing Human and Financial Resources

People and money are the two most important elements that managers and leaders of nonprofit organizations must maintain and cultivate if their organizations are to survive and be successful. But wise stewardship of these resources in the nonprofit environment presents many special challenges, not the least of which is that time and money that are contributed voluntarily constitute key components of the overall resource base of many organizations in this sector. Indeed, volunteer labor represents more than 40 percent of employment in the nonprofit sector, while private contributions account for more than a quarter of the annual funds flowing to these organizations. These figures greatly contrast with those of business or governmental organizations where the dependencies on volunteer labor and charitable contributions are quite low. Thus, the management of voluntarily contributed resources is a prime focus of the chapters in this section.

In Chapter Six, E. Gil Clary and Mark Snyder analyze the recruitment of volunteers. These authors focus on the use of media strategies to attract volunteers, recognizing that individuals choose to volunteer for a variety of reasons. Some individuals volunteer to gain new knowledge, and others seek to advance career prospects, express their values, gain social approval, or deal with personal feelings and problems. Thus, media messages must be customized to the functional motivations of different targeted groups. Clary and Snyder show that by using a new instrument that differentiates among the various motivations for volunteering, media-based recruitment programs may be designed more effectively.

Jeffrey L. Brudney focuses on the paid staff who manage volunteer programs, in Chapter Seven. Based on a broad survey of these volunteer administrators, he finds that nonprofit organizations generally do not devote sufficient attention and priority to the position of volunteer administrator. In particular, Brudney learns that few administrators of volunteer programs received special training for their responsibilities prior to assuming their positions, although most of these administrators do believe they can count on support from their organizations to attend programs of continuing education while on the job. Brudney finds that administrators of volunteer programs are a highly educated and committed group of people, and he presents their ideas for further educational opportunities and research that would help them become more effective managers of volunteer workforces.

In Chapter Eight, Cynthia D. McCauley and Martha W. Hughes turn our attention more broadly to the leadership challenges of chief executives of nonprofit organizations in the human services. Based on an extensive survey, these researchers identify twelve key challenge dimensions for executive leadership, ranging from the utilization of limited resources and building support for change to dealing with time pressures, improving volunteer resources, and coping with uncertainty. These challenges are found to vary in intensity according to organizational characteristics such as agency size, diversification of funding base, age, and other variables. McCauley and Hughes conclude by identifying key competencies that help nonprofit executives deal effectively with their special challenges. High on the list of competencies are flexibility and resourcefulness in leadership and problem-solving behavior.

Margaret A. Duronio and Bruce A. Loessin, in Chapter Nine, study the critical function of fundraising in nonprofit organizations, focusing specifically on institutions of higher education. Based on a statistical analysis of 575 institutions, these authors analyze, in depth, the practices of ten institutions selected for their fundraising success by having exceeded statistical predictions. They find that the success of these outstanding programs is particularly related to institutional leadership and commitment to fundraising. Duronio and Loessin go on to examine how the management of the fundraising function per se is related to its success — in the areas of information and communication systems, staff development, and planning and evaluation.

6.

Persuasive Communications Strategies for Recruiting Volunteers

E. Gil Clary
Mark Snyder

As even the most casual observer can see, a multitude of problems face our society, as well as other societies around the world. To name but a few, there are the problems associated with violence, poverty, hunger, illiteracy, and destruction of the environment. These problems are fundamentally human problems and as such require action on the part of human beings, both individually and collectively, if solutions are to be found and implemented. It seems, however, that there is yet another human problem to be added to our abbreviated list: the problem of inaction, or lack of participation with respect to involvement in solving social problems. Whether in considering some form of political activism (Fiske, 1987; Verba and Nie, 1972), in recycling materials on a regular basis (Gallup Organization, 1988), or even in the seemingly simple act of voting (Bureau of the Census, 1989), we find large numbers (and often the vast majority) of U.S. citizens doing nothing.

Note: Portions of the research described in this paper were supported by a grant from the Gannett Foundation.

In contrast to this pattern of lack of involvement is the phenomenon of volunteerism: people involved, on an ongoing basis, in an activity designed to help others and doing so without pay. The Gallup polls conducted for INDEPENDENT SECTOR have provided detailed information regarding Americans' participation. Looking especially at volunteerism during the 1980s, we find the rate of participation hovering around 50 percent in 1980, 52 percent (Gallup Organization, 1981); in 1985, 48 percent (Gallup Organization, 1986); in 1987, 45 percent (INDEPENDENT SECTOR, 1988); and in 1989, 54 percent (INDEPENDENT SECTOR, 1990). These rates, it should be noted, were obtained with a definition of volunteerism that included both formal (for example, regular participation with an organization) and informal (for example, helping neighbors or ad hoc work with an organization) volunteer activities.

Reflecting on the variety of problems facing society, and the level of action and inaction exhibited by the citizenry, the question of how to increase the rate of participation in more formal organized efforts arises, especially efforts where people engage in coordinated actions with others. More to the point, one important task facing the leadership of organizations in the independent sector, and in society more generally, is the recruitment and development of committed volunteers. Essentially, this is an issue of social influence, of attempting to encourage people to spend some of their time engaged in activities designed to benefit someone else, and/or society as a whole (in addition to any benefits accruing to the volunteer). We should hasten to add that the problem is one of action, not attitude. According to the 1987 survey (INDEPENDENT SECTOR, 1988), by a three to one margin respondents agreed that "persons should volunteer some of their time to help people elsewhere" even though the rate of actual participation in volunteer work (45 percent in 1987) fell short of these favorable attitudes. In this chapter, we begin by considering some of the strategies that are available for encouraging social and community activism; we then take a more detailed look at one technique—that of persuasive communication.

Social Influence for Social Activism

Having conceptualized the problem as one of utilizing social influence strategies to encourage participation in volunteer work, we find that a large assortment of techniques is available for influence attempts. We begin by considering how current volunteers came to be involved in volunteer work. The INDEPENDENT SECTOR surveys conducted during the 1980s included an item asking volunteers how they first learned about their current volunteer activity. Consistently, these surveys found that the two most frequently cited ways of learning about the activity were being asked by someone and prior participation in an organization (using the 1989 survey as an illustration, the percentages were 42.4 and 41.3 percent, respectively; INDEPENDENT SECTOR, 1990). These were followed by having had a family member or friend benefit from the activity, having sought out the activity on their own, and having seen an advertisement (these percentages for 1989 were 27.8, 21.0, and 6.0 percent, respectively; multiple responses were allowed). Overall, then, these surveys strongly suggest that volunteers learned about their volunteer activities primarily through their existing social contacts and networks and rarely through mass media communications.

It is important to ask, however, if the picture regarding the influence of media-based persuasive communications is always so pessimistic. In fact, from some of our own research, a more optimistic view emerges. As part of our work investigating the motivations of volunteers, we have also asked them how they became involved with their current volunteer activity. (We should note that our item followed a free-response format and respondents gave only one response, while the INDEPENDENT SECTOR survey provided response options and allowed for multiple responses.) In one investigation with approximately 500 volunteers working in one of six organizations (this investigation is described more fully in Clary and Snyder, 1990), we found that the most frequently reported response was advertising, with one-third of these volunteers citing ads on television, radio, newspapers, and magazines, as well as brochures, posters, and church bulletins. This was followed by "word of mouth" (26.5 percent), self-initiation (17 percent), participation in another organization (5 percent), academic coursework (4.5 percent), benefiting a family member or friend (3.5 percent), and being a former recipient of the service (1 percent); finally, 9 percent of the respondents provided no response. Thus, our research with volunteers participating in very formal volunteer settings found that media communications played an important role in recruitment efforts.

Although there are a number of reasons for the discrepancies between our research and those of the Gallup surveys, some important points can also be drawn from this set of findings. In addition to the potential efficacy of media-based campaigns for recruiting volunteers, our research also points to another important route to recruitment, namely that of relying on existing social networks. Our research found that the second most frequent means of recruitment was word of mouth and combining this with involvement in other organizations, academic requirement, and benefit to family and friends, approximately 40 percent of our volunteers pointed to some feature of their existing social network as being responsible for their involvement in their current activity. Similarly, the Gallup surveys found that the three most frequently cited means of recruitment were through one's social network: (1) being asked by someone, (2) being involved in another organization, and (3) being influenced by family or friends who have benefited from the activity. The critical point here is not whether recruitment via advertising is more or less important than recruitment via social networks but rather the likelihood that the most successful recruitment occurs through a coupling of these two strategies.

To summarize, responses from current volunteers point to utilizing a multipronged approach to the recruitment of volunteers. Most obvious from our discussion thus far is the combination of media-based persuasive communications with personal contacts through an individual's existing social network. Therefore, we emphasize that leaders of organizations and communities should think in terms of coupling these two recruitment strategies with others if possible, rather than relying exclusively on one technique or the other. (Parenthetically, this multiple-strategy approach to social change is precisely the one recommended by researchers on social marketing, for example, Kotler and Roberto, 1989.) Having provided this broader context for this approach to volunteer recruitment, the remainder of the chapter will be devoted to a more detailed examination of the strategy of media-based persuasive communications. Specifically, our approach to recruitment via advertisements builds on our earlier work on the motivational foundations of people's involvement in volunteer work.

The Functional Approach to Volunteers' Motivation

Our research on the motivations behind people's participation in volunteer work is based on a functional analysis of volunteer behavior (see Clary and Snyder, 1991). A functional analysis considers the reasons, needs, or motives that underly people's beliefs and behaviors and argues that these beliefs and behaviors serve important personal and social needs and goals. Furthermore, the functional approach emphasizes that different people may satisfy different functions through the same behavior. Applied to the case of people engaged in volunteer work, the functional approach seeks to determine the motives and goals that individuals may satisfy through their involvement with volunteer activities, with the expectation that different individuals will be involved in the same activities for very different motivations.

Our initial work identified five motivational categories. Through participation, a volunteer may seek to satisfy a *knowledge function* (to learn, to gain a greater understanding of people, to practice skills and abilities), a *career function* (to enhance one's job and career prospects, to gain experience and contacts), a *value-expressive function* (to act on important values such as humanitarian values, altruistic concerns, or desires to contribute to society), a *social-adjustive function* (to fit into important reference groups, to gain social approval/avoid social disapproval), and/or an *ego-defensive function* (to reduce feelings of guilt, to resolve or escape from one's own personal problems). With this conceptual understanding of volunteers' motivations, we developed an inventory to measure the five functions served by volunteering (the Volunteer Functions Inventory, or VFI). As reported by Clary and Snyder (1990), a factor analysis of volunteers' responses to the first version of the VFI identified factors corresponding to our five motivational categories, as well as one additional factor. A sixth group of items emerged that appear to involve *esteem enhancement,* whereby volunteers seek to satisfy psychological growth and development needs (for example, enhance self-worth and self-confidence and expand their social network). For this reason, we currently work with a revised version of the VFI (VFI-R), which consists of six scales, and evidence to date indicates that the inventory possesses adequate psychometric qualities (Clary, Snyder, and Ridge, 1992).

At this point in our research, we have some understanding, on both a conceptual and empirical level, of the nature of the motivations that underlie participation in volunteer work. Furthermore, perusal of the literature on volunteers' motivations reveals findings consistent with the functions we have identified (Clary and Snyder, 1990, 1991). In addition, several key points of this functional approach are supported by the literature on volunteerism. Specifically, the functional approach is in agreement with others on the point of "multiple motivations" (see Van Til, 1988): that is, as discussed earlier, the same activity may serve very different functions for different people, and involvement in an activity by one individual may well serve more than one function or motive for that individual. Finally, the functional approach shares with other theories the view that human behavior is goal directed and purposive (see, for example, Moore, 1985).

The Functional Approach to Persuasion

There is, of course, much more to the functional approach than simply identifying the various functions that beliefs and behaviors might serve. In fact, the functional approach arose within psychology as a theoretical perspective on attitudes and persuasion (Smith, Bruner, and White, 1956; Snyder and DeBono, 1987, 1989). As an approach to understanding attitudes, functional theorists asked: "Of what use to people are their attitudes?" and responded by considering the ways in which attitudes might help meet needs, execute plans, and achieve goals. More important for our purposes here is the functional perspective on persuasion. According to these theorists, attempts to influence people should take into account the psychologically important needs and goals of the individual recipient (or group of recipients), seek to determine the important motives, and then present a communication targeted directly at those particular motives.

The functional theorists, and particularly Katz (1960), have recommended how one might arouse and change attitudes based on different functions, identifying specific strategies for specific functions. It should be pointed out, however, that Katz and the other functional theorists were especially interested in cases where the goal was changing attitudes, that is, encouraging those with unfavorable attitudes to adopt favorable ones, or vice versa. In the case of promoting volunteer work, however, it appears that changing attitudes is unnecessary, given research (cited earlier) that suggests that most people's attitudes toward volunteering are already highly favorable. The challenge facing us here is one of finding out the motives or functions that are most important to the individual and urging him or her to translate those favorable attitudes into volunteer action. Fortunately, therefore, the logic of the functional perspective on changing attitudes and behaviors also applies to arousing action.

To illustrate this approach, consider the case of college students. Our previous research with the VFI suggests that the career function is especially important to younger people, at least relative to other groups. Knowing nothing else about a particular group of college students, we recommend that attempts at promoting volunteer work among this group should emphasize the ways in which volunteer work can satisfy career-related concerns. For example, some volunteer activities allow one to explore potential careers, to gain career-relevant experience, and/or to provide an additional item for one's resume. The prediction, of course, is that college students will find volunteer work more appealing following exposure to this kind of message, while other groups, especially where members are already in satisfying careers, would be less persuaded by such ads.

In the sections that follow, we discuss two studies designed to examine the functional approach to promoting participation in volunteer work.

Study 1: Video Ads

Our first investigation involved the creation of video messages, with each message corresponding to one motivational category (Ridge and others, 1991). (When we were conducting this study, we were working with the first version of the VFI, which consisted of five motives; thus this study included five, not six, messages.) For all advertisements, the message was delivered by the same "collegiate-looking" young woman, lasted approximately one minute, and included the same opening and closing lines. We wanted to create ads that differed only in the content of the message. Thus, in the *value-expressive ad*, the actress discussed how volunteer work provided the opportunity to act on her concerns for others; the *knowledge ad* emphasized several things one could learn by participation in volunteer work; the *career ad* discussed career-relevant experiences gained through volunteering; in the *social-adjustive ad*, the actress mentioned strengthening her current social network, as well as expanding her social circle; and the *ego-defensive ad* emphasized the ways in which volunteering can alleviate unpleasant psychological states (for example, reduce guilt, work through problems).

These messages were then viewed by a sample of college students in a laboratory setting, with each student viewing only one advertisement. Each ad was viewed several times, and each viewing was followed by a set of questions. Prior to the experiment itself, each student completed the VFI, so that we knew which motives were most important to each of them. In delivering a message to each individual, then, the ad presented was one that appealed to a motive that was of great importance *or* one of little importance to the person. For example, the social ad was shown to some students who were extremely high and to some who were extremely low in the social function; the same thing occurred in the remaining four messages as well. Our primary interest here was in comparing people who received a message *appropriate* or relevant to those who received a message *inappropriate* or irrelevant to their psychological needs. We predicted that individuals receiving the appropriate message would perceive that message as more appealing and persuasive than those receiving the inappropriate message.

The results confirmed this expectation. First of all, students were more likely to perceive motive-appropriate messages as serving their personal goals. As compared to students who viewed a message that was not tailored to a motive important to them ($n = 43$), those who viewed an advertisement that did engage a motive important to them ($n = 63$) found the advertisement more effective. More specifically, motive-appropriate messages were rated higher in overall quality and, more important, more motivating in getting them to volunteer (on an index of four items); these differences were statistically significant. Finally, in the motive-appropriate message conditions, more positive emotional reactions were elicited, and the model (actress) was viewed in more positive terms; interestingly, no differences were observed with respect to perceptions of the model's expertise and power.

To summarize, the video experiment supports the central prediction of the functional approach to persuasion: persuasive messages are more effective if the specific message addresses psychological motives, needs, goals, or functions important to the individual receiving the message. We must also note that the effect of appropriate versus inappropriate message (for an individual) was stronger within some message conditions than others; the differences were greatest for the ego-defensive and careerist ads, and to a lesser extent, the value-expressive ad.

Study 2: Brochure Messages

In our second investigation, we again sought to test the functional hypothesis that an advertisement's persuasiveness depends on whether the message appeals to a motive important to the recipient of the message (Ridge and others, 1991). There were a number of important changes in this study. The most critical was that, because it appears that (based on our continuing work with the VFI) there are six (not five) functions served by involvement in volunteer work, this study involved all six motives. In addition, the second study utilized a different medium; whereas the first study used video messages, in the second we created brochures or flyers, the kinds of ads one might send through the mail, distribute on the street, or make available at some central location. Thus, these messages followed a print format.

As in the video study, we attempted to make the messages comparable in all other respects: on the front page of each brochure, three key phrases were printed; on the inside, each message was prefaced by the same introduction. More specifically, each began with the words: "You're probably thinking that if you become a volunteer, you'll have to give and give and give. But guess what? While you're helping others, volunteering can be doing important things for you. You'll be surprised at how much you can GET out of volunteering. As a volunteer, you can . . . " This was followed by a message designed to show how volunteering could serve specific psychological functions or motives; there were six messages, each corresponding to one of the six volunteer functions.

As in the previous study, a sample of college students ($n = 59$) completed several questionnaires, one of which was the VFI-R, before exposure to the messages. In this study, all six messages were presented to each student and the task was to indicate on a 100-point scale the persuasiveness of each message; participants could distribute their ratings as narrowly or broadly as they saw fit. Finally, the study as a whole was presented as one concerned with advertising in general, and as such, the task was to evaluate some ads.

In this study, we expected evaluations of the effectiveness of the messages to be guided by the importance of volunteer-relevant motivations. To examine this hypothesis, we obtained for each subject a correlation between their scores on the VFI and ratings of the six messages. Thus, the critical data point here was the intra-subject (or within-subject) correlation of VFI scores and ratings of the messages. For the fifty-nine subjects participating in this study, an average intra-subject correlation of .71 was obtained, and inferential tests revealed that this association was significantly greater than zero. Thus, the strength of individuals' motivations was associated with evaluations of the persuasiveness of the messages, so that a message was rated as effective when the corresponding motive was strong and as less effective when the corresponding motive was weak.

In addition to obtaining the correlation between the six VFI scores and ratings of the corresponding brochures for each student individually (the intra-subject correlation), we also examined the correlations between each scale on the VFI and its corresponding brochure for the group as a whole (for example, the correlation between scores on the values function and ratings of the values brochure, the career function and ratings of the career brochure, and so on). Our expectation here was that the greatest degree of association would occur between corresponding and noncorresponding scales and brochures. On the whole, our expectation was confirmed, with the highest (and statistically significant) correlation obtained when motivations and brochures corresponded. The lone exception to this rule was with the social function; here, ratings of the social brochure did not correlate with any of the six motives.

Overall, Study 2 also found the tendency for evaluations of an advertisement's effectiveness and persuasiveness to covary with the corresponding motivation. With this finding, support was again obtained for the central proposition of the functional approach to persuasion: favorable responses to the message contained in a volunteer recruitment advertisement become more likely as the message appeals to a motivation important to the target audience.

Summary

It appears that the functional approach to persuasion has been supported in the context of strategies for recruiting volunteers.

This support has been obtained in two studies that differed in several respects: different samples of college students (who are, by and large, not currently involved in volunteer work), different media (video and print), different research methods (between-subject and within-subject designs), and different versions of the functional messages. Although more research is needed (to be discussed in a later section), the present results are encouraging. Persuasive messages designed to stimulate volunteer work should seek to arouse psychological functions important to the recipient, demonstrating how these functions can be satisfied through involvement in volunteer activity.

The Role of Values

Throughout this chapter, we have suggested that persuasive attempts appeal to people's psychological self-interest. This, of course, raises questions about the role of values in efforts to promote volunteer work. Certainly, values such as humanitarian concerns, caring for others in need, and contributing to society are central features in volunteer activity. Furthermore, research on people's reasons for volunteering repeatedly places values in a prominent position. National surveys (for example, INDEPENDENT SECTOR, 1990) and our own research with the VFI consistently find the value-expressive function to be the most frequently endorsed motive for samples as a whole (for example, Clary and Snyder, 1990; Ridge and others, 1990). Given this role, an obvious implication is that one important strategy that might be used to encourage volunteer work is appealing to people's values.

In some of our earliest research on persuasive attempts at promoting volunteering, we examined the effectiveness of just this value-oriented strategy (Copeland, Snyder, Clary, and French, 1990). Here, we created four types of print ads that either emphasized abstract reasons for volunteering (for example, "for our society to work, everybody needs to do their part"), emphasized concrete reasons for volunteering (for example, "I could make a lot of new friends through a volunteer organization"), gave abstract reasons for not volunteering (for example, "volunteering is somebody else's responsibility," countered by "if everybody says that, nothing's going to get done"), or presented concrete reasons for not volunteering (for example, "I don't have the time," countered by "maybe I could rearrange my schedule to fit it in"). Each ad consisted of four reasons, with all reasons within an ad being of the same type. In two studies with college students, one using largely nonvolunteers and the other using a known group of volunteers, students were shown all ads and asked to rate them in terms of overall effectiveness. Across the two studies, the results consistently indicated that the two most effective ads involved countering abstract reasons for not volunteering and emphasizing concrete reasons for volunteering; and the least effective was the ad emphasizing abstract reasons for volunteering. In the second study with known volunteers, we included some other ratings, in addition to overall effectiveness. When asked specifically about which ads would be most effective in *attracting new volunteers,* the results were quite similar to those cited above. When asked about which ads would be most effective in *keeping current volunteers,* the "emphasizing abstract reasons for volunteering" message was now rated as the second most effective advertisement.

In sum, our research is consistent with related work in suggesting that values play an important role in volunteer activity. Our research further suggests, however, that value-centered persuasive attempts may be more effective at particular points. More specifically, our working hypothesis is that the promotion of volunteer work might be viewed as a two-step process, whereby the initial recruitment of volunteers appeals to psychological motives and needs important to the individual and communicates to individuals the ways in which volunteering can serve these functions. In the second phase, where one seeks to retain current volunteers, it seems important to develop and/or strengthen values relevant to volunteer activities. In other words, in attempting to cultivate committed volunteers, these activities need to be made meaningful, and one important way to create meanings is by connecting the work to broader, more abstract values, such as showing compassion for others and contributing to the common good (Brickman, 1987).

Into the Future

To date, our research has created a foundation for one approach to questions surrounding the motivations of volunteers. Through the development of, and research with, the VFI, we have some understanding of the nature of people's motivations underlying participation in volunteer activity. Furthermore, this understanding can be useful in attempting to persuade people to engage in volunteer work. In seeking to encourage volunteer activity, the functional approach recommends that persuasive communications appeal to psychological motives and needs important to the recipient of the communication. Thus far, studies examining the validity of this hypothesis have been supportive of our functional approach. In the process, we have also created initial versions of advertisements appealing to each of six psychological functions, which can serve as models for practitioners in the volunteer community to develop strategies for drawing on volunteers' motivations in recruitment and retention efforts.

There is, as always, more research that could be conducted. Up to this point, our persuasion studies have all been in the controlled environment of the psychological laboratory, certainly a necessary condition in the initial phases of this kind of research. We are approaching the point, however, where our messages must be tested outside the laboratory where it is possible to examine whether or not people actually sign up for volunteer work. Along a parallel path, research on the VFI continues, as we further test and refine our revised version of the inventory and the theory on which it is based. As in our laboratory studies, the VFI will merge with our research on persuasion, with the VFI identifying motivations important to particular groups and then using this information to select the most appropriate functional message.

In concluding, we wish to return to our point of departure. In the beginning, we suggested that those interested in encouraging volunteer activity among members of our society have a wide assortment of social influence strategies at their disposal. Our research has focused on media-based communications and the importance of tailoring messages to motivations, yet this is only one strategy. As we suggested earlier, the most successful campaigns for promoting volunteer activity will most likely be those that utilize multiple strategies and, here again, the functional approach might offer some guidelines. That is, just as specific advertisements can be designed to appeal to specific functions, there may also be specific influence techniques that work best for specific psychological functions.

Toward this end, we offer some initial suggestions. It may be that processes involved in education may be most useful for those high on the knowledge function. Programs in career development may be used with the career function. Direct contact between a communicator and target may work best for those high on the social function. Personal development activities might be coupled with the esteem-enhancement function. Therapeutic processes may offer some suggestions about influencing those with ego-defensive motives. And religious and spiritual processes may prove useful with the value-expressive function. The point here is that we can draw upon processes, programs, and techniques developed in other domains to create effective ways for promoting volunteer activity. Furthermore, some of these processes and techniques may possess a unique connection to specific functions. The fundamental message remains the same, however; to effectively recruit volunteers, one should tailor one's message to the motivations and functions important to the individual potential volunteer.

References

Brickman, P. *Commitment, Conflict, and Caring.* Englewood Cliffs, N.J.: Prentice-Hall, 1987.

Bureau of the Census. *Statistical Abstract of the United States.* (109th ed.) Washington, D.C.: U.S. Department of Commerce, 1989.

Clary, E. G., and Snyder, M. "A Functional Analysis of Volunteers' Motivations." Paper presented at INDEPENDENT SECTOR's Spring Research Forum, Boston, Mass.: Mar. 1990.

Clary, E. G., and Snyder, M. "A Functional Analysis of Altruism and Prosocial Behavior: The Case of Volunteerism." In M. S. Clark (ed.), *Prosocial Behavior*. Newbury Park, Calif.: Sage, 1991.

Clary, E. G., Snyder, M., and Ridge, R. "Volunteers' Motivations: A Functional Strategy for the Recruitment, Placement, and Retention of Volunteers." *Nonprofit Management and Leadership,* Summer 1992.

Copeland, J., Snyder, M., Clary, E., and French, S. "Promoting Volunteerism: Some Alternatives to Appeals to Humanitarian Values." Paper presented at the annual meeting of the American Psychological Society, Dallas, Tex., June 1990.

Fiske, S. T. "People's Reactions to Nuclear War: Implications for Psychologists." *American Psychologist,* 1987, *42,* 207–217.

Gallup Organization. *Americans Volunteer 1981.* Washington, D.C.: INDEPENDENT SECTOR, 1981.

Gallup Organization. *Americans Volunteer 1985.* Washington, D.C.: INDEPENDENT SECTOR, 1986.

Gallup Organization. "Household Waste Threatening Environment; Recycling Helps Ease Disposal Problem." *Gallup Report,* Dec. 1988, *280,* 30–35.

INDEPENDENT SECTOR. *Giving and Volunteering in the United States: Findings from a National Survey, 1988 Edition.* Washington, D.C.: INDEPENDENT SECTOR, 1988.

INDEPENDENT SECTOR. *Giving and Volunteering in the United States: Findings from a National Survey, 1990 Edition.* Washington, D.C.: INDEPENDENT SECTOR, 1990.

Katz, D. "The Functional Approach to the Study of Attitudes." *Public Opinion Quarterly,* 1960, *24,* 163–204.

Kotler, P., and Roberto, E. L. *Social Marketing.* New York: Free Press, 1989.

Moore, L. F. (ed.). *Motivating Volunteers: How the Rewards of Unpaid Work Can Meet People's Needs.* Vancouver, Canada: Vancouver Volunteer Center, 1985.

Ridge, R., Snyder, M., Clary, E., and Associates. "The Volunteer Functions Inventory: Toward an Understanding of the Motives to Volunteer." Paper presented at the annual meeting of the American Psychological Association, Boston, Mass., Aug. 1990.

Ridge, R., and others. "Matching Messages to Motives in Persuasion: A Functional Approach to Promoting Volunteerism." Paper presented at the annual meeting of the American Psychological Society, Washington, D.C., June 1991.

Smith, M. B., Bruner, J., and White, R. *Opinions and Personality.* New York: Wiley, 1956.

Snyder, M., and DeBono, K. "A Functional Approach to Attitudes and Persuasion." In M. Zanna, J. Olson, and C. Herman (eds.), *Social Influence: The Ontario Symposium.* Hillsdale, N.J.: Erlbaum, 1987.

Snyder, M., and DeBono, K. "Understanding the Functions of Attitudes: Lessons from Personality and Social Psychology." In A. Pratkanis, S. Breckler, and A. Greenwald (eds.), *Attitude Structure and Function.* Hillsdale, N.J.: Erlbaum, 1989.

Van Til, J. *Mapping the Third Sector: Voluntarism in a Changing Social Economy.* New York: Foundation Center, 1988.

Verba, S., and Nie, N. *Participation in America: Political Democracy and Social Equality.* New York: HarperCollins, 1972.

7.

Strengthening Volunteer Administration Through Continuing Education and Research

Jeffrey L. Brudney

The involvement of volunteers in nonprofit organizations is one of the distinguishing features of the independent sector and a growing phenomenon in the public sector. Most nonprofit organizations and many government agencies are vitally dependent on volunteer labor for their internal functioning and for the provision of important goods and services to clients. In turn, the quality and effectiveness of volunteer performance, as well as the overall direction and coordination of this component of the organization, rests with a key official: the administrator of volunteer services. Yet few studies have examined empirically the support of host organizations for the volunteer administrator, especially in relation to this official's need for training and research.

This chapter analyzes the results of a national survey of volunteer practitioners completed in 1990 that was intended,

Note: I am grateful to Mary M. Brown, doctoral candidate in public administration at the University of Georgia, for assistance with data processing and analysis.

in part, to address these issues. The chapter explores the degree of organizational support for continuing education in volunteer administration, the interest of volunteer services managers in enhancing their professional background, and the subjects these managers consider most important for further training and research in volunteerism. It concludes with a discussion of the implications of the findings for leaders and managers in nonprofit organizations.

Background

In contrast to the study of nonprofit organization and management, a field that has witnessed explosive growth in research, journals, and academic programs over the past decade, relatively little scholarly attention has been directed to administrators of volunteer services. Three recent and highly useful compendia of literature on the voluntary, nonprofit sector offer testimony to this conclusion. Although citations to studies in volunteer administration appear in *Voluntary Associations: An Annotated Bibliography* (Pugliese, 1986), *Philanthropy and Voluntarism: An Annotated Bibliography* (Layton, 1987), and *The Literature of the Nonprofit Sector: A Bibliography with Abstracts,* Volume I (Derrickson, 1989), these compendia evidently do not consider research on the topic sufficiently voluminous or noteworthy to warrant a distinct chapter, subject heading, or review.

In the extant literature in this area, three themes emerge of special relevance for assessment of the training and research needs of volunteer services administrators. The most striking is that, in general, organizations do not seem to provide great support to these officials or the programs they lead. Noted volunteerism authority Ivan H. Scheier makes the point most forcefully. In a series of articles published in the *Journal of Volunteer Administration* in 1988–1989, Scheier (1988a, 1988b, 1988–1989) argues that organizations often fail to appreciate the range of important tasks performed by volunteer administrators and tend to trivialize their accomplishments. He calls for "empowerment" of these individuals and their profession, which he defines as "enhanced status and respect accorded the volunteer administrator and the volunteer program by the host organization as well as more generous resource allocation to this effort" (Scheier, 1988–1989, pp. 50–51).

Empirical research supports Scheier's observations. Results of a survey of 269 volunteer managers in five northwestern states and two Canadian provinces by Appel, Jimmerson, Macduff, and Long (1988) suggest that volunteer administrators are stretched among various organizational functions. Job titles notwithstanding, just one-third of the sample were able to devote all their work time to managing the volunteer program. Due to other work responsibilities, nearly four in ten (38 percent) spent less than half their time on this obligation. Scheier (1988a, p. 33) reports similar findings based on a smaller sample of volunteer administrators, as do the authors of a study based on volunteer practitioners in Rhode Island (Ostrowski and Sehl, 1990).

A Survey on Employer Recognition sponsored by the Association for Volunteer Administration (AVA) further questions the status of volunteer services administrators in host organizations (Patton, 1990). The survey observed an "air of second-class citizens, which the volunteer administrators from the nonprofit sector frequently display" (p. 7). Although confident of their own professionalism, respondents voiced concerns about employers sharing that appraisal. The study concluded that these officials like their work, are committed to working with volunteers, and would stay in the field of volunteer administration as a career were "all necessary supports in place" in the organization (p. 7).

Although the AVA study left ample room for interpretation of its disturbing conclusions, a survey of 463 full-time and salaried administrators of volunteer programs by Harold W. Stubblefield and Leroy Miles (1986) presents many more specific instances of the difficulties that these officials may encounter in host organizations. Approximately one-third of the volunteer administrators in their survey believed that they did not have great influence on staff-related policies, their salary was lower than for officials in comparable positions in the agency, other administrators in the agency enjoyed more job security, and other staff members did not regard their position as a professional occupation (Stubblefield and Miles, 1986).

Research based on the public sector offers analogous findings. A national survey of local governments by Sydney Duncombe (1985, p. 363) found that only about one-fifth (21.9 percent) of a sample of 534 cities with volunteer programs even had an official designated as head of this effort. In many of these cities, moreover, the agency had simply appended the responsibilities for volunteer management onto the existing job description of an administrative assistant, personnel analyst, public services assistant, or others in like positions. The chief qualification for leadership of the volunteer contingent often appeared to be the individual's willingness to take on additional duties (Duncombe, 1985).

The burden of this research is that host organizations do not routinely place a high value on the position of volunteer administrator. As intimated by the results of Duncombe's (1985) survey, they may assign the position and its new duties while assuming that the occupant will continue with the present job, and with no adjustment to salary. A leading expert on volunteer programs, Marlene Wilson (1976) writes, "It is frequently difficult to ascertain if this assignment should be regarded as a promotion or demotion" (p. 16).

A second theme derived from the literature anticipates differences in support of the volunteer program contingent on organizational auspices in the nonprofit or public sector. Based on a comprehensive review, Brudney (1990) determined that nonprofit agencies, more often than governments, possess attributes that make them receptive to volunteer efforts. These characteristics include a tradition of working with volunteers and a recognized need for their involvement, increased flexibility and less fragmentation in approach, closeness to the field and a smaller scale of operations, greater capacity to focus on the full range of client needs and tailor services to them instead of concentrating on isolated problems, fewer unionized employees, and significant diversity in both the content of services and the institutional framework within which they are provided. To the degree that nonprofit rather than public organizations possess these characteristics, they are more likely to extend greater support to administrators of volunteer services. Even though the level of agency support for these officials as a group may not be high (as indicated by the research reviewed above), this factor can be expected to vary systematically by organizational auspices.

A lack of support for the position of volunteer administrator presents an anomaly, for these managers commonly possess relatively high levels of formal education, which should command respect and commitment in employment. In the study of volunteer practitioners in the northwestern United States and Canada, for example, virtually the entire sample (96 percent) had completed at least some college; two-thirds (66 percent) held a bachelors degree; and nearly one-quarter (23 percent) had a graduate degree (Appel, Jimmerson, Macduff, and Long, 1988). In the survey of full-time and salaried volunteer program administrators, two-thirds (67.4 percent) had completed at least a bachelors degree, and more than one-quarter (28.4 percent) had attained a masters or doctorate; another one-fifth (21.2 percent) were working on a higher academic degree than the one currently held (Stubblefield and Miles, 1986). In a survey of the membership of the Association for Volunteer Administration (1987), 58.7 percent of respondents reported that their current position requires a minimum of a bachelors degree. In the Rhode Island study, nearly three-fourths of the volunteer administrators (74.2 percent) had at least a bachelors degree, and over one in ten (12.4 percent) had a graduate degree (Ostrowski and Sehl, 1990). A final theme evident in this literature, then, is a pronounced trend toward higher education among volunteer practitioners.

This review of prior research suggests three hypotheses for further investigation. First, host organizations will not usually invest substantial resources in the position of administrator of volunteer services. Second, the support that is forthcoming for the position will likely be higher in nonprofit agencies than in government. And third, because volunteer administrators appear to be well educated, they should express a solid commitment to furthering their professional background. These hypotheses are examined empirically below.

Data Collection and Sample

In October 1989, the AVA board of directors called for the dissemination of a survey to elicit opinions on the status of continuing education programs in volunteer management and to provide direction to future initiatives. Endorsed by both AVA and the National VOLUNTEER Center, the resulting mail survey, Educational Needs in Volunteer Administration, was conducted in late 1989 and early 1990. Responses to the survey form the empirical basis for this study.

Although no comprehensive enumeration of volunteer administrators exists, the survey embraced a very broad constituency. Groups receiving the questionnaire included the AVA membership, which numbers approximately 1,750; directors of voluntary action centers, about 320 in all; and another 1,200 practitioners, assembled from mailing lists provided by educators and directors in volunteer administration. The possibility of overlap across the various lists precludes a firm estimate of total sample size, but the survey probably reached some 3,000 professionals and leaders in volunteer administration.

Of this number, 765 returned the questionnaire, for a response rate of 25 percent. This figure is not especially high, yet it is still quite acceptable for a mailed survey that included neither a preaddressed envelope for the completed instrument nor the necessary postage for return mail. Regardless of the exact parameters of the sampling frame, the survey qualifies as one of the largest such undertakings ever in the field of volunteer administration.

The sample of volunteer administrators yielded by the survey is not only substantial but also several indicators suggest that it is broadly representative. First, the questionnaires received came from every state and from most Canadian provinces. Second, 73 percent of the respondents are involved in nonprofit organizations and 7 percent in "other" institutions; the remaining 20 percent work in government volunteer programs. This distribution is consistent with findings from major national surveys indicating that the great bulk of volunteering occurs in nonprofit organizations, with about one in five volunteers assisting public agencies. Third, in response to an open-ended question, the administrators named as the focus of their program thirty-four different substantive areas, bridging the spectrum from corporate-sponsored projects to religious institutions. These results, too, are quite similar to those obtained in national surveys on volunteerism (for example, Hodgkinson and Weitzman, 1990).

Findings

The Educational Needs Survey contained two items that allow examination of the hypothesis pertaining to organizational support for administrators of volunteer programs. Given the overall purpose of the survey, the items are rooted in educational issues. The first inquired whether respondents had received any training in volunteer management prior to beginning work in the field. The second asked the administrators: If you were to attend a major training program on volunteer management, would the training costs be paid by your agency, by you, or by a combination of both.

The results of the survey show that just one-quarter of the sample (24.5 percent) had undergone training in volunteer administration before beginning work in the field. As expected, host organizations do not appear to be very concerned about the preparation of individuals to lead the volunteer program — at least not initially. This finding offers evidence for the first hypothesis of a general lack of support for the volunteer manager position.

The administrators' responses concerning possible organizational backing for continuing education opportunities seem to place agencies in a more positive light. More than half the practitioners (56.7 percent) anticipated that if they were to attend major training, their agency would underwrite the full cost; another 34.9 percent expected that the organization would share the expense. Only 8.4 percent of the sample said that training costs would fall to them alone. Because the item asked respondents to speculate on how the costs of future training would be paid, one must exercise caution in interpreting the results. Nevertheless, over 90 percent of the volunteer administrators anticipated that the institution would bear at least a portion of the training expense.

The second hypothesis proposed that nonprofit agencies would give stronger backing to the volunteer administrator position than would government. Based on the items examined above, the hypothesis garners limited support. Managers working in nonprofit organizations, more often than their counterparts in government agencies, had accumulated training in volunteer administration before beginning work in the field, 26.2 percent versus 20.4 percent. In addition, the nonprofit organizations appeared more willing than government to underwrite the costs of continuing education for the managers. Of the volunteer administrators involved in the nonprofit sector, 58.4 percent said that their organization would assume the full expense of training, compared to 53.2 percent of the public sector managers.

The results are consistent and suggestive of the expected linkage between nonprofit auspices and support for these officials, yet they are not sufficiently robust to infer that a definite relationship exists in the population of volunteer administrators. The chi-square test indicates that the associations between nonprofit status and prior training in volunteer administration ($p < .1674$) and anticipated agency sponsorship for continuing education ($p < .2147$) approach statistical significance but do not warrant rejection of the null hypothesis at conventional levels. More detailed statistical analysis of the first two hypotheses would have been desirable to specify and elaborate the findings. However, because the authors of the Educational Needs Survey did not ascertain demographic information from the volunteer administrators or background information regarding their organizations, further statistical breakdowns are not possible.

Finally, as proposed by the third hypothesis, the survey leaves little doubt regarding the commitment of the administrators to enhancing their preparation in volunteer management. Fully 91 percent of the sample said that they would have appreciated the chance to attend relevant training before or soon after they had entered the field (as opposed to the 24.5 percent who had actually received prior training). Four out of five of the administrators (83 percent) indicated that they would now appreciate the chance to attend an advanced course on volunteer management. Virtually the same number (82.1 percent) expressed interest in an in-depth seminar on specific topics in the field, such as volunteer involvement in local government or innovative program design. These officials professed keen interest in augmenting their professional background.

Areas for Coverage in Training and Research

The Educational Needs Survey asked the sample of administrators to list subjects they thought should be addressed in a basic seminar on volunteer management, as well as in an advanced seminar, and to name areas in volunteer management in which they recommended that further research be conducted. All three questions were presented in an open-ended format, so that the managers were able to give their views without constraint. As many as four possible responses were coded on each question. In all, the administrators offered a total of 2,180 comments concerning the basic seminar, 1,826 comments on the advanced seminar, and 597 suggestions for further research. Detailed perusal of this great wealth of information led to the creation of an original coding scheme consisting of approximately 100 distinct subject areas.

To facilitate analysis and interpretation, the specific categories have been aggregated according to general topics in volunteer administration and management. Space limitations restrict discussion here to the ten areas on each question mentioned most frequently by the managers. The "top ten" account for 82.4 percent of all comments made regarding a basic seminar in volunteer management, 74.4 percent of the comments for an advanced seminar, and 68.1 percent of the preferences expressed for further research. Table 7.1 presents the results.

As might have been anticipated, respondents identified the essentials of volunteer management as most vital for coverage in the basic course. The area mentioned most frequently was recruitment of volunteers (17.2 percent of comments). The next three priorities for training were motivation, recognition,

Table 7.1. Top Ten Preferences of Volunteer Administrators
for Subjects to Be Addressed in Basic Seminar, Advanced Seminar,
and Further Research in Volunteer Administration.*

Subject Area	Basic Seminar		Advanced Seminar		Further Research	
	Percentage	Rank	Percentage	Rank	Percentage	Rank
Volunteer recruitment	17.2	(1)	4.2	(9)	7.9	(3)
Motivation, recognition, retention	13.7	(2)	6.2	(5)	10.9	(1)
Screening and placement of volunteers	10.1	(3)				
Supervision and management of volunteers	8.2	(4)	10.2	(2)	5.5	(7)
Professional skills	7.7	(5)	15.1	(1)	6.9	(5)
Planning and evaluation	7.1	(6)	8.8	(3)	6.9	(5)
Training employees and volunteers	5.7	(7)				
Job design for volunteers	5.0	(8)				
Record keeping	4.5	(9)				
Marketing and publicity	3.2	(10)	5.0	(7)		
Organizational change and development			6.6	(4)	3.4	(10)
Fund and resource raising			5.5	(6)		
Director of volunteer services			4.4	(8)	7.0	(4)
Budget and accounting			4.2	(9)		
Empowerment/political			4.2	(9)	10.2	(2)
Nontraditional volunteers					5.5	(7)
Substantive areas					3.9	(9)
Percentage of all comments	82.4		74.4		68.1	
Total comments	2180		1826		597	

*Table presents the percentage of administrators' comments made in each area and the ranking of the areas according to the frequency of comments received.

and retention of volunteers (13.7 percent); interviewing, screening, and placing volunteers in organizational positions (10.1 percent); and supervision and management of volunteers (8.2 percent). Professional skills (7.7 percent), embracing such areas as time management, leadership, ethics, communication, conflict resolution, counseling and coaching, team building, and networking, rounded out the top five subject areas. The second group of five areas consisted of planning and evaluation of the volunteer program (7.1 percent); training employees for collaboration with volunteers and volunteers for the responsibilities assigned to them (5.7 percent); designing jobs for volunteers (5.0 percent); maintaining records for the volunteer program (4.5 percent); and publicizing the program through marketing, advertising, and the media (3.2 percent).

The topics identified most often for a basic course focused primarily on building the volunteer program, but the administrators felt that developing the skills and position of the volunteer manager should receive greater emphasis in an advanced seminar. They gave top priority to the acquisition of professional skills, recommended in 15.1 percent of their comments. Issues pertaining to the director of volunteer services, including training, organizational status, compensation, and board of director relations, commanded 4.4 percent of the suggestions. Another 4.2 percent of comments centered on empowerment and political factors, such as involving volunteers in program management, building organizational support for volunteers, and honing the political skills and savvy of the volunteer administrator. The sample also endorsed treatment of several of the fundamental skills selected for the basic course, but the subject areas preferred for the advanced seminar moved beyond them to encompass organizational change and development, including organizational needs assessment and development, new programs and innovation, and future trends (6.6 percent of comments), funds and resource raising (5.5 percent), and budgeting and accounting (4.2 percent). According to these responses, a substantial portion of advanced training should be devoted to enhancing professional competencies of the volunteer administrator.

Finally, the volunteer managers called on the academic community to conduct research on questions both enduring and novel. By the frequency of their comments, they would most appreciate studies of volunteer motivation and retention (10.9 percent of suggestions), as well as recruitment (7.9 percent) and management of volunteers (5.5 percent)—surely among the most fundamental topics in all of volunteerism. But they also recommended research on nontraditional volunteers, for example, those who are handicapped or court referred (5.5 percent), and on volunteering in particular substantive domains, such as in the schools or hospitals (3.9 percent). The administrators place relatively great importance on research to address issues whose resolution will challenge the resources and commitment of their profession and host organizations well into the future: volunteer empowerment (10.2 percent) and the status of the director of volunteer services position (7.0 percent). These issues have been central to the present analysis.

Implications

The results of this analysis carry important implications for administrators of volunteer services as well as for leaders and managers of the nonprofit and public organizations that house the programs they direct. Findings from the Educational Needs Survey show that only one-quarter of the sample had undergone training in volunteer administration prior to beginning work in this field. Yet nine out of ten of the volunteer practitioners believe that their organization would be willing to subsidize at least a portion of the cost of their continuing education. Although the two items are not directly parallel (the former solicits factual information and the latter asks for a projection), the differences in response invite explanation. What might account for the apparently marked increase in the percentage of organizations interested in training for the administrator of volunteer services since the entry of these officials into the field?

One explanation suggests a more enlightened corps of leaders and managers in host organizations, who through observation, experience, or interaction may have come to appreciate more fully the benefits of the volunteer program and its administrator. The increasing professionalism of the field of volunteer management over the past decade may have facilitated such awareness.

Many of the volunteer practitioners included in the survey entered the field some time ago: nearly one-third of the sample (31.3 percent) have worked in volunteer management for ten years or more and another 25.4 percent for six to ten years. During this period, volunteer administration has continued its rise toward professional status. The field now boasts a variety of support resources, including membership associations; international, national, and regional conferences; technical assistance and consultation; coursework and some degree programs offered by universities; and AVA-sanctioned certification. If, as suggested by the findings of the Educational Needs Survey, leaders and managers of nonprofit and public organizations have become more supportive of the position of volunteer services administrator, the reasons may lie in these developments. The field of volunteer management has grown more active and visible. As a result, potential employers are better able to identify organizational needs in this area and to locate, hire, and support appropriate individuals through continuing education.

A fully compatible interpretation focuses on the role of the volunteer services administrator in promoting such awareness among agency leaders and managers. Organizations are most likely to learn about continuing education in volunteerism — indeed, about the entire field — from these officials. Thus, volunteer administrators need to devote a significant component of their job to advocacy for their position and program.

In this regard, findings from the Educational Needs Survey are quite optimistic. With the burden on them to persuade the agency, the sample of volunteer administrators express remarkable confidence that host organizations will appreciate the merits of further training and, thus, support it financially. Similarly, the AVA Survey on Employer Recognition discussed above found that when volunteer managers took the initiative, organizations were often forthcoming in endorsing and subsidizing training. When they failed to take the lead, however, a more likely outcome was frustration and missed opportunities (Patton, 1990).

If the degree of lack of organizational support for volunteer administration lamented in the literature is to improve, these results suggest that the volunteer manager must play a key part. As the data in Table 7.1 illustrate, issues of empowerment and political and professional skills appear to weigh heavily on the minds of these officials. Not only do they strongly endorse these topics for treatment in advanced training seminars but also for greater attention in scholarly research.

Administrators of volunteer services cannot build this support on their own, however. They require assistance from leaders and managers in nonprofit and public sector agencies who have the authority to make policy and allocate resources accordingly. As discussed above, agency leadership may have grown more aware of and receptive to efforts to upgrade the volunteer administrator position. Yet much progress must still lie ahead.

The 1986 survey conducted by the Association for Volunteer Administration (1987) found that 80 percent of its members earned less than $30,000 (the average salary was $24,169). Some five years later, a national survey of 704 nonprofit organizations by the Technical Assistance Center (1990) estimated the average salary of a volunteer coordinator at $20,863. Not only did this figure rank low compared to earnings of other professional positions in the sample of nonprofit agencies, but also it intimates that salary for volunteer administrators remained flat over the latter part of the 1980s. Despite relatively high levels of formal educational attainment, these officials tend to believe, with some apparent justification, that they earn less than occupants of comparable positions in their organization (Stubblefield and Miles, 1986). To strengthen the position of the volunteer services administrator, leaders and managers of nonprofit and public organizations should address the compensation issue. They also need to consider elevating this official in the organizational hierarchy and ensuring full participation in decision making and policymaking relevant to the volunteer program.

Conclusions

Despite the importance of volunteer services administrators to most nonprofit and many government organizations, these officials have been the subject of little systematic research. To address this gap, the present study has proposed and examined empirically several hypotheses pertaining to volunteer administrators. Analysis based on a very broad sample of 765 volunteer practitioners in the United States and Canada, surveyed in 1989 and 1990, revealed an abiding commitment on the part of these officials to continuing education in volunteer management. According to the views expressed by the administrators, most host organizations appeared willing to subsidize such training.

As expected, nonprofit organizations seemed somewhat more supportive of the position of administrator of volunteer services than did government agencies, but these results did not attain statistical significance. Research has started to appear with an explicit focus on contrasts (and similarities) between public and nonprofit organizations (Cnaan and Goldberg-Glen, 1990; Sundeen, 1990). As in the present study, findings are not conclusive, but they do suggest the importance of organizational auspices for volunteer involvement. Given the likely influence of organizational context factors on such processes as volunteer recruitment and retention, the nature and extent of citizen participation, and the scope and quality of services to clients, institutional differences merit increased attention from scholars and practitioners in volunteerism. So, too, does the crucial role played by leaders and managers of nonprofit organizations, as well as the volunteer administrator, in developing support for this position and the volunteer program.

References

Appel, M. A., Jimmerson, R. M., Macduff, N., and Long, J. S. "Northwest Volunteer Managers: Their Characteristics, Jobs, Volunteer Organizations and Perceived Training Needs." *Journal of Volunteer Administration*, 1988, 7(1), 1–8.

Association for Volunteer Administration. *Profile: 1986 Membership Survey.* Boulder, Colo.: Association for Volunteer Administration, 1987.

Brudney, J. L. *Fostering Volunteer Programs in the Public Sector: Planning, Initiating, and Managing Voluntary Activities.* San Francisco: Jossey-Bass, 1990.

Cnaan, R. A., and Goldberg-Glen, R. "Comparison of Volunteers in Public and Nonprofit Human Service Agencies." *Nonprofit and Voluntary Sector Quarterly,* 1990, *19*(4), 345-358.

Derrickson, M. C. *The Literature of the Nonprofit Sector: A Bibliography with Abstracts,* Vol. 1. New York: Foundation Center, 1989.

Duncombe, S. "Volunteers in City Government: Advantages, Disadvantages and Uses." *National Civic Review,* 1985, *74*(9), 356-364.

Hodgkinson, V. A., and Weitzman, M. S. *Giving and Volunteering in the United States: Findings from a National Survey.* Washington, D.C.: INDEPENDENT SECTOR, 1990.

Layton, D. N. *Philanthropy and Voluntarism: An Annotated Bibliography.* New York: Foundation Center, 1987.

Ostrowski, J. S., and Sehl, F. "How Are We Doing? A Look at the Compensation Levels of Rhode Island Volunteer Administrators." *Journal of Volunteer Administration,* 1990, *9*(1), 9-19.

Patton, J. H. "Association for Volunteer Administration Survey on Employer Recognition: A Report to the Membership." *Journal of Volunteer Administration,* 1990, *9*(1), 1-8.

Pugliese, D. J. *Voluntary Associations: An Annotated Bibliography.* New York: Garland, 1986.

Scheier, I. H. "Empowering a Profession: What's in Our Name?" *Journal of Volunteer Administration,* 1988a, *6*(4), 31-36.

Scheier, I. H. "Empowering a Profession: Seeing Ourselves as More Than Subsidiary." *Journal of Volunteer Administration,* 1988b, *7*(1), 29-34.

Scheier, I. H. "Empowering a Profession: Leverage Points and Process." *Journal of Volunteer Administration,* 1988-1989, *7*(2), 50-57.

Stubblefield, H. W., and Miles, L. "Administration of Volunteer Programs as a Career: What Role for Higher Education?" *Journal of Voluntary Action Research,* 1986, *15*(4), 4–12.

Sundeen, R. A. "Citizens Serving Government: The Extent and Distinctiveness of Volunteer Participation in Local Public Agencies." *Nonprofit and Voluntary Sector Quarterly,* 1990, *19*(4), 329–344.

Technical Assistance Center. *1990 National Nonprofit Wage and Benefits Survey.* Denver, Colo.: Technical Assistance Center, 1990.

Wilson, M. *The Effective Management of Volunteer Programs.* Boulder, Colo.: Johnson, 1976.

8.

Leadership in Human Services: Key Challenges and Competencies

Cynthia D. McCauley
Martha W. Hughes

Personnel psychologists have long been concerned with how to best select individuals to fill positions in organizations, how to train and develop them, and how to evaluate their effectiveness in these positions. They believe that to do any of these things well requires a good job analysis: an in-depth understanding of what people in these jobs do, what they have to deal with, and what skills and abilities help them perform their jobs well.

Because of the potential leadership roles played by managers in organizations, a considerable amount of research has been devoted to the analysis of managerial jobs. Some of this research has focused on the demands placed on individuals in these positions (for example, Tornow and Pinto, 1976), while

Note: The research described in this article was supported by a grant from the Kellogg Foundation. Mark Sills and Chris Troxler of the Human Service Institute provided invaluable advice on research design and access to human service administrators.

other research has looked more closely at the skill or personal quality requirements of the job (for example, Boyatzis, 1982). When these studies are integrated, a coherent picture of the tasks managers face and the competencies needed to deal with these tasks begins to emerge (Stewart, 1989; Yukl and Lepsinger, 1991).

However, most studies of the challenges involved in running an organization and the competencies necessary to do this effectively have taken place in the corporate sector. Because the nonprofit sector has some unique characteristics, we cannot necessarily generalize research results on corporate managers to managers in this sector. Nonprofit organizations' missions, governance structures, funding sources, and reliance on volunteers create differences in their internal dynamics and external relationships (Young, 1987; Herman and Heimovics, 1989).

Because selection, training and development, and evaluation are equally as important for managers in the nonprofit sector, more attention to the development of job analysis information in this sector is warranted. Increased research and systematic thought on the critical managerial challenges and competencies of running nonprofit organizations have recently emerged (Heimovics and Herman, 1989; Herman and Heimovics, 1989; INDEPENDENT SECTOR, 1989; National Assembly, 1989; Rubin, Adamski, and Block, 1989).

In this chapter, we present findings from our own research focused on understanding the jobs of managers of human service agencies. By "human service agency" we mean local nonprofit agencies (both public and private) that provide services to meet the social needs of the community, such as health, social services, arts, and recreation. Our research questions included:

1. What do human service administrators see as the challenges in their leadership positions?
2. Does the prevalence of these challenges vary across different types of agencies?
3. What do human service administrators see as the competencies most important for success in their positions?

Methods

We began by interviewing twenty-seven directors of human service agencies in North Carolina. The interviews, which consisted of a number of open-ended questions that focused on managing relationships, setting agendas, and career issues, served as the basis for designing a more comprehensive survey.

The major section of the survey contained sixty-eight leadership challenge items, each item representing a specific challenge we had heard from two or more directors in the interview process. In responding to each item, the administrator used a five-point scale to indicate how much he or she experienced the challenge in his or her position. Another section asked administrators to select eight of sixteen qualities they considered most important for success in their positions. The qualities reflected scales on a research-based management development questionnaire (McCauley, Lombardo, and Usher, 1989).

The survey also contained questions about the characteristics of the administrators' agency, including the number of years in existence, the current annual budget, the number of board members, whether the agency was public or private, whether it was affiliated with a national organization, and which funding sources it relied on (foundations; local, state, and/or federal government; United Way, community or civic groups; churches; fees for products or services; and contributions from individuals).

We sent the survey to a sample of 300 human service administrators, a list that was obtained from three different sources: participants in a workshop for hospice organizations in the eastern United States, a representative selection of administrators in North and South Carolina acquired from the mailing list of the Human Services Institute, and directors of United Way agencies in a large midwestern metropolitan area.

A total of 161 managers participated in the study, representing a 54 percent return rate. Seventy-four percent of the organizations were private agencies; 40 percent were part of a national organization. Of the total, 134 were executive directors and 27 were managers at other levels. Sixty-three percent of the group were female. On the average, the managers had held their current position for five years, had been managers for eleven years, and had worked in the human service field for sixteen years. Counseling, education, and health care were the most frequently mentioned primary services of the agencies surveyed.

Results and Discussion

Leadership Challenges

Our first task was to define the core leadership challenges represented among the sixty-eight different challenge items by grouping together challenge items that were statistically highly related with one another and looking for a common theme across the items within groups. Our assumption was that these homogeneous groups of items represented the underlying distinct dimensions of leadership challenges. A variable clustering technique was used to divide the sixty-eight leadership challenge items into groups that could be interpreted as primarily unidimensional. A twelve-cluster solution was chosen as most closely meeting statistical and interpretability criteria.

Each dimension consisted of three to eleven challenge items. The twelve dimensions resulting from the analysis provide a framework for understanding the core leadership challenges faced by human service administrators.

1. *Utilizing resources and building support for change.* Human service agencies must be responsive to the changing needs of their client groups and to the innovative ideas generated within the agency. But this often translates into the need to do things differently, which staff may resist. Thus one task the leaders of these organizations face is getting staff support and the necessary resources to create needed changes or experiment with new approaches. One aspect of this task for the manager is building his or her credibility within the organization.

2. *Directing and motivating staff.* For most human service agencies, people are their main assets. To maximize this asset, the manager has to make good hiring decisions, set clear expectations for staff, get them to see "the big picture" and work cooperatively, and deal effectively with performance problems when they arise.

3. *Building outside support and understanding.* The human service agency is embedded in a community that it depends on for support and that, at the same time, it is trying to make a proactive impact on. The human service administrator often spends considerable time increasing public awareness of the agency and the issues it deals with, building cooperative relationships with funders, and constructively handling competition with other agencies. The mission of the organization may also require advocacy work on the part of the leader.

4. *Improving an agency's performance.* As with other types of organizations, when an agency is experiencing major problems, a manager is brought in and charged with turning around the performance of the troubled organization. In many of these cases, the manager's basic challenges are to establish priorities and improve financial accountability.

5. *Time pressures.* Multiple agency objectives combined with small staffs create a great deal of time pressure in human service administrators' jobs. They are challenged to manage their time more effectively and to balance their work and personal life. Time pressures are particularly acute when an agency is experiencing rapid growth.

6. *Lack of supportive working environment.* The working environment is a potentially important motivator in the nonprofit agency. If it does not provide peer support or developmental opportunities, then the leader must find ways to improve it. A supportive working environment is also a critical ingredient in combating burnout.

7. *Clashes with the board.* The director of a human service agency has an important interface with the agency's board and from time to time must handle conflicts with the board due to

disagreements over major decisions, lack of role clarity, personality differences, or too much board control.

8. *Problems with clients and external groups.* Leaders of human service agencies also must deal with conflicts with individuals or important liaison groups external to the agency: clients with unmet needs or unrealistic expectations, government organizations, regulatory agencies, or various funders who create conflicting demands for accountability.

9. *Reconciling diverse demands.* The presence of multiple objectives and diverse constituencies requires a balancing act on the part of the human service leader. He or she must deal with diverse client needs, coordinate among different programs and/or parts of the organization, and balance between people concerns and task concerns.

10. *Uncertain or limited resources.* Human service administrators face yearly uncertainty in levels or sources of funding, which leads to a large amount of time spent in fundraising. They are also challenged by the inability to pay competitive staff salaries.

11. *Volunteer involvement.* Volunteers are another source of uncertain resources. Recruiting volunteers and motivating them are other major challenges faced by human service leaders.

12. *Lack of knowledge or experience.* Many leaders of human service agencies have backgrounds in helping professions with little preparation for management. Thus the new human service administrator operates with the additional challenge of building a knowledge and experience base for carrying out the responsibilities of his or her job.

The five-point ratings on the questionnaire items that made up a dimension were averaged to obtain an overall score on that dimension. Thus each participant in the survey received a score on each of the twelve leadership challenge dimensions. By averaging these dimension scores, we were able to rank the challenges from most to least prevalent among the human service administrators in our sample.

Challenge	Mean	S.D.
Time pressure	3.29	.89
Uncertain or limited resources	3.23	.93
Reconciling diverse demands	2.66	.81
Lack of supportive work environment	2.65	.78
Building outside support and understanding	2.64	.68
Volunteer involvement	2.44	.95
Problems with clients and external groups	2.44	.66
Utilizing resources and building support for change	2.43	.83
Directing and motivating staff	2.35	.76
Improving an agency's performance	2.28	.96
Lack of knowledge or experience	2.14	.71
Clashes with the board	1.73	.69

Time pressure and uncertain or limited resources were by far seen as the strongest challenges faced in our sample. These challenges are likely more constant parts of the human service world than are the lowest-rated challenges. Improving an agency's performance, lack of knowledge or experience, and clashes with the board may occur sometime during a leader's tenure but are more intermittent.

Differences Across Agencies

Research in corporations indicates that managerial jobs differ according to their settings (Stewart, 1989), and we felt that this was likely true in human service agencies as well. We wanted to see if we could uncover any systematic variations between the leadership challenges and some important agency characteristics.

To look for patterns in the variability of challenges across agencies, the leadership challenge dimension scores were correlated with characteristics of the administrator's agency (see Table 8.1) and the agency's funding sources (see Table 8.2). A number of variables in these tables are dichotomous. In these cases, presence of a state or condition (for example, agency is part of a national organization) was coded 1 and absence was coded 0. (Thus a positive correlation indicates that the challenge is associated with the agency characteristic while a negative correlation indicates that the challenge is associated with the *absence*

Table 8.1. Leadership Challenge Dimensions Correlated with Agency Characteristics.

Dimension	Private Agency	National Affiliate	Years in Existence	Size of Budget	Diversity in Funding	Size of Board
Utilizing resources and building support for change	.13	.02	.07	.18*	.11	-.07
Directing and motivating staff	.07	.08	.01	.17*	.23**	-.09
Building outside support and understanding	-.01	-.01	-.02	.04	.03	-.16*
Improving an agency's performance	.09	-.13	.11	-.03	.09	-.11
Time pressures	.08	.01	-.08	-.04	.02	-.20**
Lack of supportive work environment	-.07	.03	-.07	.05	-.02	-.11
Clashes with the board	-.05	-.04	-.01	-.09	.07	-.09
Problems with clients and external groups	-.02	.10	.05	.26**	.22**	-.11
Reconciling diverse demands	.05	.09	-.05	.01	.10	.01
Uncertain or limited resources	.13	.10	-.16*	-.11	.10	-.13
Volunteer involvement	-.15*	-.02	-.16*	-.27**	-.11	-.07
Lack of knowledge or experience	.02	.03	-.06	-.14	-.07	-.12

*p < .05.
**p < .01.

Table 8.2. Leadership Challenge Dimensions Correlated with Funding Sources.

Dimension	Local Government	State Government	Federal Government	Foundations	United Way	Community Groups	Churches	Individual Contributions	Fees
Utilizing resources and building support for change	.19*	.19*	.03	.01	.16*	-.10	-.07	-.06	.18*
Directing and motivating staff	.31**	.27**	.09	.03	.07	.04	.05	-.03	.18*
Building outside support and understanding	.05	.13	-.05	-.06	.03	.01	.05	-.11	.11
Improving an agency's performance	-.03	.17*	-.03	.02	.18*	.07	.00	-.08	.11
Time pressures	-.10	-.05	-.07	.08	.02	.00	.06	.06	.01
Lack of supportive work environment	.05	.10	.02	-.13	-.08	-.03	-.03	-.03	-.02
Clashes with the board	.02	.10	-.07	-.05	.10	.05	.06	-.02	.04
Problems with clients and external groups	.24**	.24**	.12	.03	.11	.03	.01	-.12	.25**
Reconciling diverse demands	.09	.13	.05	-.03	-.05	.05	.08	.04	.07
Uncertain or limited resources	.02	.01	-.21**	.11	.09	.12	.23**	.08	-.04
Volunteer involvement	-.11	-.05	-.18*	.03	.07	-.01	.03	-.05	-.20*
Lack of knowledge or experience	-.12	-.14	-.14	-.08	-.02	.15*	.15*	.04	-.12

*p < .05.
**p < .01.

of the characteristic.) The number of funders variable was created by summing the number of responses checked on the funding source list.

As shown in Table 8.1, seven of the twelve dimensions were significantly related to one or more of the agency characteristics examined. Administrators in public agencies are challenged more than those in private agencies by volunteer involvement, which is not surprising since volunteers are less likely to be attracted to these agencies and their boards are generally appointed by the government rather than made up of recruited volunteers. Younger agencies experience more resource challenges, both funding and volunteers, than do more established ones. This finding is also not too surprising since older agencies are more likely to have developed relationships with volunteers and funders, built up a revenue base, and established a committed board that takes on major fundraising responsibilities.

Although directors of larger agencies (in terms of size of budget) have fewer problems than smaller agencies with volunteer involvement, they tend to be more challenged by building support for change, directing and motivating their staff, and handling conflict with external groups. Larger organizations lose some of their flexibility and adaptability, and larger numbers of staff members and external interfaces require more energy directed toward working with these groups. In addition, larger organizations are more visible, which perhaps causes more conflict with external groups.

Interestingly, having larger boards is associated with less challenge from the need to build support outside the agency and from time pressures. A reciprocal effect is probably taking place: more board members can create larger support in the community and well-supported agencies easily attract more board members. More active board members may also ease some of the workload on an agency director, decreasing pressures from time constraints, for example, by fundraising, representing the agency at special functions, making presentations, and raising public awareness.

Table 8.2 shows that a majority of the challenges are also associated with the agency's primary funding sources. Directors of agencies depending on local and state government funds report higher challenges from building support for change, directing and motivating staff, and problems with external groups. It is interesting to note that those receiving federal funds report less challenge from uncertain or limited resources while those receiving financial support from churches report more of this challenge. Receiving United Way funds is associated more strongly with utilizing resources and building support for change and with improving an agency's performance, perhaps because both of these have aspects of performance accountability within them. Also, charging fees for services is related to several of the dimensions, including building support for change and problems with clients and external groups; both of these dimensions are related to being adaptable to client needs and the external environment.

It is also important to note that three of the challenges — lack of supportive work environment, clashes with the board, and reconciling diverse demands — were not related to any of the agency characteristics we examined, indicating that they are as likely to occur in one type of agency as another.

Competencies Important for Success

Another way of analyzing the job of human service administrator was to look at what incumbents thought were the most important competencies for success in their positions. Below we have rank-ordered the qualities presented in the questionnaire by the percentage of respondents who chose that quality as one of their top eight. (*Note:* We felt that all the qualities were important in general; we wanted to know which were *most* important in their particular situation.)

1. *Acting with flexibility.* (84%) Being able to behave in seemingly opposite ways, being tough and at the same time compassionate, leading and letting others lead
2. *Resourcefulness.* (80%) Being a flexible problem solver, handling pressure and ambiguity, being a strategic thinker
3. *Leading subordinates.* (74%) Motivating subordinates, delegating to them, setting clear performance expectations

4. *Integrity.* (70%) Not blaming or abusing others, relying on substance and straightforwardness
5. *Setting a developmental climate.* (64%) Encouraging growth, leading by example, providing challenge and opportunity
6. *Hiring talented staff.* (59%) Recruiting the best
7. *Team orientation.* (58%) Focusing on others to accomplish tasks, not being a loner
8. *Building and mending relationships.* (48%) Getting the cooperation of peers and clients, negotiating well, not alienating others
9. *Doing whatever it takes.* (47%) Persevering through adversity, taking full responsibility, seizing opportunities
10. *Balancing personal life and work.* (42%) Balancing work priorities with personal life so that neither is neglected
11. *Compassion and sensitivity.* (40%) Caring about the hopes and dreams of others, being sensitive to the needs of others
12. *Self-awareness.* (34%) Recognizing strengths and weaknesses, seeking corrective feedback
13. *Putting people at ease.* (34%) Having personal warmth and a good sense of humor
14. *Decisiveness.* (33%) Displaying a bias for action and calculated risks
15. *Being a quick study.* (22%) Quickly mastering new knowledge and skills
16. *Confronting problem subordinates.* (13%) Moving quickly to remedy performance problems

Being flexible and resourceful were most frequently chosen as important qualities. Four of the next five top qualities were all related to the administrator's interface with his or her staff: hiring them, leading them, setting a developmental climate, and having a team orientation. Integrity was also a frequently chosen quality.

Conclusions

The current research has provided two frameworks for understanding the jobs of human service administrators: one challenge based, the other competency or quality based. The two frameworks clearly are related to one another. Flexibility is critical for being able to reconcile diverse demands. Resourcefulness helps one deal with time pressures and uncertain or limited resources. Setting a developmental climate combats a lack of supportive work environment. Leadership skills help one direct and motivate a staff. Being a quick study is an important quality when one is in a job where he or she lacks knowledge or experience. Looking at the rank-ordering of challenges and of competencies, the challenges and competencies that are interrelated appear at about the same place on their respective lists (for example, flexibility is highly ranked as is reconciling diverse demands). The one exception to this is a high ranking for leading subordinates but a lower ranking for directing and motivating staff.

The challenge-based framework contains more components that are clearly illustrative of the unique features of the nonprofit sector. Although time pressures and directing and motivating staff are issues in any organization, other dimensions (for example, uncertain or limited resources, volunteer involvement, clashes with the board) are more unique to the human service agency. All organizations have to manage an external interface, but the dimensions in the framework related to this task (that is, building outside support and understanding, problems with clients and external groups) also focus more distinctly on nonprofit issues.

As we mentioned in the beginning, job analysis frameworks are useful in a number of human resource management tasks, and different frameworks may be useful for different tasks. A challenge-based framework may be more useful for providing prospective executive director candidates with a realistic job preview or for doing an annual performance appraisal. A competency-based model may be more useful for designing a broad-based training program for the development of nonprofit leaders.

This study also suggests that the importance of the various dimensions in a framework will vary from situation to situation. An important step is figuring out what pieces of a framework are most applicable to one's own situation. When creating networks of human service administrators or delivering training programs to them, one must also keep this variability in mind (and find ways to capitalize on it).

Finally, we do recognize the limitations of this study. Validating our results with larger and more geographically diverse samples and integrating these findings with other emerging frameworks mentioned in the introduction are the valuable steps that must follow.

References

Boyatzis, R. E. *The Competent Manager: A Model for Effective Performance.* New York: Wiley, 1982.

Heimovics, R. D., and Herman, R. D. "The Salient Management Skills: A Conceptual Framework for a Curriculum for Managers in Nonprofit Organizations." *American Review of Public Administration,* 1989, *19*(4), 295–312.

Herman, R. D., and Heimovics, R. D. "Critical Events in the Management of Nonprofit Organizations: Initial Evidence." *Nonprofit and Voluntary Sector Quarterly,* 1989, *18*(2), 119–132.

INDEPENDENT SECTOR. *Profiles of Excellence: Studies of the Effectiveness of Nonprofit Organizations, Executive Summary.* Washington, D.C.: INDEPENDENT SECTOR, 1989.

McCauley, C. D., Lombardo, M. M., and Usher, C. J. "Diagnosing Management Development Needs: An Instrument Based on How Managers Develop." *Journal of Management,* 1989, *15*(3), 389–403.

National Assembly of National Voluntary Health and Social Welfare Organizations. *A Study in Excellence.* Washington, D.C.: National Assembly, 1989.

Rubin, H., Adamski, L., and Block, S. R. "Toward a Discipline of Nonprofit Administration: Report from the Clarion Conference." *Nonprofit and Voluntary Sector Quarterly,* 1989, *18*(3), 279–286.

Stewart, R. "Studies of Managerial Jobs and Behavior: The Ways Forward." *Journal of Managerial Studies,* 1989, *26*(1), 1–10.

Tornow, W. W., and Pinto, P. R. "The Development of a Managerial Job Taxonomy: A System for Describing, Classifying, and Evaluating Executive Positions." *Journal of Applied Psychology,* 1976, *61*(4), 410–418.

Young, D. R. "Executive Leadership in Nonprofit Organizations." In W. W. Powell (ed.), *The Nonprofit Sector: A Research Handbook.* New Haven, Conn.: Yale University Press, 1987.

Yukl, G. A., and Lepsinger, R. "An Integrating Taxonomy of Managerial Behavior: Implications for Improving Managerial Effectiveness." In J. W. Jones, B. D. Steffy, and D. W. Bray (eds.), *Applying Psychology in Business: The Handbook for Managers and Human Resource Professionals.* Lexington, Mass.: Lexington Books, 1991.

9.

Management Effectiveness
in Fundraising

Margaret A. Duronio
Bruce A. Loessin

Philanthropy in the United States entered the 1990s as an enterprise generating more than $114 billion in gifts in 1990 (McMillen, 1990b), an increase of more than 100 percent over just $49 billion in 1980 ("Challenges for the 1990s," 1990). The growth of philanthropic activity during the 1980s and developments foretelling continued growth in the 1990s indicate that fund raisers will face stiffer competition in all areas of the nonprofit world. In every area, major campaigns proliferate, some with astounding goals. For example, Cornell, Harvard, and Yale Universities are planning campaigns expected to exceed goals of $1 billion each (McMillen, 1990a). Campaigns actually under way (Allbright, 1990) include the United Jewish Appeal and Federation of Jewish Philanthropies of New York City campaign for $1.2 billion; the national Presbyterian Church campaign for $150 million; the United States Holocaust Memorial Museum campaign for $147 million; and the Juvenile Diabetes Foundation campaign for $100 million.

Note: Some material in this chapter has been published in *Effective Fund Raising in Higher Education.* Copyright © 1991 by Jossey-Bass Inc., Publishers.

Fundraising has become a multimillion-dollar expenditure for higher education and all other nonprofit organizations. One recent estimate (Fisher, 1989) sets average higher education fundraising costs at about eight cents per dollar raised for private institutions and at about twelve cents per dollar raised for public institutions. Using these cost estimates, higher education institutions alone may have spent as much as $864 million to raise the $9 billion given in voluntary support to higher education in 1990. Overall fundraising costs are likely to increase as fundraising technology rapidly expands to enable fund raisers to reach greater numbers of donors with more personalized appeals. Because of both more significant consequences for organizations and escalating costs, there is a need for better understanding of the factors that affect fundraising results.

Fundraising Effectiveness and Potential for Success

Little systematic research has been done on fundraising effectiveness. (For a comprehensive review and insightful analysis of such research, see Brittingham and Pezzullo, 1990.) Defining effectiveness is a primary problem in studying fundraising. The amount of money raised by a school has been the most widely used measure of effectiveness, but this measure is inadequate because no norms have been established for comparing dollar amounts. Using money raised as the criterion without norms for systematic comparison eliminates consideration of the differences between schools in institutional resources for fund raising and provides no assessment of how a given year's results compare with an institution's potential for raising money. If an institution raises $5 million one year and $6 million the next year, does that 20 percent increase represent success? If two institutions, one a state university in a rural area with 7,000 students and the other a private college in a major city with 600 students, raise $1.5 million each, are these two institutions performing equally well? These questions are impossible to answer without information about what the individual institutions might be expected to raise.

In an effort to better determine institutional potential for fundraising success, we conducted our first study (Duronio and

Loessin, 1990; Loessin, Duronio, and Borton, 1988) to describe the relationships between institutional characteristics and dollars raised and to determine if these relationships varied across different types of institutions. Ten types of institutions were included in the original analysis of 575: private and public research, doctoral, and comprehensive universities; and private and public baccalaureate and two-year colleges.

The basic institutional characteristics we studied in our early research, in addition to type of institution and private or public status, were those most often linked in the literature to fundraising success: educational and general expenditures, endowment, expenditures per student, cost of tuition, alumni of record, enrollment, and age of institution. For measures of fundraising results, we used data reported for publication in the annual report *Voluntary Support to Education* (Council for Aid to Education, 1984, 1985, 1986).

Merely scanning the data confirmed our commonsense knowledge that, overall, the types of institutions that raised the most money (private and public research universities, for example) also had the most institutional resources. However, when institutions were sorted by type, with private research universities compared only with other private research universities and public two-year colleges compared only with other public two-year colleges, for example, it became clear that not all institutions with high levels of resources had high fundraising totals. Conversely, institutions with the lowest resources were not always the ones with the lowest totals. For all types of institutions, we found all possible combinations of levels of institutional resources and fundraising outcomes. Studying fundraising by comparing basic institutional characteristics and results does not fully explain why some institutions raise considerably more money in voluntary support than do other institutions of the same type with roughly equivalent resources. Although this early research demonstrated that some institutional characteristics (such as type of institution, endowment, and overall institutional budget) are highly correlated with dollars raised in many institutions, these findings are not particularly useful to administrators seeking to improve fundraising programs, because they

•

do not have the ability to change such factors. This initial study confirmed that it is not possible to fully understand either effectiveness or potential for success in fundraising by studying quantitative factors alone.

Case Study Methodology

In the second study, on which this chapter is based, we turned from a quantitative study of basic institutional characteristics and fundraising totals in 575 institutions to the study of qualitative characteristics commonly associated with fundraising success in just ten institutions. (Full results of this study of ten institutions appear in Duronio and Loessin, 1991a.)

Our operational definition of fundraising effectiveness is based on the idea that such effectiveness is a measure of how well an institution realizes its full potential in fundraising. Potential is an abstract concept, not well defined or easily measurable, but we know that wealthy, large, prestigious institutions have greater potential for raising money than institutions with more modest enrollments, financial resources, and reputations. Multiple regression analysis is a statistical procedure that can be used to predict what a given institution with a given set of institutional characteristics might be expected to raise in voluntary support. Institutions that actually raise an amount greater than predicted may be making good use of their resources and potential. Therefore, our operational definition of an effective fundraising program is one in which actual results exceed predicted results.

To select the ten institutions for intensive study, we sorted institutions from our original group of 575 by type, used multiple regression analysis to predict fundraising results, and calculated a score for total voluntary support. This score was obtained by dividing the actual results by the predicted results. Thus the score is greater than 1 if actual results exceed predicted results or less than 1 if predicted results exceed actual results. For example, if actual results equal $1.8 million and predicted results equal $1.3 million, the score is 1.38. If actual results equal $1.3 million and predicted results equal $1.8 million, the score is .72. We selected one institution of each of the ten types from

a pool of about 100 institutions with effective fundraising programs, that is, with scores above 1. Table 9.1 presents a summary of some basic characteristics of these ten institutions, including total dollars raised.

The ten institutions in this study are nationally representative, located in eight different states in New England, the
Southeast, the Midwest, the Southwest, and the West Coast.
They include institutions in urban and rural settings, and, among
the private institutions, some with religious affiliations and some
without. We avoided institutions with well-known reputations
for success in fundraising on the grounds that their high visibility in fundraising is a factor that now contributes to their continuing success and makes them less representative of all insti-

Table 9.1. Ranges and Medians for Institutional Characteristics
and Total Voluntary Support for Ten Institutions.

Characteristic	Private Institutions (5)	Public Institutions (5)
Educational/general expenditures	$165,490,000–$2,800,000 Median = $36,669,000	$348,153,000–$12,452,000 Median = $108,280,000
Endowment	$243,552,000–$9,761,000 Median = $17,820,000	$41,100,000–$1,346,000 Median = $1,081,000
Expenditures per student	$20,931–$4,590 Median = $6,665	$12,760–$1,917 Median = $7,091
Cost of tuition	$12,100–$3,600 Median = $7,500	$1,900–$840 Median = $1,200
Alumni of record	82,500–6,400 Median = 52,600	125,000–9,800 Median = 56,500
Enrollment	7,900–500 Median = 5,500	30,900–6,500 Median = 15,300
Age of institution	162–30 years Median = 130	120–24 years Median = 103
Total voluntary support	$28,120,000–$809,000 Median = $4,935,000	$27,905,000–$322,000 Median = $4,700,000

tutions of that type. In some cases, we chose institutions with fundraising results below the median for institutions of their types but which nevertheless had actual results that exceeded the statistical prediction. (This means these institutions were doing very well with what they had, even if dollars raised were not as high as for some other institutions of the same type.) The selected institutions are very diverse in fundraising results, resources, and institutional personalities, as well as in such factors as maturity of fundraising programs and institutional fundraising histories.

We collected data by making site visits of one to four days' duration to each institution and interviewing more than 100 people important to successful fundraising efforts, including presidents and other administrators, chief development officers, and other fundraising staff. We also reviewed relevant documents and materials. To provide a framework for studying each institution's fundraising program, we developed a list of qualitative and descriptive characteristics from a review of the literature on fundraising effectiveness (Glennon, 1986; Leslie, 1969; Pickett, 1977; Willmer, 1981) and on excellence in higher education institutions (Gilley, Fulmer, and Reithlingshoefer, 1986). The list includes

Characteristics of Institutions

Presidential leadership
Trustees' participation
Institution's commitment to fundraising
   Resource allocation
   Acceptance of need for fundraising
   Definition and communication of institution's niche and image
   Institutional fundraising priorities and policies

Characteristics of Fundraising Programs

Chief development officer's leadership
Successful fundraising history
Entrepreneurial fundraising
Volunteers' roles in fundraising
Emphasis on management of the fundraising function

Information and communication systems
Planning, goal setting, and evaluation
Staff development, training, and evaluation
Staff commitment to institution
Emphasis on constituent relations

These descriptive and qualitative characteristics provide information about the context in which the program occurs and are those commonly related to success in fundraising literature.

Overall Results

Data from the site visits were analyzed in two ways: case by case and across cases. (For a case-by-case description of results, see Duronio and Loessin, 1991a.) A summary of the overall results of the study appears in Table 9.2, which presents the number of institutions judged by us and the persons we interviewed to be outstanding in each characteristic. No institutions

Table 9.2. Number of Institutions Outstanding in Each Characteristic.

Characteristic	Number Outstanding
Institution's commitment to fundraising	10
Presidential leadership	9*
Entrepreneurial fundraising	9
Chief development officer's leadership	8**
Definition and communication of institution's niche and image	8
International fundraising priorities and policies	8
Acceptance of need for fundraising	7
Information and communication systems	7
Resource allocation	7
Emphasis on constituent relations	4
Emphasis on management of the fundraising function:	4
planning, goal setting, and evaluation	4
Volunteers' roles in fundraising	4
Staff commitment to institution	3
Staff development, training, and evaluation	3
Successful fundraising history	3
Trustees' participation	3

*The presidency was vacant in one institution.
**The position of chief development officer was vacant in two institutions.

were outstanding in all characteristics; some were doing very well with strengths in only a few. Although all had strengths in one or more of these characteristics, no single pattern emerged for all institutions. The characteristics most consistently found to be outstanding in these successful programs were related to leadership and institutional commitment to fundraising efforts. Among the characteristics least consistently found to be outstanding were those related to volunteers and trustees. Although the overall results of the study generally confirm much of what makes up the current conventional wisdom about fundraising, the results also indicate that success is more complex and more varied than conventional wisdom might suggest.

In keeping with the subject of this book, the rest of this chapter focuses on a discussion of findings for the specific characteristic of emphasis on management of fundraising function and the three related subtopics: information and communication systems; planning, goal setting, and evaluation; and staff development, training, and evaluation.

Management of the Fundraising Function

In the widely read book *Academic Strategy: The Management Revolution in American Higher Education* (1983), Keller noted that higher education institutions are "among the least business-like and well-managed of all organizations" (p. 5) and "alone among major institutions in the United States . . . have steadfastly refused to appropriate the procedures of modern management" (p. viii). Although Keller equated "least business-like" with not "well-managed," the debate about whether higher education organizations should be measured against business corporations is a long-standing one in the literature.

There is some agreement in the literature that the academic institution is unique among organizations. Baldridge, Curtis, Ecker, and Riley, 1978; Cohen and March, 1974; Dressel, 1976; Keller, 1983; Millett, 1978; and Tuckman and Johnson, 1987 have cited major differences between higher education institutions and businesses regarding such aspects as purposes, outcomes and goals, technology, the shared power of the president and faculty, the autonomy of individual departments, and the influence of external constituencies. The issue of how higher education outcomes and goals are different from those of corporations is of particular relevance in a discussion of fundraising. For instance, in a recent text on college management, Tuckman and Johnson (1987) wrote that it is difficult to translate principles of management from a business setting to higher education, noting that there are difficulties in defining excellence and specifying outcomes in educational settings. "What is the educational counterpart of profits?" (p. 2) they asked. They also noted that it is difficult to link student outcomes, a kind of bottom line in higher education, directly to faculty behavior and concluded that a university has no measure of outcomes or effects to compare with a corporation's "reasonably constant inflow of information on profits" (p. 3).

However, it is obvious that fundraising has goals that are similar to those of a corporation. Although fund raisers will point out that campaigns usually have goals that are more than monetary, such as to recruit new volunteers or to increase broad-based advocacy of the institution, most fund raisers will also insist that dollars raised is the most appropriate criterion for measuring the effectiveness of a fund-development program. Also, fund raisers believe that fundraising skills, efforts, and technology are primarily responsible for the annual growth of philanthropic dollars and that they should be evaluated on these factors.

Therefore, because fundraising in most institutions is driven by a focus on concrete, bottom-line results and is one of the most businesslike functions within educational institutions, we expected to find evidence of what one author called a "positive management ethic" (Matthews, 1982) in these successful programs. In general, this was not the case. Senior staff in only four institutions emphasized the importance of management in the success of fundraising programs. In most institutions, management was perceived, at best, more as a routine housekeeping chore than as a critical factor affecting overall fundraising performance. If fundraising is still generally considered to be a necessary evil on many campuses, management is just as necessary an evil in higher education fundraising.

Generally, administrators in academic institutions have been described as having a stronger focus on process than on results (Balderston, 1974; Lutz, 1982; Whetten and Cameron, 1985). Higher education fundraising managers, however, may have a stronger focus on results than on process, which is indicated not only in the generally weak connection most participants made between fundraising success and management but also in the division of labor in most of the offices in this study. In most institutions visited, most managers also had significant fundraising responsibilities. In five institutions, the entire management staff had such responsibilities, which consumed most of their time and attention. In the majority of instances, staff members who had both management roles and fundraising responsibilities felt considerable conflict about remaining on campus "minding the store" versus "being out there raising money."

Sometimes these managers were in conflict because of pressure from more senior managers. For example, the director of development in one of the most effectively managed programs in the study had supervisory responsibility for the entire development staff of about thirty members and accountability for reaching goals amounting to more than $20 million annually. He believed success was the result of his careful monitoring and coaching to ensure coordinated, cooperative efforts among staff members. Having also been an accomplished fund raiser, he experienced continual pressure from his superiors to spend more time on direct fundraising and less time on managing staff and programs. He spoke at length of his role in enhancing the effectiveness of the overall program by leveraging his expertise across the entire fundraising staff, but he was still being evaluated, at least in part, on the number of dollars he raised directly.

Sometimes this conflict was more personal, when enthusiasm for fundraising far exceeded interest in managing. For example, at another institution, a fundraising manager with supervisory responsibility and accountability for a large staff and multimillion-dollar annual goals experienced more internal conflict about the demands on her time. She accepted the need to spend time on managing and clearly perceived the benefits to the overall department resulting from her managerial contributions, but she derived much less satisfaction from being a good manager than from cultivating prospects and securing major gifts.

Some managers who did not specifically identify management as important to fundraising success were nevertheless good managers. Among some other managers we spoke with, there appeared to be a gap between the management values they expressed and their practices. For instance, managers in seven institutions emphasized that teamwork was important to fundraising success at their institutions, but only in four institutions did managers actually provide structures or processes to ensure and facilitate effective teams. Without considerable and specific management support and direction, effective teams do not just happen. It is an organizational fact of life that individual staff members can experience conflict between successfully completing their own work assignments and contributing to the overall success of the group. These kinds of conflicts of interest abound in fundraising and are well understood. What is not as well understood is that strong, visible management practices are critical to foster and guide appropriate resolutions of these conflicts as they occur. Promoting teamwork is not the only way to resolve them, but they will not usually be effectively resolved without deliberate management practices and policies designed to address them.

One fundraising manager at a mid-sized institution in the study showed particular understanding of the role of good management in fundraising effectiveness. A highly successful fund raiser with recently expanded supervisory and managerial responsibilities, she had carefully planned for her own professional development, building on her expertise as a practitioner, and for the professional development of the staff. She spoke with insight about the differences between being effective in a trade in one's own right and being effective in helping others to be successful in that work and about the need for good management and ongoing staff development to continually enhance the effectiveness of the overall fundraising program.

In general, strong, deliberate professional management is not particularly characteristic of these successful fundraising programs. In the institutions without an emphasis on professional management, other factors and characteristics have substituted in the past—factors such as extensive longevity and stability of a small staff, for example. To look at specific aspects of management in these fundraising programs, we examined in particular three broad areas: (1) information and communication; (2) planning, goal setting, and evalution; and (3) staff development, training, and evaluation.

Information and Communication

Information and communication is the strongest management area in these ten institutions with effective fundraising programs. Most fund raisers in this study emphasized that good systems to collect, store, access, and communicate information were essential. They need information about donors, frequent reports to monitor progress and activity, and clear directives about what is expected of them to function effectively. Additionally, they emphasized the importance of good communication both vertically across organizational levels and laterally among fundraising colleagues, within the development office and with the rest of the institution, and with external constituencies. How well staff members communicate with each other is strongly influenced by management directives, support, and modeling.

Senior managers in three institutions were exceptionally noted for how well they conveyed performance expectations to staff. In seven of the ten institutions, fundraising staff were generally satisfied with overall information and communication processes. Three institutions had problems in one or more of the areas related to information and communication and efforts were under way to address these problems.

Planning, Goal Setting, and Evaluation

We expected that formal planning, goal setting, and evaluation would be integral to effective fundraising because of (1) the need to take a more market-oriented view of opportunities and expenditures, circumventing "lockstep" annual percentage increases in fundraising goals and budgets; (2) the increased complexity and cost of fundraising technology and increased competition for philanthropic dollars; (3) the need for long-term investments in fundraising for maximum outcomes; and (4) the increasingly critical role of fundraising in setting and achieving overall institutional mission. In general, planning, goal setting, and evaluation were not particularly characteristic of fundraising programs in these ten institutions. No institution conducted formal comprehensive evaluations of these programs.

Although only two institutions had no formal plans, only four institutions had comprehensive plans that were used as working tools. The approaches to planning and goal setting varied. One program had concrete goals for dollars to be raised and activity level in all program areas; programs in three institutions were based on plans that set overall percent change and conceptual goals (examples of conceptual goals are "improve alumni involvement" or "increase personal solicitations"); programs in four institutions were based on conceptual goals only; and two had no goal setting.

Regardless of whether planning was formal or not, development managers at these institutions nevertheless all had a strategic focus, conceptualizing fundraising as a long-term process and not as a year-to-year or campaign-to-campaign function. Major campaigns promote more intensive and more formal planning: all institutions currently or previously engaged in major campaigns had such formal plans. Development managers at institutions not engaged in campaigns indicated that formal planning would precede upcoming campaigns.

In spite of our thinking that formal planning would help eliminate lockstep annual percentage increases in goals, for the most part, staff in well-established programs essentially set goals by looking at past years' results and adding a certain percentage increase. The amount of increase usually was more intuitively than scientifically derived, reflecting the optimism that regular annual increases in overall giving to higher education have generated. If and when the trend reverses and giving to higher education stabilizes or begins to drop, managers in all institutions will have to become more methodological and strategic in their planning and goal setting. In newer programs, when specific goals were set, staff most often indicated that they were guided by results achieved in what they considered to be peer institutions. Some fund raisers thought it was better to set high goals and fall somewhat short if necessary; some thought it was better (particularly as perceived by donors and volunteers) to have more reasonable goals and be certain of achieving them.

Staff Development, Training, and Evaluation

Of particular significance in a field where most practitioners do not have formal training for the job, fundraising managers in only three institutions strongly emphasized staff training and development. Three institutions held yearly staff retreats for staff development, program planning, and/or team building. Staff in the six largest institutions received merit raises based on performance evaluations. Many managers indicated that competition for experienced staff was currently a more serious problem to them than direct competition for funds. As competition continues to grow, more and more institutions will be forced to hire staff members with limited or no direct fundraising experience. On-the-job training and systematic staff development programs in development offices are therefore likely to increase as this trend continues.

Discussion and Recommendations

Higher education is not an industry noted for excellence in management. But because fundraising is among the most business-like activities conducted on any campus, we expected to find what Young (1987), writing about the lack of a strong management tradition in nonprofit organizations, called "explicit recognition of management as a critical area of activity" (p. 177). In our study, most participants, including many of those who actually manage effective fundraising programs, did not generally identify management as a critical factor in success.

In addition to the fact that the institutional environment in most higher education organizations does not demand or support systematic management and evaluation of fundraising efforts (as indicated in our study), several related factors contribute to both the lack of a strong emphasis on management as critical to success and the gap between management values and practices in fundraising offices.

1. *Fundraising managers are not sure if programs are well managed or not.* Fundraising managers know very little about the results they achieve, as very little empirical research and systematic knowledge underlie most fundraising programs operating today. Few programs are based on such tools as cost-benefit analysis or analysis of dollars raised against the potential for success. Most of these managers do not know how to assess the potential for success in their institutions and how their fundraising programs do or do not fully tap that potential. Most do not know if there are ways to spend the same amount of money to raise an even higher amount, or if less money could be spent in raising higher totals.

2. *The best fund raisers tend to be promoted to the highest management roles.* This is a phenomenon that occurs in many areas in nonprofit organizations generally and in higher education institutions specifically. Many managers in higher education also continue to carry some responsibility for functioning in practitioner roles as well. The best practitioners become managers, and they are expected to be as effective as managers as they were as practitioners, even though they may not have any specific training or preparation for the complex skills good management requires (McCorkle and Archibald, 1982; Tuckman and Johnson, 1987). This is typically what happens in higher education, where fund raisers promoted to management positions are expected to continue to raise money themselves as well as manage the function and staff, and where there is little or no formal preparation for the management role.

3. *There are very few systematic, formal educational or credentialing programs for professional fund raisers.* Although the number of such programs has grown in the last decade, most fund raisers practicing today learned on the job. No one would argue that

on-the-job training is not critical in preparing practitioners, but it is a limited vehicle for providing the skills and insights needed for management, especially as actual job conditions change, which is commonplace in this period of high turnover and mobility in the fundraising field. Furthermore, because of a lack of formal educational experiences, fundraising managers are not exposed to the literature on nonprofit organization and management, economics and finance, and the philanthropic tradition.

4. *There is a rapid growth of the fundraising field in higher education.* As indicated in the opening paragraphs of this chapter, this growth in the 1980s was astounding. The rapid expansion of fundraising programs and the steep rise in competition during this era left very little time for careful reflection; a worsening economic situation, tightening budgets, and escalating costs left very little operating money to spend on any activities not directly and specifically related to increasing revenues.

Because the programs in this study were all operationally defined as successful, we cannot assert that they suffered as a result of perceptions of management, nor can we assert that they were in fact poorly managed. Nevertheless, we continue to believe that fundraising success, if it is to be sustained over time, will more and more come to depend upon effective, deliberate, professional management of staff, resources, and processes. Although it is not the only area in which fundraising management must improve, we emphasize here the need for managers to become more scientific about expenditures and the relation of their various levels to levels of success.

We did not include fundraising costs in this particular research, but we have done so in other studies (Duronio and Loessin, 1991b; Duronio, Loessin, and Nirschel, 1989). Our efforts to collect valid, reliable data on fundraising expenditures have been only minimally successful because of highly idiosyncratic accounting systems across institutions and because most institutions do not have good cost data for fundraising efforts. Paton (1986) wrote that "no other single accomplishment will improve research about development so much as identification of practical methods for monitoring development expenditures routinely" (p. 37), and that this process cannot proceed until efforts to gather performance data *within* individual institutions improve. The Council for the Advancement and Support of Education, working with the National Association of College and University Business Officers (1990), has recently prepared recommended guidelines for more uniform accounting procedures, but they are not yet in widespread use.

There are both what Levis (1991) called "legitimate concerns and negative attitudes toward fundraising costs" (p. 261). The legitimate concerns are related to widespread financial exigencies and isolated instances of fundraising abuses. Negative attitudes about costs exist because people are uncomfortable about the fact that it costs money to raise money. This discomfort, we believe, stems primarily from a critical lack of fundamental knowledge about costs among donors and organizational administrators who control budgets.

Levis maintained that the rapid increase in voluntary support required in many nonprofit organizations, including higher education institutions, will not occur without increased investment in fundraising, but how can fund raisers expect increased budgets while such strong objections prevail? It is our contention that managers in many institutions are not as prepared as they must be to defend the need for increased expenditures.

Fund raisers contend that the process is too complicated to draw a direct connection between dollars spent and dollars raised, citing differences in the costs associated with acquiring gifts of different magnitude and from different types of donors. They point to the fact that current fundraising revenues are the result of past expenditures and that some current expenditures will not show benefits until some time in the future. These phenomena are well known in the field and are very real. The fact is that monitoring and evaluating these complex factors is not impossible, but most fundraising managers do not have the financial or accounting acumen to do these procedures. Economists and cost-benefit accountants do know how, and several very straightforward, well-grounded schemes have appeared recently in the literature (Paton, 1986; Levis, 1991; Steinberg, 1991)—a literature that most fundraising managers and practitioners will never see.

National leaders in the field as well as managers fighting hard to corral the resources they need to meet higher and higher performance expectations need to become the spokespersons for urging increased financial know-how among fundraising practitioners. Professional fund raisers need to take more responsibility for what they do not know and to promote more systematic study of these issues across the field. Practitioners must demand more and better training opportunities from their professional organizations and overcome whatever awkwardness or embarrassment they feel, not about the fact that fundraising costs money but about their inability to articulate and defend this assertion with cold facts and hard data. Doing these things will not only enhance the professionalization and reputation of fundraising, which most practitioners with a commitment to the field care deeply about, but will literally make it possible for higher education institutions to continue to depend on the lifeline of voluntary support.

References

Allbright, T. "A Capital Campaign Sampler: Status of 219 Drives." *Chronicle of Philanthropy*, Mar. 6, 1990, pp. 8–9.

Balderston, F. E. *Managing Today's University*. San Francisco: Jossey-Bass, 1974.

Baldridge, J. V., Curtis, D. V., Ecker, G., and Riley, G. L. *Policy Making and Effective Leadership: A National Study of Academic Management*. San Francisco: Jossey-Bass, 1978.

Brittingham, B. E., and Pezzullo, T. R. *The Campus Green: Fund Raising in Higher Education*. ASHE-ERIC Higher Education Report no. 1. Washington, D.C.: George Washington University, 1990.

"Challenges for the 1990s." *Chronicle of Philanthropy*, Jan. 9, 1990, pp. 1, 12–14, 16–20.

Cohen, M. D., and March, J. G. *Leadership and Ambiguity*. New York: McGraw-Hill, 1974.

Council for the Advancement and Support of Education and the National Association of College and University Business Officers. *Expenditures in Fund Raising, Alumni Relations, and Other*

Constituent (Public) Relations. Washington, D.C.: Council for
the Advancement and Support of Education, 1990.

Council for Aid to Education. *Voluntary Support of Education 1982–
1983.* New York: Council for Aid to Education, 1984.

Council for Aid to Education. *Voluntary Support of Education 1983–
1984.* New York: Council for Aid to Education, 1985.

Council for Aid to Education. *Voluntary Support of Education 1984–
1985.* New York: Council for Aid to Education, 1986.

Dressel, P. L. *Handbook of Academic Evaluation: Assessing Institutional Effectiveness, Student Progress, and Professional Performance
for Decision Making in Higher Education.* San Francisco: Jossey-
Bass, 1976.

Duronio, M. A., and Loessin, B. L. "Fund Raising Outcomes
and Institutional Characteristics in Ten Types of Higher Education Institutions." *Review of Higher Education,* 1990, *13,*
539–556.

Duronio, M. A., and Loessin, B. L. *Effective Fund Raising in
Higher Education: Ten Success Stories.* San Francisco: Jossey-Bass,
1991a.

Duronio, M. A., and Loessin, B. L. "Fund Raising Effectiveness in Higher Education Institutions." Unpublished report
prepared for the Lilly Endowment, Apr. 1991b.

Duronio, M. A., Loessin, B. L., and Nirschel, R. J. "The Price
of Participation." *Currents,* Apr. 1989, pp. 39–44.

Fisher, J. L. "Establishing a Successful Fund Raising Program."
In J. L. Fisher and G. H. Quehl (eds.), *The President and Fund
Raising.* New York: Macmillan, 1989.

Gilley, J. W., Fulmer, K. A., and Reithlingshoefer, S. J. *Searching for Academic Excellence: Twenty Colleges and Universities on the
Move and Their Leaders.* New York: American Council on Education and Macmillan, 1986.

Glennon, M. "Fund Raising in Small Colleges: Strategies for
Success." *Planning for Higher Education,* 1986, *14,* 16–19.

Keller, G. *Academic Strategy: The Management Revolution in American Higher Education.* Baltimore, Md.: Johns Hopkins University Press, 1983.

Leslie, J. W. *Focus on Understanding and Support: A Study in College Management.* Washington, D.C.: American College Relations Association, 1969.

Levis, W. C. "Investing More Money in Fund Raising—Wisely." In D. F. Burlingame and L. J. Hulse (eds.), *Taking Fund Raising Seriously: Advancing the Profession and Practice of Raising Money.* San Francisco: Jossey-Bass, 1991.

Loessin, B. L., Duronio, M. A., and Borton, G. L. "Questioning the Conventional Wisdom." *Currents,* 1988, *14,* 33–40.

Lutz, F. W. "Tightening Up Loose Coupling in Organizations of Higher Education." *Administrative Science Quarterly,* 1982, *27,* 653–669.

McCorkle, C. O., Jr., and Archibald, S. O. *Management and Leadership in Higher Education: Applying Modern Techniques of Planning, Resource Management, and Evaluation.* San Francisco: Jossey-Bass, 1982.

McMillen, L. "Gifts to Colleges Rise 8.8% in Year; Reach Record $8.9 Billion." *Chronicle of Higher Education,* May 30, 1990a, pp. A1, A26, A27.

McMillen, L. "Americans Gave More to Charity Again in 1989; Total Topped $100-Billion for 2nd Straight Year." *Chronicle of Higher Education,* June 13, 1990b, pp. A1, A23.

Matthews, D. "Improving Management Skills in Higher Education." *Exxon USA,* 1982, *21,* 28–31.

Millett, J. D. "Professional Development of Administrators." *New Directions for Higher Education,* 1978, *6,* 51–58.

Paton, J. "Microeconomic Perspectives Applied to Development Planning and Management." In J. A. Dunn, Jr. (ed.), *Enhancing the Management of Fund Raising.* New Directions for Institutional Research, no. 51. San Francisco: Jossey-Bass, 1986.

Pickett, W. L. "An Assessment of the Effectiveness of Fund Raising Policies on Private Undergraduate Colleges." Unpublished doctoral dissertation, School of Education, University of Denver, 1977.

Steinberg, R. "The Economics of Fund Raising." In D. F. Burlingame and L. J. Hulse (eds.), *Taking Fund Raising Seriously: Advancing the Profession and Practice of Raising Money.* San Francisco: Jossey-Bass, 1991.

Tuckman, B. W., and Johnson, F. C. *Effective College Management: The Outcome Approach.* New York: Praeger, 1987.

Whetten, D. A., and Cameron, K. "Administrative Effectiveness in Higher Education." *The Review of Higher Education,* 1985, *9,* 35–49.

Willmer, W. K. *The Small College Advancement Program: Managing for Results.* Washington, D.C.: Council for Advancement and Support of Education, 1981.

Young, D. R. "Executive Leadership in Nonprofit Organizations." In W. W. Powell (ed.), *The Nonprofit Sector: A Research Handbook.* New Haven, Conn.: Yale University Press, 1987.

Part Three

Management Strategies
for Social Change

Nonprofit organizations manage in a world of change. Indeed it is widely recognized that change is at the root of many management challenges, requiring leadership, planning, and other skills to foresee and adjust organizational activity to new circumstances. But it is sometimes forgotten, though it is equally important, that nonprofit organizations also seek to bring about change, especially social change that will improve the lives of people. Indeed, many would agree with Peter Drucker that making a difference in the lives of people is the real "bottom line" for nonprofit organizations.

In this section, we focus on the management of organizations that are explicitly devoted to bringing about progressive social change and helping people cope with rapid changes in their societies. Chapter Ten, by Susan A. Ostrander, is a study of the Haymarket Peoples' Fund, an organization whose intent is to fund social change groups and to redistribute power and wealth through the ways in which it does its own business. According to Ostrander, the Haymarket fund demonstrates by example that it is possible to do philanthropy in a manner that calls into question existing relations of power and uses philanthropy to challenge them. In particular, Ostrander identifies the practical procedures and strategies that Haymarket uses to achieve diversity in its own ranks and democratization in its decision making. She also introduces the concepts of fundraising and grantmaking as exercises in organizing for social change, thus integrating donors and grantees more closely into the operations of the foundation and with each other.

Robert W. Hunt, in Chapter Eleven, focuses on the catalytic role of voluntary agencies in international relief and development efforts around the world. Here the focus is on the evolution of strategic initiatives by local and international voluntary relief and development organizations. Hunt describes how voluntary agencies are becoming the linchpins to economic development and improving the lot of the world's poor by moving from short-term, technical approaches to meeting basic needs of the poor, to enterprise and job creation, to even wider approaches that incorporate the whole set of stakeholders in a given region or activity. He observes that voluntary organizations have become mediators among competing public and private sector organizations and important facilitators in the emergence of effective civil societies around the globe.

The changing demographics of American society provides the context for Krisna Abhay's study in Chapter Twelve of mutual assistance associations serving Southeast Asian–American immigrants. Abhay analyzes how these associations are organized to bring their communities into the American mainstream. He notes that they are built on the extended family model, reflecting the culture from which they emerge. While this model brings a core of strength to these organizations, it also precipitates the managerial struggles facing them as they grow and become more significant players in their communities. Traditional leadership (elders) must yield to professional management, boards with traditional members may conflict with staff, and struggles between external funders and traditional leadership may ensue. Abhay notes that these organizations must attend to principles of innovation, participation, and pluralism if they are to continue to develop and effectively serve their constituencies.

10.

Diversity and Democracy in Philanthropic Organizations: The Case of Haymarket Peoples' Fund

Susan A. Ostrander

Haymarket Peoples' Fund, a small social change foundation in Boston, was established in 1974. Now nearly two decades old, Haymarket is unusual in two respects. First, it is one of a small number of foundations that makes grants only to social change groups; second, Haymarket uses the way it does philanthropy — the structure and process of philanthropy — to redistribute power as well as wealth in the wider society. Haymarket's philanthropy, then, is both about funding social change groups and about changing the way philanthropy is done so that it is itself a part of wider change.

The aims of my overall project are to (1) describe closely and explain the day-to-day practice of a particular social change foundation, (2) develop guidelines for future practice at Haymarket and other interested foundations and similar organizations, and (3) construct a theory of social change philanthropy that is part of thinking and acting about organizing for social change in general.

The focus of this chapter is on two issues about which a number of charitable foundations are presently concerned and to which Haymarket has been especially dedicated: first, building a multicultural, multiracial organization that is inclusive of groups often excluded from decision-making positions, which I will refer to here as *diversity;* and second, giving recipient or grantee groups more of a voice in the philanthropic process while still continuing to involve donors, which I will refer to here as *democratization.*

Diversity is fundamental to democratization. Democratizing philanthropy, as Haymarket practices it, involves turning over the power to decide where the money goes to community activists recruited from recipient or grantee groups. Democratization also involves attempting to create a partnership between these activists and Haymarket's donors. The main question here is what kinds of organizational policies and practices seem important to developing a more diverse and democratic philanthropic organization. I also begin to lay out some ideas toward a general theory of the relationship between philanthropy and social change.

This chapter is in the spirit of an ongoing dialogue with the people at Haymarket. The notion of the relationship between researchers and those one is studying as a dialogue is gaining general currency in social science (Giddens, 1987). It is quite different from models that assume that application of research findings and implementation of recommendations will automatically enable practitioners to more effectively accomplish already established ends. Contrary to this static and instrumental view, a more dynamic research model based in dialogue starts from a premise that practitioners already have a substantial base of knowledge that guides their practice. This practical knowledge is largely taken for granted and may not be explicitly or clearly articulated (Berger and Luckmann, 1966). A task of the social scientist is to articulate taken-for-granted knowledge into another kind of knowledge, theoretical knowledge (Schön, 1983). Once articulated, theoretical knowledge can change practical knowledge, bringing about a more informed practice. The social scientist thus develops knowledge by reflecting what people in everyday life do and how they think about it, bringing together thought and action, scholarship and activism. Sociologist Patricia Hill

Collins argues that this is one way that theoretical knowledge has the potential to transform taken-for-granted knowledge, thus bringing about social change by affecting practice (Collins, 1990).

I have been engaged in the project at Haymarket Peoples' Fund since February 1990, gathering information at the foundation's offices. At this writing, I have attended and taken detailed field notes at over sixty meetings, representing nearly 200 hours of observation and recording. I have reviewed documents back to Haymarket's 1974 founding and begun to analyze interviews with members of the staff, governing board, and funding boards, and with other key persons. The most valuable source of information has been my presence at meetings — being there, seeing what actually happens, and hearing how people make sense of it.

Data for this project are being analyzed according to established procedures in qualitative social science research. This method involves repeated reviewing of materials, the development of themes or patterns, and the use of these themes as coding categories for systematic analysis and organization of the material (Strauss, 1987). This chapter draws on all the information gathered to this point, with the themes and arguments to be further developed in a book-length manuscript under preparation.

Philanthropy, Social Change, and the Example of Haymarket Peoples' Fund

Research on social change philanthropy, including foundation funding, is extremely scarce. Still, I think we know enough to say that philanthropic support in the United States for social change activities is very small. Drawing on his own systematic study on foundation funding for social movements from 1955 to 1980, sociologist Craig Jenkins concludes, "Foundations that fund social movements are innovative and relatively unconventional actors within their own world. Foundation support goes overwhelmingly to established charities and nonprofit institutions" (Jenkins, 1989a, p. 294). By a social movement, Jenkins means "any collective effort to bring about progressive social change on behalf of some marginal or excluded interest through innovation or rebellious means" (Jenkins, 1989b, p. 2).

In a 1990 book on social change philanthropy, Alan Rabinowitz, using what he considers Jenkins's generous estimate that less than 1 percent of foundation funding goes to support social change activities, estimates that of the total $6 billion given in grants by private foundations in 1986, less than $50 million went to support social change activities (Rabinowitz, 1990). Rabinowitz defines these as activities aimed toward "the changing of social institutions so they don't produce the very problems that 'charity' tries to alleviate" (Rabinowitz, 1990, p. xi). To this, Rabinowitz adds $5 million in social change grants made by what he calls "a growing number of progressive public foundations, many of them members of the Funding Exchange, and the smaller number of such grants that might be expected from corporate and community foundations" (Rabinowitz, 1990, p. 31). (Haymarket Peoples' Fund is a founding member of the Funding Exchange.)

One does not need to share the radical vision of Haymarket Peoples' Fund to be concerned about the paucity of these figures. Waldemar Nielsen, for example, in his encyclopedic book on the major foundations, *The Golden Donors,* is critical of most mainstream foundations for being so conventional, so devoted to what he calls "social continuity, not change," and he urges them to fund more social reform activities (Nielsen, 1985, p. 423). What can be learned from a close look at Haymarket's practice can be useful to more mainstream foundations who are open to responding to Nielsen's challenge.

What do we know about why foundations grant so little of their total funds for social change? Although Nielsen cites their timidity and fear of taking risks that might alienate some of their more conservative constituencies, it is also true that foundations that do support social change have been subject to criticism from every part of the political spectrum (Jenkins, 1989a). From the center, political moderates like Nielsen have claimed that foundations' overly cautious grantmaking ends up advancing the interests of the more advantaged groups (Carey, 1977; Tully, 1977). From the right, conservatives have accused foundations of abusing their tax-exempt privileges when they become em-

broiled in political issues (Brownfield, 1969; Hart, 1973; Metzger, 1979; McLlaney, 1980). A recent example is criticism lev-
eled against the Boston Foundation for making grants to organizations opposing a proposed tax-cutting bill (Greene, 1990).
Critics from the left have claimed that foundation funding for
social change is a mechanism for social control and cooptation,
muting the radical edge of grass-roots insurgency by profession-
alizing social movements and centralizing movement activism
(Arnove, 1982; Roelofs, 1986). Craig Jenkins's analysis finds
some support for these leftist criticisms, though he argues that
foundation funding in the 1960s and 1970s also had a number
of positive consequences for the social movements of that time
(Jenkins, 1989a).

     This chapter contributes to this debate by taking seriously
one aspect of the leftist critique. Radical critics of philanthropy
have argued, I think persuasively, that traditional philanthropy
seems to require the presence of some kind of institutionalized
inequality—between givers and receivers, donors and grantees.
Robert Arnove, for example, said that "philanthropy has always
been the reflection of a class society, because it has depended
on a division of rich givers and poor recipients" (Arnove, 1982,
p. 1). My own research on traditional women of the old upper
class can be interpreted in this light (Ostrander, 1984). In this
common image of philanthropic giving, donors who have accumulated a relatively large share of wealth may choose to give
away a portion to those who have much less.

     If philanthropy does in fact require the existence of in-
stitutionalized inequality—of structured social hierarchies—then
a philanthropy that seeks to use fundraising and grantmaking
for social change to break down hierarchies of class, race, and
gender will strongly defy established philanthropy as currently
practiced. Using Haymarket Peoples' Fund as an example, I
show that it is in fact possible to construct a way of doing philanthropy that not only does not reinforce existing social hierarchies but actually calls into question existing relations of power
and uses philanthropy to challenge them.

     A study of Haymarket Peoples' Fund may have special
importance at this time, since Haymarket and other similar foun-

dations seem to be at some kind of turning point in their development where both their size and influence are increasing. Haymarket is presently making grants that total half a million dollars a year. This is certainly a relatively small amount of money compared to the larger foundations, but when it is compared to the $50 million that Rabinowitz estimates is the total amount of funding for social change activities in the United States, it takes on a bigger significance. The Funding Exchange, of which Haymarket is a founding member, has given away $30 million since 1979 to grass-roots activist groups working for social change. The fifteen member foundations are presently engaged in a $15 million endowment campaign intended to ensure the future of their activities. More traditional community foundations in some cities report turning to Funding Exchange member funds for advice in their areas of expertise (Greene, January 23, 1990).

Haymarket grants are made to organizations in New England that are engaged in grass-roots organizing for progressive social change. Haymarket's specific vision is of a "democratic system based on:

- collective ownership and control over society's resources and equitable distribution of wealth and power within and beyond our national borders;
- the end of all economic, political and social exploitation of one human being by another;
- respect for and protection of the environment;
- an affirmation of cultural diversity, respect for the dignity and inherent value of all individuals, freedom from all forms of discrimination and oppression including those based on class, race, ethnicity, sex, sexual orientation, age, and disability; and
- a dedication to equality, solidarity, internationalism and peace" [Haymarket Peoples' Fund Grant Application, 1989, p. 1].

Since its inception in 1974, Haymarket has made grants to over 500 groups. In 1989, the issue areas funded included affordable housing and homelessness, environment and safe energy, health, antiracism work, gay and lesbian issues, elderly issues, women's rights, peace and international solidarity, worker's rights, and rights of the disabled. The diversity and democratization that Haymarket exhibits are, therefore, deeply embedded in its vision of social change and the work of its grantees.

Diversity at Haymarket: Shifting the Power

The representation on Haymarket's funding boards and governing board is striking, especially when compared to the relative lack of diversity on mainstream foundation boards. Haymarket presently has nine regional boards that are entirely responsible for grantmaking: Boston area, Hartford, Maine, New Hampshire, New Haven, Rhode Island, southeastern Massachusetts, Vermont, and western Massachusetts. (Some consolidation is currently under discussion.) All of my figures on board diversity come from reports presented at the 1990 Haymarket annual meeting, where I was present, or, in the case of the Boston board and the governing board, from my own observations and presence at meetings.

Well over half (58 percent, thirty-one) of the fifty-four regional funding board members at Haymarket are women. Forty-one percent (twenty-one) of the regional funding board members are African American, Hispanic American, Asian American, or Native American. Seven of the fifty-four members identify themselves as gay or lesbian. The Boston area regional funding board with whom I have spent the most time is now two-thirds women (ten of the fifteen members) and 60 percent people of color (nine of the fifteen members). At least two of the Boston board identify themselves as gay or lesbian. The governing board at Haymarket, which functions legally and organizationally as the board of trustees, consists at this writing of fourteen people. Six are women (40 percent), and five are people of color (36 percent). At least one is openly gay. This is compared to the most recent figures from the Council on Foundations, which show mainstream foundation boards having 29 percent women and 7 percent minorities (Boris and others, 1990). No figures on sexual orientation are reported.

At the 1990 annual meeting of the Council on Foundations, which was devoted to diversity, then-president James Joseph, himself an African American, said, "Minorities will have to be brought into decisionmaking if the legacy of giving and caring is to continue in the next century when they will represent a majority of the country's population" (Teltsch, 1990, p. 9).

How has Haymarket achieved this diverse representation among its decision makers? The earlier-mentioned fact of diversity being embedded in Haymarket's goals and the work of its grantees is one important factor. Although most foundations do not have Haymarket's radical goals of social and economic justice, the mission statements of mainstream foundations can also build in a commitment to diversity. Another factor in the successful pursuit of diversity at Haymarket is the presence of a formal written policy with the kind of diversity desired and the means for achieving it carefully laid out.

At this writing, I have observed five day-to-day practices at Haymarket that seem to support the existence of a very diverse community working together toward shared ends: (1) constant attention and concrete action in regard to issues of diversity by everyone in the organization, (2) a demonstrated commitment in terms of spending of resources, (3) ongoing attention to group process, being aware of situations in which people most often underrepresented in positions of decision making are excluded or silenced, (4) skillful handling of conflicts that arise out of difference, and (5) humor. Let me give some examples of each of these practices as I have seen them occur in the research notes I have analyzed so far. It is important to note that these five practices emerged inductively out of my research at Haymarket.

Constant attention to issues of diversity is paid at Haymarket not only by members of groups who are often underrepresented but also by persons belonging to more privileged groups. At the 1990 Haymarket annual meeting, for example, a man expressed concern that "there was only one woman in my small discussion group. It was very male dominated." At a meeting of the governing board, another man said of one of Haymarket's committees, "We need women to join. It's mostly minority males." He then said that if there were not women presently in Haymarket that could serve on the committee, then the board would need to do a search outside, affirming the seriousness of his concern.

Attention to diversity includes noticing when a group's representation has fallen and doing something about it in a timely manner. For example, the Boston area funding board noted that their representation of people of color had declined, and so a plan and timetable were made to bring in new members. In a matter of a few months, six new members were added, all people of color.

A willingness to spend resources to ensure diverse participation is evident at Haymarket. For example, whenever meetings are held, all expenses are paid. Although the expenses are typically small, the payments make a difference to people with modest incomes. The reimbursements also affirm the value of everyone's presence.

Attention to group process helps to ensure that representatives of different social groups are not only present at the table when decisions are made but are given the space to speak and are heard when they do. Haymarket makes decisions on a carefully spelled-out model of consensus. When a decision is about to be made, disagreement is explicitly called for, institutionalizing an acceptance of dissenting voices.

I observed another aspect of group process at Haymarket when, more than once, someone was "checked" on some intrusive behavior or when someone expressed concern that another person was feeling excluded or silenced. On one occasion, for example, a woman of color had been absent a few times from board meetings. A white woman reported, "She's feeling like she's not respected and her opinions are not being heard." Another board member, a white man, agreed to call this woman to tell her how much they needed her presence and valued her views. On another occasion, when a white man was speaking and essentially restating what a man of color had just said, a white woman intervened to say, "Like [he] just said." A lack of defensiveness on the part of the person being called on his or her behavior is also something I have seen displayed at Haymarket over and over.

The handling of conflict that arises out of difference is also important. At one meeting where the program for the annual meeting was being planned, a draft of the agenda was presented that included a morning-long discussion around the issue of Central American solidarity. An African-American board member immediately objected, saying, "I'm interested in South Africa. This (program) excludes people." After listening carefully to the discussion that ensued, one of the Hispanic board members who had originally defended the program said, "Let me make a proposal. We should see this issue (Central America) as one turning point, as one opportunity to discuss strategic grantmaking, a chance to open up the general question of priorities and how we got to funding so much on Central America." Another Hispanic board member proposed a new title for the morning's program that expressed the general concern with grantmaking priorities, not naming any particular constituency. There were enthusiastic murmurs of approval, a call for dissent was made, and because none was heard, a decision was made that all seemed pleased with.

Finally, there is the matter of humor. One pattern of humor I see at Haymarket is a turnabout where the white middle- and upper-class men who are often the makers of jokes in the rest of society become the good-natured targets. For example, in a discussion of a new committee assignment, three men volunteered, and one woman laughed and said, "It's okay. It's for an unimportant job." The three men joined in the laughter. The ability of white men to make jokes about themselves is also important. Once when an African-American woman reversed the names of two white men, one of them said, "I'm the other white boy in the room. I know we all look alike." Humor takes the edge off.

I do not want to suggest here that Haymarket Peoples' Fund has these issues all worked out. It does not, but it seems to be further along the road of building what I like to call a "community of difference" than any other organization I know (Young, 1986). White, middle-class people especially have a tendency to interrupt, to speak by eye contact only to the other white people in the room, to hear only a familiar language, to move quickly along when one's own agenda is advancing well. These are all behaviors I have seen at Haymarket, behaviors familiar to people who train white people in antiracism and men in antisexism.

These, then, are some of the observations I have made so far at Haymarket in regard to the matter of diversity. Let me now consider democratization of the philanthropic structure and process, for which I have suggested that diversity at Haymarket forms the groundwork.

Democratization at Haymarket: Turning Over the Power and Building a Partnership

Very little is known about how funding decisions are made in mainstream foundations. What research does exist describes the typical method of allocation as one where staff and boards of trustees who are representative of wealthy donors decide (Odendahl, 1987; Nielsen, 1985; Jenkins, 1989a). Donors who established the foundation may have substantial influence until their death, influence that may continue to family heirs. At Haymarket Peoples' Fund, decisions are made by funding boards of community activists, typically recruited from the kinds of grantee groups Haymarket funds. The process of making grants calls into question existing relations of power, by shifting the power to decide where the money goes from donors to these community activists. If funding board members are to serve this function, it is essential that they be diverse in the ways considered above, which is what I mean by diversity laying the groundwork for democratization.

What I hear most often at Haymarket about why it is important that funding decisions be made by a community-controlled structure is what most people there call "sharing the power." I want to direct attention here, however, to three ways I have so far observed that democratization of the way grants are made contributes to effective grantmaking, ways that I believe may be of interest to mainstream foundations. The first is board members' knowledge of the grantee groups, the second is their being well informed about important community issues when setting priorities for grantmaking, and the third is their ability to actively bring in proposals from community groups that might not otherwise seek funding.

I have seen at Haymarket a number of instances of grantmaking that was made better because members of the funding board knew grantee groups well. On one occasion, for example, a potential grantee was being interviewed by members of the funding board as part of the grant process. The grantee was speaking about a drop-in center for which support funds were being sought. He said, "You have to spend a day at the center," apparently assuming he was speaking only to strangers. A board member responded, "I've spent many days at the center." In the ensuing discussion, questions were raised about how close this grantee was to his constituency. Only when these questions were answered did the board decide to make the grant. On another occasion the board considered a grant to a women's organization that some board members were not familiar with, in spite of its high visibility among feminist activists and its reputation for effectiveness around issues of women and poverty. One board member said, "For the women's community in Boston, (this) is the most respected organization working on empowering women of color. It's important for Haymarket to support it." This group received a particularly large grant that it might not have gotten without this board member's knowledge.

People making decisions about who gets the money can, of course, be too close to potential grantees. Haymarket has a clear conflict-of-interest policy, and funding board members frequently remind each other of it. One time, for example, when a board member was making a particularly impassioned plea for a group, another member said, only half in jest, "Are you in cahoots with this group?" I have, on any number of occasions, seen Haymarket board members remove themselves from the decision when a group they were very close to was being discussed.

Grantmakers who are drawn from their constituencies are well informed when it comes to setting priorities for what is called "strategic grantmaking." In one discussion of priority setting for the coming year, a new board member, a person of color from a segment of the population that had not previously been well represented on the board, said, "There's a lot of fear among minorities that there'll be an increase of violence against us, a scapegoating for the economic problems that people are facing. I think we should pay attention to the issue of hate crimes and target some groups working on that." Another new board member, also a person of color, raised questions about the extent of Haymarket's past commitment to international solidarity groups. She said, "The solidarity movement is primarily white, middle-class people, and that's why they don't make the links between local issues and international issues. It would mean looking at their own racism, and that's too close for comfort." Another woman of color affirmed the point. This funding board then decided to take a fresh look at its grantmaking, shifting some priorities.

Finally, grantmakers who are close to the community they are funding can actively bring in proposals from groups who may be doing good work but have not previously sought funding. For example, in one review of the kinds of groups funded, a board member said, "Last cycle we didn't fund any AIDS groups. This time we gave $_____ to $_____. We went out and hustled a proposal by word of mouth and charged a member of the board to invite a proposal."

I want next to consider the partnership that Haymarket is attempting to create between donors and community activists, a partnership that raises a potential for democratizing Haymarket's fundraising as well as its grantmaking. How does a foundation democratize its funding decisions by raising the voices of grantee groups and yet not silencing donors? Haymarket acknowledges the contradiction between trying to create a philanthropy that both turns the power to make funding decisions over to people who have been typically excluded from positions of power and seeks to involve donors, recognizing that donors most often come from that segment of the population that already has most of the power in the wider society.

Although one interpretation of the partnership between donors and activists at Haymarket is simply the sharing of goals, there seems to be increasing discomfort about the invisibility

of donors and a wish on the part of most parties to move toward
a fuller notion of this partnership. At present, Haymarket has
no openly identified donors on its funding boards, but in their
role as activists, a few donors may appear on these boards. One
donor representing the donor committee serves on Haymarket's
governing board, and donors are involved in various subcom-
mittees of the board, such as personnel and long-range planning. The major involvement of donors at Haymarket is in planning conferences for people with wealth. These conferences deal
with technical issues, such as investment strategies; personal issues, such as the sense of isolation that many wealthy people
feel; and political issues, such as how to become more active
around issues of concern. The planning of these wealth conferences may separate donors from funding board activists and
grantees, a separation that is increasingly seen at Haymarket
as too great. It seems likely that donors will soon have the opportunity to become more involved, perhaps occupying one position on each regional funding board.

Two other issues related to partnership between donors,
activists, and grantees are also important here and are presently
under discussion at Haymarket. One is a concern about what
is called the democratization of Haymarket's funding base, that
is, incorporating more working-class and middle-class donors.
The other is the goals for what Haymarket calls "donor services,"
such as the wealth conferences discussed above. A basic issue
here, as it should be for any foundation, is how much money
Haymarket could raise if it changed some of its current practices so that donors would be more involved in the organization. Can fundraising be done in such a way that it organizes
donors so that they not only are funding social change activities but also are more actively involved in them? Can political
education be an inherent part of the fundraising process? Or
is the goal simply to get as much money as quickly as possible
to social change organizations? Do these two approaches con-
tradict one another or are they necessarily connected? Does it
make sense for the line between donors and activists to dissolve,
or at least become substantially blurred, as donors become more
active in Haymarket (and in wider social movements) and as

activist board members donate money to Haymarket according to their particular financial abilities? These are the kinds of questions that democratizing the funding base and shifting the emphasis at wealth conferences in a more political direction bring to the fore. Let me consider each of these two issues very briefly.

People at Haymarket, as at any other funding organization, are concerned about expanding the base of donors. Haymarket, however, was originally established by younger people of inherited wealth who wanted to direct a portion of their money toward groups working for radical social change, and it has a history of attracting money especially from this group. Although everyone would like to bring in more money to Haymarket, some want to focus more on smaller contributions from middle- and working-class people, while others want to continue focusing on inherited-wealth donors because they see that as Haymarket's strength. As one governing board member said, "We know how to involve people with money and how to get them to give." The shift to attracting money to Haymarket from working-class and middle-class people would be labor intensive, both because more smaller contributions are more work than fewer large ones and because it would involve shifting Haymarket's image. As one wealthy donor put it, "The media has been very interested in radical rich kids giving away money. We've been willing to go along with that and it works, but it (also) gives the image of Haymarket as accepting only big gifts of $10,000 or more."

The other issue is "donor services." Since 1975, Haymarket has organized weekend conferences for people with inherited wealth or extra earned income. Although no solicitation for Haymarket is done at these conferences, most of the contributions come from people who have attended at least one of them. The concern has been raised that some conference participants may give money to Haymarket largely because of the personal support they receive and the social relationships they form with other wealthy people and with Haymarket staff members at the conferences. Questions have been asked about how well informed and how committed conference participants who then become

donors are to Haymarket's goals and to its particular social vision. The issue is how Haymarket can be doing more political
organizing of wealthy people to bring them into playing an active part in its work for social change. More involved donors
might also contribute more money. They would, as one funding board member put it, "feel like part of the movement rather
than only giving away their money to the movement." This organizing donors might be worth the extra time and energy, in
terms not only of building social movements but also increasing funding.

Both of these issues — the democratization of Haymarket's
funding base and the mobilization of donors to become more
involved in social change activities — point to central ideas in
a beginning framework for connecting social change philanthropy to more general organizing for social change. I will begin to consider these ideas after summarizing the research and
drawing some implications for other organizations concerned
with diversity and democratization.

Conclusions and Implications

My research at Haymarket Peoples' Fund makes clear that it
is possible for foundations and similar organizations to reach
and sustain a diverse representation of people in terms of race,
class, gender, and sexual orientation. It appears that one primary
requirement is an explicit commitment to diversity as an integral part of the organization's mission statement, not as an
add-on but built in to what the organization seeks to accomplish and its reason for being. In the case of charitable foundations, this means that a clearly articulated relationship between
diversity and effective fundraising and grantmaking needs to
be made. It seems possible to do this in a variety of ways. A
concrete written plan for achieving and maintaining diversity
is also important.

A number of day-to-day practices seemed especially useful in sustaining diversity at Haymarket, increasing the involvement of members of typically underrepresented groups. These
practices would likely be useful in other organizations. One is

constant attention to diversity concerns on the part of all members of the organization. Women and minorities report that they tire of being the only ones or the primary ones who call attention to issues of diversity. My research suggests the value of shared responsibility in this regard. A willingness to take explicit and immediate action is important, for example, seeking new members when representation of any particular group falls. A demonstrated commitment to spending the organization's time and money to sustain diversity contributes considerably to the goal. It is valuable to pay attention to group dynamics and notice when members from typically underrepresented groups are silent or seem to feel excluded. The causes of such behaviors include being interrupted or not feeling heard. Women, people of color, or low-income people may feel unheard when what they have already said is repeated by others and attended to in a way it was not when they said it originally. People may also be silenced by nonverbal behaviors, such as being excluded from the eye contact that a speaker makes when talking to a group. One useful way to call out people who have not spoken is to ask specifically for disagreement when it appears on the surface that everyone agrees and to wait to give people a chance to formulate their thoughts. People also need to be willing to keep tabs on each other to learn new behaviors that encourage more inclusive interactions. Humor may be especially useful here in taking off the edge. Finally, a skillful handling of conflicts that may arise out of diversity concerns, done in a way that does not gloss over such conflicts but rather allows them to be voiced in a manner that is respectful to all points of view is a requirement of success.

At Haymarket, diversity of representation lays the groundwork for a democratization of grantmaking decisions that seems to contribute in observable ways to effective grantmaking. Funding boards drawn from the kinds of groups to whom the organization makes its grants have considerable knowledge of the groups, which improves grantmaking. Legitimate concerns about conflicts of interest can be resolved. Funding board members drawn from the communities targeted for grantmaking know the priorities of those communities and when priorities are shifting in ways that the foundation's grantmaking plans must reflect. These kinds of board members can also do effective outreach, bringing in grantees who without this kind of connection might not submit proposals even though they are doing good work in the community.

Diversity and democratization in the structure and process of Haymarket's grantmaking are well established. They are the very heart of the alternative philanthropy that Haymarket represents. It is a kind of philanthropy that not only provides funding for social change groups but also shifts power to groups who have typically been excluded from exercise of power. Two issues arising out of current discussions at Haymarket about fundraising raise additional challenges for social change philanthropy: establishing relationships between donors and grantees and activists and democratization of the funding base to include more middle- and working-class people and community activists. This would blur the boundaries between donors and grantees, contributing further to Haymarket's aim of using philanthropy to call into question existing relations of power and to redistribute wealth and power. It would also blur the boundaries between donors and activists, thus bringing donors into networks for organizing so that they become active participants in movements for social change beyond only supporting such movements with their money.

These ideas have a theoretical base in some existing work on the new sociology of money that shows that money has a social (and I would add political) value as well as an economic one (Zelizer, 1989). That is, it can create, maintain, and call into question social relationships and relationships of (political) power. My ideas about a theoretical and practical connection between social change philanthropy and more general organizing for social change also draw on earlier work of which I have been a part that conceptualizes philanthropy as carrying the potential for creating social relationships between donors and recipients (Ostrander and Schervish, 1990). Because donors and recipients may come from different and unequal class and race groups, the establishment of such relationships will be across class and race and other social hierarchies.

There seem to be several ways to further extend this notion of doing both fundraising and grantmaking so that these activities are themselves organizing for social change. For one thing, when donations are solicited, some form of political education of donors takes place. This is to some extent inevitable, since donors cannot very well be persuaded to give to some issue or constituency without being convinced of its importance. Doing fundraising as organizing would also mean putting progressive donors in touch with one another, as the Haymarket conferences for people of wealth do, and connecting them to activists and grantees, as Haymarket is beginning to talk about doing more. Doing grantmaking in such a way that the process itself is part of social change organizing can also include bringing grantees together, especially grantee groups who are working in the same issue area or who are struggling to meet similar kinds of challenges. Haymarket already does some of this. This kind of grantmaking can also mean being very conscious about the requirement that a grant proposal be laid out to facilitate the grantee's development as a group in order to succeed. For example, grantees may be required to be clear about goals and how they are going to reach them. This is probably fairly standard in the grants process in mainstream foundations as well as alternative ones, but the challenge may be especially important when the goal is social change. The process may also include setting priorities for funding that then actively affect the directions that social movements take, and doing so in a way that is grounded in a very close connection to the diverse grantee–activist community being funded. Haymarket has been hesitant to set granting priorities beyond the broad visions quoted early in this chapter because it sees itself following, not leading, movements for social change. In the absence of a well-organized national progressive movement, however, Haymarket and similar organizations with access to a wide network of progressive activists are being called upon to take more of a leadership role.

It appears, then, that there are a number of fruitful directions to explore in regard to the relationship between social change philanthropy and social change in more general terms. My continued writing about Haymarket Peoples' Fund will have much more to say about a framework for thinking about philanthropy and social change. There is a great deal more to learn.

References

Arnove, R. F. (ed.), *Philanthropy and Cultural Imperialism*. Bloomington: Indiana University Press, 1982.

Berger, P. L., and Luckmann, T. *The Social Construction of Reality*. New York: Doubleday, 1966.

Boris, E. T., and others. *1990 Foundation Management Report*. Washington, D.C.: Council on Foundations, 1990.

Brownfield, E. *Financing Revolution*. Washington, D.C.: American Conservative Union, 1969.

Carey, S. "Philanthropy and the Powerless." *Research Papers 2*, Commission on Private Philanthropy and Public Needs (Filer Commission). Washington, D.C.: U.S. Government Printing Office, 1977.

Collins, P. H. *Black Feminist Thought: Knowledge, Consciousness, and the Politics of Empowerment*. Boston: Unwin Hyman, 1990.

Giddens, A. *Social Theory and Modern Society*. Stanford, Calif.: Stanford University Press, 1987.

Greene, E. "The Boston Foundation: Educator or Advocate?" *Chronicle of Philanthropy*, Sept. 18, 1990, pp. 4–11.

Greene, S. "Group That Aids Grassroots Activists Enters Second Decade with Big Plans." *Chronicle of Philanthropy*, Jan. 23, 1990, p. 5.

Hart, J. "Foundation and Public Controversy: A Negative View." In F. Heiman (ed.), *The Future of Foundations*. Englewood Cliffs, N.J.: Prentice-Hall, 1973.

Haymarket Peoples' Fund. Grant Application. Boston: Haymarket Peoples' Fund, 1989.

Jenkins, J. C. "Social Movement Philanthropy and American Democracy." In R. Magat (ed.), *Philanthropic Giving*. New York: Oxford University Press, 1989a.

Jenkins, J. C. "Foundation Funding of Progressive Social Movements (Revisited)." In J. R. Shellow and N. C. Stella (eds.), *Grantseekers Guide*. Mt. Kisco, N.Y.: Moyer Bell, 1989b.

McLlaney, W. H. *The Tax-Exempt Foundation*. Westport, Conn.: Arlington House, 1980.

Metzger, P. *The Coercive Utopians: Their Hidden Agenda*. Denver: Public Service Company of Colorado, 1979.

Nielsen, W. *The Golden Donors: A New Anatomy of the Great Foundations.* New York: Dutton, 1985.

Odendahl, T. *America's Wealthy and the Future of Foundations.* New York: Foundation Center, 1987.

Ostrander, S. A. *Women of the Upper Class.* Philadelphia: Temple University Press, 1984.

Ostrander, S. A., and Schervish, P. G. "Giving and Getting: Philanthropy as Social Relation." In J. Van Til (ed.), *Critical Issues in American Philanthropy: Strengthening Theory and Practice.* San Francisco: Jossey-Bass, 1990.

Rabinowitz, A. *Social Change Philanthropy in America.* New York: Quorum Books, 1990.

Roelofs, J. "Do Foundations Set the Agenda? From Social Protest to Social Service." Unpublished paper, department of political science, Keene College, Keene, N.H., 1986.

Schön, D. A. *The Reflective Practitioner.* New York: Basic Books, 1983.

Strauss, A. L. *On Qualitative Analysis for Social Scientists.* Cambridge, Eng.: Cambridge University Press, 1987.

Teltsch, K. "At Foundations, the Voice of Women and Minorities Remains Faint." *New York Times,* Apr. 7, 1990, p. 9.

Tully, M. J. "Who's Funding the Women's Movement." *Research Papers 2,* Commission on Private Philanthropy and Public Needs (Filer Commission). Washington, D.C.: U.S. Government Printing Office, 1977.

Young, I. "The Ideal of Community and the Politics of Difference." *Social Theory and Practice,* Spring 1986, *12*(1).

Zelizer, V. A. "The Social Meaning of Money: 'Special Monies.'" *American Journal of Sociology,* Sept. 1989, *95*(2), 342–377.

11.

Voluntary Agencies and Global Development: Emergent Strategies of Leadership and Management

Robert W. Hunt

The story of the role of voluntary agencies in development is a formidable one. For decades, thousands of international agencies, and tens of thousands of local organizations within developing nations, have been active in providing relief and longer-term, developmental resources (Bolling, 1982). The fact is that much of the changing and dynamic history of national and international development might be written from the perspective of these organizations. Moreover, voluntary agencies are currently at the center of challenges and opportunities likely to change the nature of global development radically in the coming decades. This chapter will deal with some of this story, beginning with an introductory discussion of the main actors and issues in global development over the past four decades. Then, the body of the chapter will deal with the historic role of voluntary agencies in a critical area of activity: the promotion of business enterprise and community economies and how this reflects challenges and changes in international development. A concluding discussion will deal with the prospect that voluntary agencies may play a large role in promoting a strategic global dialogue on development — building on past activities and forming bridges among levels and sectors of society to promote a more integrated set of development options nationally and globally.

Development in Isolation: Initiatives Without Dialogues

In the first decades after World War Two, worldwide economic development activities were characterized by "highly bounded" visions. Development was something for economists to plan and for states with technically skilled administrators to carry out. Industrial development and modern infrastructure and communications were the matrix out of which benefits were created and subsequently distributed (So, 1990). Those isolated from the first benefits of modernization were to be provided with palliatives, by public welfare agencies and private voluntary associations or through clan and family largess.

These activities led to great frustration and failure. Economic development waxed, then waned, for much of the developing world. Even successfully industrializing nations found troubling gaps between rich and poor and saw them expand. Welfare from state agencies, and development programs in general, were often stymied by perpetual budget crises. International agencies offered financial and technical assistance. These often contributed to excess expenditure and debt, or called for great sacrifices for those least benefited by the processes of industrialization in the first place. Questions arose about the capacity of modern states to promote and manage development that could reach all sections of society and that was sustainable (Hettne, 1990). The poorest nations were further handicapped by deep-seated weaknesses in governing capacity, dominated by personalistic politics and by a shortage of experienced personnel for managing development activities (Gamer, 1982; Staudt, 1991).

Reformers in the 1970s and afterward stressed two dominant strategies. On the one hand, they looked for ways of promoting market efficiencies and increasing state capabilities for efficient and effective management. Alternatively, they stressed means for promoting more participation on the part of the most affected segments of the population and a broadened concept of participation to include sharing in the benefits of development activity (Michalopoulos, 1987; Uphoff, Cohen, and Goldsmith, 1979).

The primary strategy of the major international donor agencies was represented by the concept of "structural adjustment," which stressed the need for policy reforms likely to stabilize economies and promote incentives for private initiative and enterprise. At the same time, this strategy called for reducing obstacles to free market mechanisms and the productive energies of populations viewed as long handicapped by excessive, inefficient, and often corrupt leadership. These reforms, aimed at "getting the prices right," saw development as largely economic in nature and individual entrepreneurship as a primary source of energy. Previous development failures were seen as due, in considerable measure, to the existence of excessively centralized, bureaucratized efforts at planning and policymaking.

Alternative visions focused on the failure to promote effective development efforts among those who were least wealthy and powerful. The importance of their participation was stressed, particularly in managing and maintaining development projects. It was felt that more effort should be dedicated to meeting the basic human needs of the whole of society, partly by increasing attention to rural and agricultural development. Concomitant changes were needed to support the smaller, simpler economic activities with which the rural (and urban) poor were likely to be involved. Development should be more open, more a mutual process involving both state and private sector energies and institutions (Owens and Shaw, 1972).

Propagators of both types of reforms continued to perceive development as "technical" and apolitical. Structural adjustment programs, though aimed at the whole of society, stressed economic transformation and had little to say about the contingent impacts of such changes on politics and society. Participatory alternatives did promote wider public involvement and posed tasks for organizations involving the poor, but they continued to define development tasks largely in terms of economic expansion, with related "modernizing" goals. Participation by the poor, and the meeting of their basic needs, might be good in and of itself—but its value needed also to be measured through the resulting probability for successful economic development. Activities by the poor that reflected popular sentiment but not rational economic goals (for example, through pursuit of certain ethnic group goals) were not taken as signs of development (So, 1990).

Yet the significance of these changes at the top, and throughout the institutional base of society, was great. The dynamic processes both critiques reflected—and unleashed—remain powerful. They established a wider arena for deliberation and provided space for divergent visions of development and its processes. They recognized and helped legitimize activities that brought a wider range of traditional values into the planning for, and the management of, change. Most important, they promoted discussion and deliberation that helped produce clearer visions of the contradictions in modernization theory.

To be sure, these contradictions were made visible as well by continuing changes in the global political economy. Mounting debt, the growth of ethnic politics, and the associated decline in the capacity of nations to generate legitimate and effective development programs underlined the failures of existing bureaucratic systems and development theories. Moreover, the emergence of "second-world" competitors for scarce development resources threatened the fragile prospects of many Third-World nations. The "fall" of the Berlin Wall and the emergence of European claimants for global resources produced a decisive threat to Third-World claims for a share in these already limited capital supplies. Finally, technological changes that have erased borders and given the power of advocacy and coordination to disparate groups with limited interests in state programs and policies have further reduced the power of governments to set national agendas.

Still, the vision of industrial modernization, and the assumption that economic development is the primary requisite for stable societies, continues to dominate the development dialogue. Moreover, bilateral and multilateral development agencies will continue to set the basic agenda for action in these terms. However, the debate about the appropriateness of ultimate development goals, and means to achieve them, is real and significant. How quickly challenges may be mounted and become effective — as new paradigms for development — is uncertain. It seems likely to turn in substantial degree, however, on the extent to which institutional resources available to the least wealthy half of the world's people can become vehicles for promoting their interests. It also depends on the extent to which these often-private institutions and networks are able to promote a productive dialogue with the public and private bureaucratics now dominating development planning on "structural adjustments" that incorporate issues of equity, ecology, and politics.

The Voluntary Sector: Historic Development Role

To assess the prospects for such a transformation of the processes of development, it is useful to review efforts over the past three decades to promote viable employment and income options — efforts targeted mainly at those who have been most marginalized by previous development activities. At the center of these efforts have been international and indigenous voluntary agencies. Some of their work has been palliative, aimed at reducing the worst effects of poverty, and much of it has been uncreative and repetitious, but a large and growing effort has promoted a range of small to medium businesses, capable of operating in a global marketplace. And a growing number of voluntary agencies have committed considerable time and resources to learning lessons from failures and limited successes. Subsequently, some of the work of voluntary organizations in business and group development has been highly entrepreneurial and strikingly successful, comparing favorably to the best of development projects (Kilby and D'Zmura, 1984). But successes have also produced questions about making the efforts more cost effective and about means for converting local victories into productive outcomes beneficial to the wider society. These questions, and the response to them, are posing possibilities for an even more extensive role for voluntary agencies, and networks of these agencies, as a means for bridging the divergent approaches to development. This is nothing short of articulating participatory and "structural adjustment" efforts within the context of a global process of transformation.

Voluntarism and Small Business
Development: Beginning Strategies

In the 1970s, North Atlantic–based private voluntary organizations (PVOs) began to move away from the short-term relief activities for which they were most known: dealing with problems of famine, natural disasters, and disease. They looked for ways of dealing with the fundamental sources of poverty and moved toward longer-term involvement with development activities. Among the most important tasks were the promotion of income and jobs, including assistance for self-employment and small business enterprise. By the end of the 1970s, perhaps a quarter of the largest international voluntary development assistance agencies had significant small enterprise components (Technical Assistance Information Clearing House, 1982). Many had credit programs, reflecting the assumption that the major obstacle to enterprise start-up and viability was the shortage of fixed and working capital assets. Simple to extensive training was commonly provided, sometimes as a precondition for borrowing. Experimental work was done with entrepreneurial selection and training emphasizing psychological characteristics associated with entrepreneurship (Gupta, 1990). PVO efforts and goals were similar to those advanced previously in government programs: they stressed the need to meet specific obstacles to business success and assumed that business start-up and survival were, by themselves, signs of development. They were, in short, part of efforts to deal with critical components or bottlenecks in development; they were involved in "bounded" exercises, too.

Evaluations of these projects suggested that they did promote new and expanded business activity (Hunt, 1982; Bhatt, 1986). However, little if any evidence indicated what more business might mean for a community, or whether for every new job created another was lost. Moreover, while many poor people were being reached by development projects, the very poorest often were not. Costs of getting to remote rural areas were great, and start-up costs for new firms among those with little experience were high. Voluntary agency projects, as was the case with most government development projects, were aimed primarily at providing valued assistance to prospective and existing businesses, with little knowledge or concern about what new business meant in terms of wider economic activity or the income levels of the poorest.

Voluntary agencies also provided many of the voices critical of these approaches. Some PVOs argued for adding a stronger social component to projects for enterprise development, including with this more generalized critiques of public development efforts for their failures to produce positive social outcomes as well (Agency for International Development, 1985). Work in the 1970s, some of it supported by the U.S. Agency for International Development (A.I.D.) introduced a more participatory component to rural and urban small business projects (Mann, Grindle, and Shipton, 1989; Berg, 1987). Moreover, A.I.D.-sponsored studies demonstrated that the smallest rural and urban enterprises were often quite efficient, and capable of competing with larger and more technically developed firms (Chuta and Liedholm, 1979). Projects that integrated social and economic components became a hallmark of many PVO small enterprise and community development efforts.

Projects of organizations such as Overseas Education Fund (OEF) in Latin America, Asia, and Africa and the Working Women's Forum in India focused on providing "life skills" for very poor women and on beginning a longer-term effort at income generation through group development. Group-centered efforts among urban borrowers introduced the concept of "solidarity groups," where group lending and peer pressure for repayment reduced administrative costs and sometimes generated impressive improvements in income. In Africa, Opportunities Industrialization Centers, International (OICI) business projects in southern Africa and the National Council of Churches in

Kenya (NCCK) projects provided group backstopping for vocational and business education programs. OICI in particular spent time developing and nurturing advisory groups and governing boards that were likely to provide information and other forms of assistance for sponsored enterprises. Evaluations of these more socially centered and integrated projects found strong potential for income improvements and equity in the group projects, particularly when they were well designed and associated with preexisting social and political relationships and institutions (Kilby and D'Zmura, 1984; Farbman, 1981).

Some PVOs saw these efforts providing strong justification for their special capabilities in the area of small enterprise development. Their self-descriptions focused on a capacity for longer-term, more intimate support activities, of the variety that group development projects required. They also expressed a commitment to the type of participatory project management that would generate continuing economic benefits and the growth of political resources among the neediest, including women. This was clearly development and not relief; but it was also presented as a more complex and enduring form of development, beyond what governments could provide, more fully incorporating a segment of society that was otherwise ignored but could make, as well, significant economic contributions to the nation. Moreover, PVOs often viewed their projects as more experimental, because they tended to emerge in a participatory way out of the experiences and needs of the beneficiaries themselves. They were lower in cost, due to the differences in operating style of voluntary agencies as compared with major bilateral and multilateral agencies (Van Heemst, 1981; Berg, 1987). Surely they could provide the "reach" throughout the lower ranges of society that structural adjustment programs could not.

A thorough review of the evaluations that these private agencies themselves conducted, however, indicated that many of these claims were spurious. The level of participation in design, management, and evaluation of development programs by targeted individuals was commonly minimal, and little local ownership of projects could be seen. PVO project innovation was, at best, limited. Costs were often higher per unit of desired outcome (for example, jobs created) than in larger programs, especially when the true costs of replacing underpriced voluntary inputs were calculated in as part of assessments of project sustainability (Tendler, 1982). Whether the money loaned or the skills provided would contribute to the alleviation of poverty in a given community, or even to the attenuation of existing local markets, and whether improvements would be widely shared and sustainable were not seriously considered. Nor was consideration given to whether those helped were the most deserving, or whether the new enterprises had backward and forward links to other local economic activities.

In addition, with the diversity of international and indigenous agencies working with small enterprises, little hope of replication and "scaling up" could be seen. What had emerged were large numbers of divergent projects and little prospect that they could have broad, let alone national or regional, impacts. Voluntary agencies were best described as smaller, often less efficient versions of conventional, statist programs and were more often ameliorative than developmental. They continued to focus on the short term and to be limited in terms of systemic assumptions, which was partly related to the continuing sense that the businesses they were mainly working with were, in any event, transitional institutions. They could hardly have a future, as societies modernized, and would eventually be driven aside by more modern economic activity promoted in the wake of structural adjustments and attendant development policy reforms. Thus, for PVOs and their critics a strong suspicion remained that they were really "relief" agencies.

In the early 1980s, critics both inside and outside the PVO community considered their limits. In addition, the interests of a conservative American administration, reflected through the major bilateral programs of the U.S. Agency for International Development, and a worldwide recession encouraged a search by many PVOs for less intrusive, more cost-effective ways for promoting competitive economic activity among the world's poor. The social compulsion remained. Most voluntary sector agencies working with income-generation projects did not wish to turn to an emphasis on "the best bets" among the potential sources of assistance; nor did they favor expanded government programs seeking breadth and coherence at the expense of political development and equity (Small Enterprise Education and Promotion Network, 1987). They may have been presently unable to promote widescale increases in jobs and income to the degree they would like, but they continued to feel their potential for this was greater than was possible through governmental mechanisms (Agency for International Development, 1985).

The Voluntary Sector: Joining the Dialogue

The result has been a slow but promising growth by voluntary agencies in experimentation with a more catalytic, more systemic set of approaches. This in turn rests on a broader concept of management: the need for managing systems of relations among clients and among "input" and "implementing" institutions (Korton, 1990). This perception encompasses a sense of a need for connections involving individuals and small enterprises, outward through institutions at all levels of society. Some examples may be useful.

Opportunity International's (OI) project for setting up credit institutions in Asia and Latin America offers one such example. It began over a decade ago as an organization for American businesspeople supportive of the creation of lending institutions linked to evangelical Christian communities in Latin America and has evolved to a program of impressive institutional range and complexity. It once focused on the provision of credit and on training managers for credit institutions, approaches typical of the earlier PVO efforts. Now, prior to the provision of funds for starting a revolving fund, OI spends a great deal of time in the creation of local boards with a strong sense of ownership and commitment to equitable development. These boards are expected not only to take early leadership in directing the lending process and promoting local entrepreneurs but to gain skills in management and fund raising needed to sustain (and expand) the lending agency. Where OI's programs have most clearly followed this path, in the Philippines, the partner agencies in the country have themselves become lead agencies for the development of additional boards and lending bodies (Lassen, Moser, and Jelinek, 1987).

Another example comes from southern Asia and the Sarvodaya Shramadana program in Sri Lanka. For over thirty years, the Sarvodaya program has provided support for participatory planning and integrated development in thousands of villages (Ariyatrane, 1985). The Sarvodaya approach calls for beginning rural development with activities likely to encourage participation through the development of a variety of interest associations (for women, men, youth, and occupational activities) and the promotion of community planning through village associations. Buddhist monks are often active participants, and stress is placed on "right livelihood" and simplicity in life style. More recently, Sarvodaya work has expanded to include some small enterprise projects, and research indicates that the holistic approach, which is the hallmark of Sarvodaya programs, has not prevented its programs from achieving cost-effective impacts, even while stressing community integration over strictly economic values. One study of a Sarvodaya project for developing village stores — where the processes for setting up the stores and selecting the management stressed community-based values more than economic rationality — found that most of the stores quickly became profitable (Feldstein and Hunt, 1985). Because of Sarvodaya's emphasis on creating community linkages, it is likely these stores will also have some backward and forward impacts on neighboring rural economies.

Sarvodaya's approach is self-consciously directed toward strategic planning and participatory approaches that enhance the self-confidence of community members and build on local resources, thereby reducing the possibilities for political conflict with national and regional elites. Skills needed are more likely to be those that are widely available and widely shared.

PVO efforts of this more incorporative sort can sometimes be promoted by outside agencies from the international voluntary sector, and even by governments. A recent A.I.D. rural industries and employment project in Thailand, for instance, combined standard government-based credit and extension services with what amounted to a program for promoting institutional development and political pluralism from below, among small business entrepreneurs (Eisendrath, Brown, Hunt, and

Gregory, 1989). Resources that were expected to assist extension workers in the creation of five associations for small, rural
businesses produced over seventy. Moreover, through another
component of the project, the instituting of a joint government-
business policy committee, these small associations have begun
to challenge existing political arrangements. Surprisingly, local
governors indicated to interviewers that they appreciated these
new business associations as an influence that would assist them
in exerting pressure on the highly centralized Thai bureaucracy
(Eisendrath, Brown, Hunt, and Gregory, 1989). As with the
case of the Sarvodaya program, the results generated not only
inputs helpful to new and existing businesses but opportunities
for participation and for influence within the relevant policy environment. Small businesses in this sense are not those envisaged
in early programs but those more capable of being integral to
the search for economic and social change.

In a recent work summarizing the findings of research
sponsored by the Agency for International Development on micro
and small business development projects, success was attributed
in large measure to the relative managerial capabilities of development institutions, mainly international and indigenous voluntary agencies. Small enterprise projects with the maximum potential for benefiting owners and workers—and for communitywide
impacts—were those with *strategic, technical, administrative,* and *communication* (or *political*) capacities. This meant that the institutions involved in a project needed capacities to establish goals
and priorities and to adapt operating policies in light of changing circumstances to ensure that targets are achieved. Such accomplishments in turn required the selection, training, and support of committed and effective staff members with the ability
to assess current experiences, to learn from experience, to maintain autonomy from sponsors, and to make informed decisions
about strategy and programs. Sensitivity to the environment was
critical and called for a capacity to work effectively with other
organizations, public and private, that had a stake in the project
and its outcomes (Mann, Grindle, and Shipton, 1989).

Over the past few years, therefore, small enterprise project
success has been increasingly disassociated from isolated tech-

nical inputs, such as the delivery of credit and training, or from the mere opening of new firms. Contemporary micro and small income-generation efforts are associated with a variety of activities and are integral components of work for systemic change. Perhaps the best known model of this new approach, one fully targeted to income generation and the linkage of beneficiaries to a wider set of social relationships, is the micro enterprise program of the Grameen Bank of Bangladesh. Launched in 1979, the bank, which is government owned but which operates largely autonomously, has become an important means for providing credit for the rural poor. Those with assets worth less than an acre of land are eligible to join in groups of five with their own elected officers, who call weekly meetings. The groups' first meetings are training sessions, focused on credit management and on group development (in part through physical exercise). Members then take loans for any productive activity, to be repaid in weekly installments. Future loans to any in the group depend on regular repayment by group members. Members are also expected to save money, providing the bank with funds for additional lending.

The program is now national in scope, providing well over a quarter of a million borrowers with loans that average less than a hundred dollars each. About 70 percent of the borrowers are women, and loan arrearage has remained at less than 5 percent (Timberg, 1988). It is advanced as a "minimalist" approach, in that it spends relatively little on training and extension services and has developed a strong pattern of repayment, making growth possible (though it continues to receive funds from outside the nation as well). Its group component provides means for linking borrowing to mutual assistance work (in part to ensure that all members are able to repay loans) and to collective efforts supportive of wider community activities. The Grameen project appears to have many of the managerial capabilities found effective in promoting income-generating activities, with wider community impacts (Mann, Grindle, and Shipton, 1989). It has become a model program with global significance, with many group lending programs in other nations following its lead, or at least drawing on similar assumptions. For instance, the

Foundation for International Community Assistance (FINCA) "village banking" program in Central America promises both to provide group-level experiences and to promote wider deliberations toward a national business policy agenda. A recent major U.S. government grant to FINCA/El Salvador promises to provide resources to at least a fourth of the poor families in that nation, and accompanying support for a range of voluntary sector agencies capable of instituting a nationwide support network for the poor (Rotstein, 1990). Moreover, about a dozen of these Grameen and FINCA-type programs operate in North America (Mondale and Tune, 1989; Woodstock Institute, 1990).

Projects to promote enterprise and income among the world's poor have thus been dramatically transformed over the past two decades, with voluntary organizations in rich and poor nations playing a leading role in changing the definitions of enterprise development: its contexts, its beneficiaries, and its antecedents. Voluntary agencies began with short-term, technically fragmented approaches to assisting the poor to meet basic needs through enterprise and job creation. They have moved to a much wider sense of how business and community impacts may be part of one package, needing attention that incorporates the whole set of stakeholders in any region of activity. David Korton describes this in terms of three stages of voluntary association development, with the type of activity represented by the Grameen Bank, Opportunity International, and the Sarvodaya Shramadana movement moving away from short-term, project-centered efforts and approaching the problems of poverty through efforts to catalyze local capabilities and to assist in linking disparate local and sectoral changes within a systemic framework (Korton, 1990). In the important sense described some years ago by the economist Harvey Leibenstein (1968), this puts voluntary development associations into the category of the "entrepreneurial" in their search for means for "filling gaps" and "completing inputs" in still highly fragmented societies, where political systems and economic markets remain disjointed.

Still, whether these efforts are now, or can become, more complete mechanisms for filling the gaps and helping with the articulation of national economies remains to be seen. Similarly, whether small business and associated community development voluntarism can build networks and find connections with associations working with other public issues (for example, ecology, human rights) and whether they can collectively become partners with large-scale business and government to pursue a more integrated set of "structural adjustment" initiatives is also unclear. The answers to these questions may well determine the prospects for an emergent "civil society" in developing areas, intermediate between government and individual citizens and well articulated with both.

Voluntary Agencies and the Future of Global Development

The dramatic changes in Europe over the past two years, apparently intractable problems with inequity and capital shortages in the global economy, and the universal concern for environmental limits have posed new opportunities for thinking about the future role of income-generation and "jobs" projects, and of the role of private and voluntary people's organizations in promoting them. The news media and professional journals report daily on the emergent claims, activities, and projects of voluntary ecological, human rights, women's, disarmament, and related agencies throughout the world (Stremlau, 1987). Alan Durning, of the Worldwatch Institute, suggests that this sort of emergent "micro-planning" for development may increasingly be recognized as part of a larger process of global transformation. He has traced the evolving connections among groups working for ecological balance and those dealing with problems of rural poverty and foresees a much more significant push from below for a more environmentally grounded process of development (Durning, 1989).

There may be an additional step in that direction. Regional voluntary agencies are increasingly seeking to become mediators among competing public and private sector organizations in seeking new policy choices and consensus — commonly rooting their efforts in the universal needs posed by income-enterprise-community development projects. In a recent Asian study, the consortium of private voluntary organizations called PACT (Private Agencies Collaborating Together) has assessed the potential of national and regional voluntary agencies it calls "Voluntary Resource Organizations" or VROs (Private Agencies Collaborating Together, 1989). These institutions serve as coordinating and service delivery agencies and assist individual or groups of associations with strategic facilitation. They are, in short, resources and brokers for the voluntary sector, connecting its members to each other and external agencies and serving as a means for finding common ground among these agencies. Studies in Bangladesh, Indonesia, Nepal, Sri Lanka, and Thailand revealed the growth of VROs, many deeply involved in problems of unemployment and poverty. In Thailand alone, where a specific survey was conducted, some forty of these resource organizations existed. Typically, they had begun to develop a wide range of interests and the potential for promoting a "policy network" to confront a significant range of public issues — issues with local, national, and global significance.

   The emergence of this diverse but increasingly significant structure of authoritative capacity in developing nations, and among the poorest elsewhere, offers nothing less than the potential for resolving the basic contradictions promoted by past development efforts. Moreover, with the dramatic changes of the past few years, it appears that national leaders are increasingly sensitive to this potential: the emergent "civil society" within most nations and across national borders. For instance, the American government, through its Agency for International Development, U.S. Information Service, the National Endowment for Democracy, and others, is now involved in a "democracy initiative." This worldwide effort promises consideration of ways for facilitating the development of competitive markets and free institutions. Already, many private voluntary organizations are involved in work with small private sector economic initiatives there (Mason, 1990). Voluntary organizations will be testing development models from Third-World settings, supporting the emergence of a more participatory political culture and civil society. Companion efforts in poor regions of North America are likely to increase in numbers, based on the successes of the

Grameen experiments in about a dozen North American settings (Woodstock Institute, 1990). Recent publications of the World Bank suggest that some in this institution—which has in the past shown little regard for voluntary or people's organizations as development agencies—are increasingly viewing the lack of institutional capability, from the government down to the village, as a primary obstacle in development (World Bank, 1991).

In short, the prospects are strong that development efforts by voluntary agencies and peoples' organizations will produce a significant "action research" agenda that articulates with that coming (finally) from multilateral and bilateral agencies. Perhaps the experiences of voluntary agencies and governments in income-generation projects can serve to promote a truly dialectical process and partnerships among varying levels of society: the global underclass, popular development agencies, and those who manage the central institutions of politics and business (Marglin, 1990; Wignaraja, 1990). In a world of shortages, where institutions of government and society are increasingly challenged, such options might well prove quite attractive. In a world where the record of response to basic human needs is so poor, they may suggest real alternatives (Hettne, 1990).

References

Agency for International Development. *Report on a Workshop on Private Voluntary Organizations and Small Enterprise Projects.* Discussion Paper no. 22. Washington, D.C.: Agency for International Development, 1985.

Ariyatrane, A. T. *Collected Works,* Vols. 1–3. Dehiwala, Sri Lanka: Sarvodaya Research Institute, 1985.

Berg, R. *Nongovernmental Organizations: New Force in Third World Development and Politics.* East Lansing: Center for Advanced Study of International Development, Michigan State University, 1987.

Bhatt, V. V. "The Entrepreneurship Development Program: India's Experience." *Finance and Development,* 1986, *23,* 48–49.

Bolling, L. *Private Foreign Aid.* Boulder, Colo.: Westview Press, 1982.

Chuta, E., and Liedholm, C. *Rural Nonfarm Employment: A Review of the State of the Art.* East Lansing: Department of Agricultural Economics, Michigan State University, 1979.

Durning, A. *Action and the Grassroots: Fighting Poverty and Environmental Decline.* Washington, D.C.: Worldwatch Institute, 1989.

Eisendrath, A., Brown, B., Hunt, R., and Gregory, P. *Evaluation of the Rural Industries and Employment Project: Thailand.* Washington, D.C.: Agency for International Development, 1989.

Farbman, M. (ed.). *The PISCES Studies: Assisting the Smallest Economic Activity of the Urban Poor.* Washington, D.C.: Agency for International Development, 1981.

Feldstein, H., and Hunt, R. *Sri Lanka Evaluation of Small Private Enterprise Projects of Private Voluntary Organizations.* Washington, D.C.: Agency for International Development, 1985.

Gamer, R. *The Developing Nations: A Comparative Perspective.* Needham Heights, Mass.: Allyn & Bacon, 1982.

Gupta, S. K. "Entrepreneurship Development Training in India." Appropriate Technology International working paper presented at the U.S. Agency for International Development meeting on microenterprise development, Washington, D.C., Mar. 1990.

Hettne, B. *Development Theory and the Three Worlds.* New York: Wiley, 1990.

Hunt, R. *A Review of Evaluations of Small Enterprise Projects Designed and Implemented by Private Voluntary Organizations.* Washington, D.C.: Agency for International Development, 1982.

Kilby, P., and D'Zmura, D. *Searching for Benefits.* Washington, D.C.: Agency for International Development Evaluation Studies, 1984.

Korton, D. *Getting to the Twenty-First Century.* West Hartford, Conn.: Kumarian Press, 1990.

Lassen, C., Moser, T., and Jelinek, R. *Building Local Institutions for Job Creation and Income Generation: An Evaluation of the Institute for International Development, Inc.* Washington, D.C.: Agency for International Development, 1987.

Leibenstein, H. "Entrepreneurship and Development." *American Economic Review: Papers and Proceedings,* 1968, *58,* 72–83.

Mann, C., Grindle, M., and Shipton, P. *Seeking Solutions: Frame-*

work and Cases for Small Enterprise Development Programs. West Hartford, Conn.: Kumarian Press, 1989.

Marglin, S. "Sustainable Development: A Systems of Knowledge Approach." *The Other Economic Summit/North America,* 1990, *6,* 5–8.

Mason, J. *A.I.D.'s Experience with Democratic Initiatives: A Review of Regional Programs in Legal Institution Building.* A.I.D. Program Evaluation Discussion Paper no. 29. Washington, D.C.: Agency for International Development, 1990.

Michalopoulos, C. "World Bank Programs for Adjustment and Growth." In V. Corbo, M. Goldstein, and M. Khan (eds.), *Growth Oriented Adjustment Programs.* Washington, D.C.: International Monetary Fund and the World Bank, 1987.

Mondale, W., and Tune, R. A. "The Good Faith Fund and the Grameen Bank: Similarities and Differences." Paper presented at the South Arkansas Rural Development Seminar, Arkadelphia, Ark., Sept. 1989.

Owens, E., and Shaw, R. *Development Reconsidered.* Toronto, Canada: Heath, 1972.

Private Agencies Collaborating Together (PACT). *Asian Linkages.* New York: Private Agencies Collaborating Together, 1989.

Rotstein, A. "Village Banking Offers Revolving Loans to Put Poor Women in Business." *Los Angeles Times,* Apr. 29, 1990, D1.

Small Enterprise Education and Promotion Network. *Monitoring and Evaluating Small Business Projects.* New York: Small Enterprise Education and Promotion Network, 1987.

So, A. *Social Change and Development: Modernization, Dependency and World System Theories.* Newbury Park, Calif.: Sage, 1990.

Staudt, K. *Managing Development: State, Society and International Contexts.* Newbury Park, Calif.: Sage, 1991.

Stremlau, C. "NGO Coordinating Bodies in Africa, Asia and Latin America." *World Development,* 1987, *15,* 213–225.

Technical Assistance Information Clearing House. *Small Enterprise Development Assistance Abroad.* New York: American Council of Voluntary Agencies for Foreign Service, 1982.

Tendler, J. *Turning Private Voluntary Organizations into Development*

Agencies: Questions for Evaluation. Washington, D.C.: Agency for International Development, 1982.

Timberg, T. "Comparative Experience with Microenterprise Projects." Unpublished report, National Technical Information Service #PB89162986XSP, Washington, D.C.: Robert R. Nathan, Associates, 1988.

Uphoff, N., Cohen, J., and Goldsmith, A. *Feasibility and Application of Rural Development Participation: A State of the Art Paper.* Ithaca, N.Y.: Rural Development Committee, Cornell University, 1979.

van Heemst, J. *The Role of NGOs in Development.* The Hague: Institute of Social Studies, 1981.

Wignaraja, P. "The Crisis of Development in South Asia." *Lokayan Bulletin,* 1990, *8*(3), 43–57.

Woodstock Institute. *Group Lending Exchange.* Report of workshop on micro-credit methodology, Chicago, Woodstock Institute, 1990.

World Bank. *Managing Development: The Governance Dimension.* Washington, D.C.: World Bank, 1991.

12.

Leadership Challenges Facing Mutual Assistance Associations: Helping Immigrants Move into the Mainstream

Krisna Abhay

This is a useful and original contribution to the literature on leadership in the nonprofit world.

— John W. Gardner
Centennial Professorship
in Public Service
Stanford University

The purpose of this chapter is to present a comparative study of Southeast Asian–American self-help groups and how they are organizing to bring their respective communities into the mainstream of American society. Prior to 1975, the number of Indochinese residing in the United States was very small. They were mostly foreign nationals here on business ventures or as univer-

Note: I am grateful to Anna Mary Portz, research associate, and Ly K. Tran, research assistant, for assistance in completing the paper.

sity students. However, the situation changed dramatically after the fall of the three countries of Indochina (Cambodia, Laos, and Vietnam) to communism. Fleeing political persecution and human rights abuses, huge numbers of refugees began pouring out of that region. Over two-thirds were resettled in the United States. Since then, many successful Indochinese communities have begun to emerge throughout the United States and are becoming important factors in the social, economic, and political evolution of American society. This is a remarkable achievement for a population that began here without the benefit of a strong anchor community and has been in the nonprofit milieu for a relatively short time.

Before the Vietnam War, the French and the English as colonial powers had the greatest influence over the cultures of Southeast Asia (causing the coining of the phrase "Indochina"). Transplanted to the United States, it was natural therefore for Cambodians, Laotians, and Vietnamese to look toward "the authorities"—the central government or individuals of traditional rank—to address the inequities and temporary impediments they faced in the new U.S. environment.

Referring to a population who had been primarily newcomers only a generation past, de Tocqueville wrote: "The Americans make associations to give entertainments, to found seminaries, to build inns, to construct churches, to diffuse books. . . . Wherever, at the head of some new undertaking, you see the government in France, or a man of rank in England, in the United States you will be sure to find an association" (Nielsen, 1985). By the 1960s, such American associations (since evolved into the so-called nonprofits) held significant influence over the fields of education and health as well as the issues of civil rights, urban affairs, foreign aid, international cultural exchange, and even national security (Nielsen, 1985). It was natural, then, for refugees interested in these same issues to form nonprofit, community-based self-help groups, which became known as mutual assistance associations. William R. Conrad, Jr. defines the nonprofit sector's "most intriguing characteristics [as] innovation, citizen participation and pluralism."[1]

The Civil Rights Movement of the 1960s established an important precedent in the development of the Indochinese-American communities. The Civil Rights Movement worked to give people of all races, creeds, and social status access to equal opportunity and created a mandate for government funding programs with an affirmative action aim. The key vehicle for the refugee community organizing effort has been the mutual assistance associations, commonly known as MAAs.

Overview of Mutual Assistance Associations (MAAs)

Since 1975, more than 1,200 MAAs[2] (approximately one per thousand refugees) have emerged from within the Indochinese-American community nationwide. Like those immigrants and refugees who came in generations past, the Indochinese and other late twentieth-century refugees have repeated the pattern of joining together in associations wherever they settled. Today, we find MAAs across the United States in various stages of development. There are perhaps a half dozen mega-MAAs (with an annual budget of $1 million or more), which differ little in outward appearance from large nonrefugee nonprofit service providers. Their income sources are diversified, with a still-significant portion coming from government grants and contracts. Other MAAs are just coalescing, especially ones focused on and led by refugee women and those in communities where the refugee population has not yet reached a critical magnitude. In between these two extremes are the majority of MAAs, many of which draw their major funding from the federal refugee program and others that continue to function based on a hard-core group of dedicated volunteers.

Many MAAs provide a range of educational, supportive, and training services to their communities, including language courses, job training programs, and cultural orientation. In her analysis, Bui (1981) divided MAAs into categories: social/fraternal, educational/cultural, religious/spiritual, professional, political, and those serving specific subpopulations (senior citizens, women, veterans, students). Mortland (1988) types MAAs as those that operate as temples, those that raise money to support resistance armies overseas, those that act as freelance entrepreneurs providing special services, and those that operate primarily as social service networks. Over the past decade, the latter interdisciplinary, refugee, service-providing type of MAA has gained increasing public recognition. Incentives often came from the federal government through initial encouragement and seed funding offered by refugee program officers. These MAA service providers, now constituting the majority of operating MAAs, are our focus here.

Understanding the cohesiveness and effectiveness of the MAAs requires understanding that Indochinese think and organize themselves very differently from Westerners. With weak public institutional structures in Cambodia, Laos, and Vietnam, and a tradition of unresponsive, centralized authoritarian governments, community social structures are patterned on the model of the extended family. When these people were transplanted to the United States in the absence of a strong anchor community (it is estimated that there were no more than 3,000 Indochinese in the United States when the great influx began in 1975), Indochinese refugees reorganized after the extended-family model—and MAAs were born.

The Extended Family:
Traditional Organizational Model

From the start, MAAs operated on a powerful principle: *the interests of the individual are better served when the interests of the group are served.* In face of adversity, the extended-family model provides a system and structure for practical application of a traditional social strategy in which relationships are formalized through a pattern of kinship obligations. There are advantages to this approach.

- A kinship-style structure allows for a traditionally acceptable and culturally understood method of pooling financial and material resources.
- In the absence of strong public educational institutions, the kinship-relationship structure provides a forum for sharing,

accumulating, combining, and transferring practical knowledge from generation to generation. With this combined know-how, the pooled financial and material resources can be put to more effective and efficient use for the benefit of all members.

- This model provides a medium for the equitable redistribution of benefits among members and a mechanism for debate and conflict resolution within the group through the council of elders or the elected officers of the MAA. It provides a means for extending group power and authority through alliances that are prearranged and sealed by marriage.

- Power and authority are usually conferred to the leaders by virtue of their skills (know-how) and accumulated resources. Since the acquisition of practical knowledge and the accumulation of assets can occur only over time, it is natural for the Indochinese communities to adopt the extended-family model as a system for formalizing leadership and social position. Under such a system, seniority becomes an important indicator of leadership, power, and authority.

- In countries like Cambodia, Laos, and Vietnam where "the power of the Emperor stops at the village gate" and the government is seen primarily as a tax collector, offering no democratic means of participation nor any central public institution for the passing on of knowledge, it follows naturally that people depend upon known and trusted individuals. The council of elders, representing the interests of many extended families, becomes an acceptable and practical form of governance for the community.

Increasingly, MAA leadership has shifted from the community's elders to those men or women, sometimes quite young, who have demonstrated the greatest capacity to function effectively in the new environment.

Stages of Organizational Development

Like any nonprofit organization (refugee or other), MAAs pass through various stages of development as they strive to meet their challenges. Pho (1988) notes that the management and leadership problems experienced by many MAAs are not uncommon in new organizations. Drawing from Paul Hershey and Kenneth H. Blanchard's *Management of Organizational Behavior: Utilizing Human Resources,* Pho explains that the stages of an organization's life can be described as evolution and revolution, with "each evolutionary period characterized by the dominant management style used to achieve growth, while each revolutionary period is characterized by the dominant management problem that must be solved before growth can continue" (1988, p. 4). The four stages of organizational growth described by Hershey and Blanchard are (1) creativity, (2) direction, (3) delegation, and (4) consolidation. The need for change is seen as four different kinds of crises, each of which must be dealt with before the organization can move on: (1) crisis in leadership, (2) crisis in autonomy, (3) crisis in control, and (4) crisis in red tape.

Pho reports that MAAs appear to be in the first stage of organizational growth — creativity. They are experiencing the need to adapt to already changing conditions: funding cutbacks, new political realities, and shifting community needs. Their founders have dominant leadership characteristics but generally lack applicable managerial experience and training. The management problems that are arising cannot be adequately handled by existing management arrangements and are outside the scope of expertise of the founding leadership.

Because for some time to come many MAAs will continue to be led by the same founding board members and key staff, Pho articulates the challenge as figuring out how each MAA can develop the management skills and experience needed to achieve its newly emerging objectives. Studies and evaluations conducted over the past five years have highlighted a variety of managerial and administrative weaknesses in MAAs. She concludes that most MAAs will require training or assistance in the following areas:

- Personnel systems, including staffing needs, job descriptions and qualifications, policies for hiring and firing, promotions, pay scales, and benefits

- Budgeting and financial management
- Strategic financial and programmatic planning
- Definition and clarification of goals and objectives
- Inter- and intraorganizational information and communication
- Methods of decision making and lines of authority
- Fundraising—both proposal writing and grants management

Adaptation to the American Context

When they began in the late 1970s and early 1980s, MAAs were characterized by their informality, devotion to a cause, and often charismatic leadership. Those that got government funds had to change in response to federal and state guidelines; management of the government-funded segment of their operation became tighter and more performance based. Often, the MAAs' ethnic board members (the council of elders) continued many of the old culturally demanded activities as well; because these were not funded, they could be run in the old, loose way. What developed was two parallel systems of accountability, which had caused tension ever since their inception. Training and technical assistance focused on program staff (who were being paid to run the government-funded program), to the virtual exclusion of the council of elders and the detriment of board governance.

Early seeds of tension emerged when MAA programs became "funder driven" and increasingly less responsive to the changing needs of the overall community. To keep getting government grants, MAAs had to focus services and attention on the "have-nots," thereby ignoring the interests and legitimate needs of those refugees who were beginning to "make it" and who could become a vital source of support for future newcomers—and for the MAA itself—in terms of volunteers, financial contributions, and advice. By 1984, former refugee program official Gregory B. Smith had already noted:

> As the organization focuses more and more on [government-funded] services delivery, this subset of the refugee population [the unemployed, those

with greatest need for English language training, day care services, and mental health crisis intervention] has become the exclusive clientele of the organization. The other 50% (who have gained a foothold in the local economy through wage employment or self-employment) have less of an interest — or stake — in the organization, *because it no longer speaks to their enlightened self-interest.* Those in greatest need become separated from those with the solutions . . . the MAA is uniquely suited to (and responsible for) *sustaining links between those who are faring well and those needing help.* How well the MAA performs this task will determine its relevance to the community in the years ahead. The MAA can succeed *only as it speaks* (through services) *to the interests and needs of both parts of its legitimate client base* [1984, pp. 4–5].

Research Findings

Since the primary impetus (beyond the Indochina Resource Action Center) for the development of MAAs was the federal government, especially the Office of Refugee Resettlement, it is not surprising that much of the research and analysis on MAA management has been generated by or for one or another government office. Periodic assessments of efficiency and effectiveness have been published; most respected among these is the work of David S. North and his associates.

Another researcher (Carol A. Mortland at the Board of Cooperative Educational Services Refugee Assistance Program in Ithaca, New York) astounded us with her conclusions on the performance of some MAAs: "The structure, activities, and evaluation processes of these organizations are created by a limited number, often only one, refugee to conform to governmental views of legitimacy and conceptions of what constitutes a fundable organization. The notion of a democratically-organized group responding to the needs of the community by obtaining funding to meet those needs is a myth. The reality is that Southeast Asian [MAAs] are created by individuals in response to government conceptions of what they should be. These individuals then perpetrate the myth of the democratically-based and run group in order to obtain continuing funds while incidentally offering services" (1988).

Additional ethnic-specific[3] research has been conducted by Pobzeb Vang, who based his organizational assessment of Lao-Hmong organizations also on Western standards rather than examining the traditional cultural patterns for models of Hmong association.

Methodology: Case Studies in Adaptation

In organizing the research, the Indochina Resource Action Center (IRAC) team looked primarily for sites with a critical population mass — a sufficient number of refugees to sustain one or more MAAs — and secondarily at sites with a "receptive" environment — presence of enlightened leadership within either the refugee or the mainstream community or both. Conducted over six months, this search yielded some dozen potential research sites, each of which was then visited over the ensuing eighteen months.

Before conducting any site visits, IRAC cast a wide net, inviting the participation of all known MAAs within each location. Included in the invitation packet was a brief, two-page survey instrument (organizational profile), which some 120 MAAs were asked to complete and return to IRAC as part of a workshop registration packet.

Although it focused on organizational planning and strategic resource development, the subsequent workshop series also included a session devoted to helping each MAA make a quick assessment of its own organizational capacity for leadership and management. The principal author asked each participating MAA to undertake a three-month process of self-assessment, using the five-page tool[4] distributed during this session. This two-stage process yielded fifty-three self-assessments, which became the basis for more in-depth research, often through the vehicle of follow-up technical assistance.

Simultaneously, because there are MAAs in smaller sites that IRAC did not plan to visit, the IRAC team engaged in a telescoped process to gather information from these as well. Some MAAs came directly to IRAC for help, others were referred by refugee program officials, some we ran into in the course of conferences and unrelated meetings, and others were contacted directly either because they were new or because an individual in the IRAC network had asked the IRAC team to help that particular MAA. To date, this ongoing process has yielded an additional twenty-two organizational self-assessments (short form).

The data gathered both in written form (the two surveys) and through group workshops, one-on-one organizational consultations, and follow-up technical assistance form the knowledge base upon which the principal author identified four different leadership/management scenarios. As composites, the MAAs described below are anecdotal; findings are not statistically significant. In fact, over the past year of research, IRAC has found some MAAs moving along from one leadership/management pattern into another. The research team feels, therefore, that the cases themselves are both explanatory and typically valid as example MAAs from our experience. As John Gardner (1989) points out, nonprofits have a tendency to coalesce around individuals with strong charismatic personalities. In MAAs, this can take one of two forms.

Case 1

These MAAs retain the traditional model of governance, by a council of elders. Board members are selected for their past social status in the home country and are the accepted heirs to the moral authority passed on through tradition. These MAAs have the following characteristics:

- Affiliation is the main criterion for leadership selection.
- They have large boards of directors.
- The leadership does not have the know-how to effectively use its organizational resources to make MAAs visible in

mainstream society. They are unable to attract outside financial support.

- They retain enough political power to influence the direction of debate in setting the community's agenda.

Case 2

These MAAs form relationships with external groups, such as mainstream nonprofits or churches sympathetic to the refugee community. Know-how is transferred from mainstream institutions to the MAAs, mostly through younger leaders because of their natural advantage in language acquisition. The council of elders is expanded to include nonrefugees in an advisory capacity as board members or members of the organization's advisory committee. This kind of MAA is more successful in obtaining grants from government to establish programs that serve its clientele and has the following characteristics:

- Nonrefugees are recruited to serve, at least in an advisory capacity.
- It is funded by and has visibility in nonprofit circles.
- It is staff driven; younger leadership with know-how is given the authority to serve and represent the interests of the community.
- Power is retained by the council of elders who keep the younger leader or executive director in line. Because the elders are generally unfamiliar with American styles of governance and management, they (as board members) withhold power from the staff leadership.
- Board/staff tension begins to appear because of the experience gap.

Case 3

The old style of governance is totally rejected in favor of the American nonprofit style. This MAA becomes service oriented and shows these characteristics:

- The budget is relatively larger.
- Its programs can serve individuals outside the traditional constituent base.
- It expands its geographic area of operation with the establishment of branch offices.
- The board composition changes to favor people with professional background over those with community connections.

Case 4

The old style of governance is adapted to the new context. Expertise (practical or academic) becomes an important criterion for leadership selection, more important than affiliation. Community development is now the organizational focus. These MAAs have these characteristics:

- Board size is decreased.
- Service programs are issue oriented rather than funder driven.
- They become more politically active in the mainstream.

Using the Research to Improve MAA Practices

Three critical issues face the Indochinese-American nonprofit leadership. All three relate to increasing the momentum toward building MAAs that are democratically based and run.

1. Defusion of board-professional staff tension is caused by the experience gap: practical knowledge acquired in Indochina by board members versus academic and technical knowledge received by professional staff trained in the United States. Increasing access to a broad range of information and training opportunities is needed to help narrow gaps between board members and organizational staff. Board members, who now form the traditional council of elders, are additionally hampered by lack of English language skills. (Also, forms of address in ethnic languages reinforce hierarchy.)

2. There is a brain drain of the U.S.-educated and technically competent younger generation who are frustrated and feel shut out of leadership because of old-style leadership dominance. Today, the rift between the old and the new styles of leadership is literally tearing many MAAs apart. The transitional younger generation, who went through elementary and perhaps junior high school in their own countries and have completed their high school and university education in the United States are beginning to break out of group-think and become more individualistic in orientation. Their exclusion from leadership and authority by the community elders has driven them to seek material success (by American standards) as a means to acquired credibility and status. "The only way to be heard is to become an MBA and drive a BMW." Timing is critical—this special bicultural generation is getting married, having children, and buying houses or planning for their nuclear family's future. Once this "bridge generation" has begun to focus on upward career mobility, they may not have energy for the community. They (and their children) will regret that community leadership opportunities were not available when they were ready to make that commitment.

3. People must deal with memories. The traumatic loss of the homelands and the continuing exodus of refugees from home countries help keep alive the political debate (armed resistance versus reconciliation and reconstruction) and remain a constant source of internal ethnic community tensions that hamper MAA effectiveness whenever such dissensions come up among the MAA leadership.

Returning to Conrad's analysis (1987), we find three key words that are critical to MAAs: innovation, participation, and pluralism. Resolving tensions between the board and professional staff will require *innovation*. A new "filtering" system that takes into account the differing perspectives, experiences, and knowledge levels can help the MAA keep the best of both the old and the new cultures. With enhanced communication skills, the MAA leadership can be in a better position to clarify the organization's ever-emerging mission and set realistic and manageable goals that will allow the organization to endure, even grow, and take full advantage of resource opportunities. As an ultimate step, the organization may want to consider innovative ways of freeing up key leadership for additional learning experiences, perhaps in the form of tailored leadership seminars or even longer-term sabbaticals.

Encouraging broader *participation* is the key to stopping the brain drain and bridging the experience gap. MAAs will need new systems for communicating with all their various constituencies. Democratization of the board recruitment and selection process is essential. With increasing mutual respect, perhaps with a mentoring process structured into the MAAs' plan, clear and constructive roles for multiple generations become possible.

The many passions within these constituencies cannot be defused without a commitment to *pluralism*. MAAs must build into their organizations a mechanism that encourages constructive discussion and debate. For an MAA to move beyond conflict requires mutual consensus that disagreement is acceptable, even healthy.

Notes

1. Only a small percentage of the 1.2 million Southeast Asian refugee population has acquired U.S. citizenship to date, but as permanent residents of this country they function in many ways parallel to citizenship.
2. The Indochina Resource Action Center maintains the most accurate national MAA listing, updated quarterly. Of the 1,200-plus known MAAs, we are in touch with 50 percent on a regular basis.
3. There are seven distinct ethnic groups who are commonly considered in the United States under the collective group of Southeast Asian or Indochinese: Cambodian, Hmong, Lao, Miem, Montanard, Thaidam, and Vietnamese.
4. Besides the usual questions about program, budget, and funding breakdown, the organizational self-assessment tool

solicited information on mission, planning system, and institutional structure for planning. The sections on board and staff composition asked about length of service, age, gender, ethnicity, professional training, area(s) of expertise or skill, and previous organizational or work experience.

References

Bui, D. D. "The Indochinese Mutual Assistance Associations." *Bridging Cultures: Southeast Asian Refugees in America.* Los Angeles: Asian American Community Mental Health Training Center, 1981.

Carver, J. *Boards That Make a Difference: A New Design for Leadership in Nonprofit and Public Organizations.* San Francisco: Jossey-Bass, 1990.

Conrad, W. R., Jr. *A Basic Nonprofit Leadership/Management Concept and Model.* Downers Grove, Ill.: Voluntary Management Press, 1987.

Downing, B. T., and Mason, S. R. *A Study of Lao Family Community, Inc. in Minnesota: An Ethnic Self Help Organization.* Unpublished paper, Southeast Asian Refugee Studies Project, University of Minnesota, 1982.

Dunlop, J. J. *Leading the Association: Striking the Right Balance Between Staff and Volunteers.* Washington, D.C.: Association Management Publications, 1989.

Gardner, J. W. *On Leadership.* New York: Free Press, 1989.

Gies, D. L., Ott, J. S., and Shafritz, J. M. *The Nonprofit Organization: Essential Readings.* Pacific Grove, Calif.: Brooks/Cole, 1990.

Hershey, P., and Blanchard, K. H. *Management of Organizational Behavior: Utilizing Human Resources.* (5th ed.) Englewood Cliffs, N.J.: Prentice-Hall, 1988.

Hofstede, G. *Culture's Consequences: International Differences in Work-Related Values.* Newbury Park, Calif.: Sage, 1980.

Houle, C. O. *Governing Boards: Their Nature and Nurture.* San Francisco: Jossey-Bass, 1989.

Hunter, P. M. "The Board Wars: Impasse, Communication, and Change." *Resource Bulletin,* 1988, *9,* 8–9.

James, E. (ed.). *The Nonprofit Sector in International Perspective: Studies in Comparative Culture and Policy.* New York: Oxford University Press, 1989.

Le Xuan Khoa, and Bui, D. D. "Southeast Asian Mutual Assistance Associations: An Approach for Community Development." In T. C. Owan (ed.), *Southeast Asian Mental Health: Treatment, Prevention, Services, Training, and Research.* Washington, D.C.: National Institute of Mental Health, 1985.

Mortland, C. A. *Southeast Asians and the American Economy: Intervening Groups.* Ithaca, N.Y.: BOCES Refugee Assistance Program, 1988.

Nielsen, W. A. *The Golden Donors: A New Anatomy of the Great Foundations.* New York: Dutton, 1985.

North, D. S., Teng Yang, and others. *An Evaluation of the Highland Lao Initiative.* Washington, D.C.: Office of Refugee Resettlement, 1985.

O'Connell, B. *The Board Member's Book: Making a Difference in Voluntary Organizations.* New York: Foundation Center, 1985.

Pho, L. "Organizational Development and Human Resources Management for MAAs." *Resource Bulletin,* 1988, *4,* 4–5.

Setterberg, F., and Schulman, K. *Beyond Profit: The Complete Guide to Managing the Nonprofit Organization.* New York: HarperCollins, 1985.

Smith, G. B. "Facing the Challenge: Refugee Community Development During the 1980's and Beyond." *The Bridge,* 1984, *1*(3–4), 3–5.

Vang, P. *The Politics of Hmong Organizations in America.* Denver, Colo.: Hmong Council Education Committee, 1990.

Part Four

Public Policy Issues

The most salient contemporary issues about nonprofits that face public decision makers include whether and how to regulate their advocacy activities, the tax deductibility of charitable contributions, policies and procedures with respect to the purchase of health and other services from nonprofits, and licensing regulations and quality standards. The chapters in this section discuss a pair of public policy issues that are not yet in the spotlight but that may be edging toward center stage: nonprofits' accumulation of equity and the application of antitrust laws to nonprofits.

Chapter Thirteen, by Howard P. Tuckman and Cyril F. Chang, starts by asking, "Who owns the equity of nonprofits under existing federal and state laws?" After analyzing why nonprofits accumulate equity—to supplement program funding, to finance capital projects, to provide a cushion in periods of economic decline, and to support growth and new initiatives—the authors discuss the positive and negative results of equity accumulation. Tuckman and Chang offer five criteria that can be used to determine whether equity accumulation is excessive and conclude by recommending alternative strategies for avoiding excess accumulation.

Richard Steinberg, in Chapter Fourteen, reflects on the growing application of antitrust statutes to the nonprofit sector, discussing their use in challenging hospital mergers, universities' reputed collusion in granting financial aid, the practices of united fundraising organizations, and nonprofits' use of price

251

discrimination and sliding-scale fees. He speculates that antitrust laws may in the future be applied to proposed mergers among day-care centers and nursing homes and to the practices of research charities. Steinberg presents three interrelated rationales for treating nonprofits differently — the nondistribution constraint, their unique outputs, and the distinctive structure of their funding — and urges that these be used as a basis for amending the antitrust laws.

13.

Accumulating Financial Surpluses in Nonprofit Organizations

Howard P. Tuckman
Cyril F. Chang

A nonprofit's decision to build its equity position has both positive and negative effects from a social perspective. Interestingly, the burgeoning nonprofit literature has paid limited attention to this aspect of nonprofit activities. Accountants define equity as the difference between an organization's assets and liabilities; as this difference widens, an organization's financial worth increases. Equity consists of the liquid and illiquid assets of a nonprofit net of its total debt. Liquid assets provide the wherewithal for supplemental funding of charitable programs, for financing new construction, for withstanding financial downturns, and for diversification and growth because these assets are readily convertible into cash (Chang and Tuckman, 1990). Illiquid assets provide either a stream of revenue (as in the case of earnings from interest or rent) or income in kind (as in the

Note: The authors would like to thank Harvey Dale, Gabriel Rudney, Gid Smith, Richard Steinberg, and the participants of the INDEPENDENT SECTOR 1991 Spring Research Forum.

case where the nonprofit occupies rent-free space in a building that it owns). In addition, the portion of illiquid assets free of debt can be pledged as collateral by organizations wishing to obtain loan finance for their activities (Tuckman, 1991). Thus, nonprofits have sound economic reasons for wishing to increase their equity position.

Several problems can arise when a nonprofit decides to accumulate equity. An important one involves the potential for contract failure between those who donate to an organization and those who oversee the use of donated funds. For example, contract failure can arise if donors provide a nonprofit with funds with the expectation that the money will be used in the immediate support of its mission when, in fact, the organization reserves the funds for an indefinite period without telling the donors. In this case, the "contract" is carried out in a manner different from that which the donor intended and contract failure results from the informational asymmetry between buyer and seller.[1] Society may also experience other difficulties if equity accumulation leads to inefficient use of capital and/or to disproportionate political and economic power.

The purpose of this chapter is to provide several thoughts as to when the equity of nonprofit organizations becomes excessive and how to avoid this problem. We begin with a discussion of who owns the equity of a nonprofit and then consider nonprofits' motives for accumulating equity. We consider the social consequences of this accumulation, and we propose several criteria for identifying when excess accumulation occurs. A number of methods are then proposed for dealing with excess accumulation.

The Legal Ownership of Nonprofit Equity

It is generally well known that federal and state tax laws preclude distribution of a nonprofit's assets to its shareholders, board of directors, and/or other administrators. Asset distributions that result in private gains can lead to the loss of the offending organization's tax-exempt status. While the statutes are explicit on this point, they are somewhat vague regarding who owns the equity that nonprofits retain.[2] It is reasonable to argue that the founders of a nonprofit are not its owners. Instead, they are caretakers for the interests of those the nonprofit serves and, in this capacity, they bear a fiduciary responsibility both to the donors and beneficiaries of the organization.[3] In fact, some state corporation statutes designate nonprofits as "nonstock corporations," in explicit recognition that increases in net worth are not permitted to accrue to the founders or officers of these organizations (Oleck, 1988, p. 5). The founders of a nonprofit have no residual claim to its assets, either while it is functioning or when it dissolves. Except to the extent that the courts decide to return donated property upon dissolution of a nonprofit, the founders cannot gain from growth in the equity of an ongoing enterprise.

Likewise, society also cannot reasonably be called the owner of a nonprofit because of the limited ownership rights that state and federal statutes confer on it. It does not receive a direct financial return when a nonprofit earns a surplus (has revenues in excess of its expenditures); it has no direct control of how a nonprofit uses its surpluses; and, except in cases where it provides contracts or grants, it has a limited voice in determining which assets nonprofits will acquire and how they will produce services.[4] Society cannot ask nonprofits for the temporary use of their assets nor can it appropriate these assets for its own use, except in cases where the nonprofit statutes have been violated. As long as nonprofits remain in business and pursue their legitimate missions, society benefits from their operation but does not own them.

Additional ownership problems arise when a charitable nonprofit terminates its existence. Such an organization is precluded from distributing its assets for private gain, but this preclusion does not mean that the state will own the assets of the dissolving nonprofit. The *cy pres* doctrine plays an important role in guiding the courts as to how the assets of a terminating nonprofit should be distributed (Oleck, 1988). Under this doctrine, the courts attempt to redirect a dissolved organization's property to a charitable use within "the general intention on the settlor" (p. 1194). The members of the charitable nonprofit are given no claim to the property but, if the defunct nonprofit is affiliated with (or is a branch or subsidiary) of a parent organization, its assets pass to the parent. For example, the assets of a closed-down church will normally revert to the entity to which it was responsible in the church hierarchy. Similarly, the assets of a defunct Boy Scout troop usually pass to a local Boy Scout council or to the nonprofit sponsor of the troop. Where no identifiable parent exists, some states will require the property to revert to the state or to the original donor. In others, the courts may choose to give the assets to a nonprofit with an unrelated but charitable purpose. Thus, even in the case of dissolution, society's claim on nonprofit property is not well defined.

Analysis of these ownership issues, together with the terms under which a nonprofit is established, suggests that the laws provide ownership rights to the nonprofits themselves. There are several ways that nonprofits can be legally recognized: as corporations, charitable trusts, and associations. For nonprofits that choose to incorporate, these rights are granted into perpetuity. Similarly, for nonprofits organized as charitable trusts, rights of ownership may also be granted for an unlimited period of time. However, the trust organizational form imposes stringent financial fiduciary obligations on the organization's trustees (Oleck, 1988). In contrast, a nonprofit organized as an unincorporated association must specify the continuity of its existence in its articles of association and vest property rights in its board of directors or trustees. The indefinite character of an organizational form can cause problems in acquiring, holding, and passing on property. Not surprisingly, most attorneys advise nonprofit organizations to choose the corporate form (Oleck, 1988).

Why Is Little Attention Paid to Equity Accumulation?

In understanding why the ownership issues have drawn little attention, it is important to recognize the central role assigned by state statutes and the federal tax code to the purpose of an organization. Along with restrictions on the distribution of assets for private gain, organizational purpose is a defining characteristic of whether an organization will be granted nonprofit status and whether it will qualify for special tax and legal treatment. Both state statutes and the federal Internal Revenue Code (IRC) require that a nonprofit be engaged in socially acceptable activities if it is to be chartered as a charitable organization. Under the IRC, organizations such as educational institutions, hospitals, and religious organizations are automatically allowed 501(c)(3) status as charitable nonprofits. A similar situation exists in some state statutes. For example, the Illinois General Not-for-Profit Corporation Act allows an organization to incorporate as a nonprofit corporation if its purpose is a sanctioned one.[5] Some scholars oppose the use of restrictive categories in determining which organizations should receive nonprofit status. For example, Hansmann (1981) offers the normative prescription that the essential role of the nonprofit should be to serve as a fiduciary in situations where contract failure exists and that restricting the purposes of nonprofit organizations "serves no obvious need that could not better be served by other means" (p. 509). This has tended to be a minority view, but the states do differ in the extent to which they seek to restrict permissible purposes. Once a nonprofit's purpose is approved, both the state and the federal government place limited restrictions on its use of funds and neither government sets forth criteria with respect to how these funds should be spent or saved.[6]

The implicit assumption underlying state and federal statutes is that since society gains from the social services provided by nonprofits, it is largely irrelevant whether these organizations accumulate surpluses over time. Interestingly, while both scholars and practitioners acknowledge that charitable organizations are free to earn a profit, little has been written regarding how these profits are to be used (for example, Hansmann, 1981). It can be argued that this is a direct result of the unwillingness of society to have strong government oversight of the nonprofit sector. An alternative argument is that a safeguard exists against the misuse of these funds because the assets of nonprofits must be used solely in support of organizational mission. Since a prohibition against private distribution of assets exists, any fund accumulations are assumed to be *ultimately* used in support of organizational purpose. Hence, the issue is not whether an organization experiences large increases in equity but rather whether it is engaged in activities of a charitable nature. Although it is not clear which of these arguments underlies existing statutes, the consequence is that these laws focus on the purposes of nonprofits rather than on their use of funds.

Institutional Ownership and the
Pervasiveness of Nonprofit Surpluses

Vestment of equity ownership in nonprofits themselves rather than in society provides an incentive for these organizations to try to save a portion of the revenue that they receive each year. In a recent article (Chang and Tuckman, 1990), we examine 4,730 nonprofit tax returns from a sample of tax filers drawn by the IRS for the 1983 tax year. The analysis reveals that 86 percent of the nonprofits in this sample reported positive surpluses and that the average surplus was $2.7 million. A similar analysis of 6,168 nonprofits in the 1985 IRS sample reveals that 85 percent of these organizations had surpluses that averaged $3.4 million (Tuckman and Chang, 1991). Unpublished data for the 1986 tax year confirm the pervasiveness of surplus accumulation among the nonprofits in the IRS sample for that year. It should be noted that the IRS data are subject to several criticisms. They tend to be biased upward because nonprofits with gross revenues under $25,000 and a large number of small religious institutions do not file a return. Moreover, the IRS includes 100 percent of the nonprofits with assets of $10 million or more in its sample. To some extent, this upward bias can be corrected by weighting the data to take into account underrepresentation of nonprofits in the under-$10-million-asset category.[7] This procedure makes the sample representative of the actual population of tax filers. When the 1986 data are weighted, the average surplus of the 112,827 tax filers is $2.5 million. Moreover, 75 percent of the nonprofits report a surplus. Although the weighted average surpluses for nonprofits in 1986 are lower than the unweighted ones, they nonetheless support our earlier finding that the vast majority of charitable nonprofits earn profits.

The Motivation to Accumulate Equity

A question arises as to why nonprofit managers want to accumulate equity (whether through persistent surpluses or through other means) if they do not experience monetary gains personally in the process. An answer to this question is presented in the form of a model that tests the assumption that nonprofits consciously seek to accumulate equity (Tuckman and Chang, 1991). We also offer several reasons why nonprofits want to accumulate equity. Some nonprofit organizations earmark the net earnings on their assets for provision of services to persons otherwise unable to afford them.[8] In this sense, net earnings on assets increase the ability to fulfill a charitable mission and can also subsidize program operations, increase equity, and/or improve the quality of offered services. Moreover, the ability of nonprofits to accumulate funds for the purposes favored by the donors of these funds improves the ability of nonprofits to attract donations from those who require the assurance that their contributions will be used in activities that they believe to be important.

Significant earnings from assets also offer nonprofit managers a degree of independence from their funding sources. Nonprofits usually must respond to donor preferences if they wish to obtain gifts and bequests (James, 1983). Those that rely on program service revenues are dependent on the buyers of their services while those that receive government grants must meet the wishes of grantors. The managers of these nonprofits find it easier to satisfy their own desires with respect to what their organization should be doing when they can make use of an earnings stream that does not require accountability to an external source. It is difficult for most nonprofits to build equity to a point where it offers them substantial freedom from outside funders, but this does not preclude their managers from trying.

Equity can also serve the interests of nonprofit administrators themselves. Managers can draw down their liquid assets to finance existing programs, to diversify into new areas, and to temporarily offset revenue shortfalls resulting from the provision of charitable care. Equity held in the form of liquid or semiliquid assets can be drawn down to finance unexpected expenditure spikes and/or unplanned declines in contracts, gifts, donations, and government grants. This reduces a nonprofit's vulnerability and increases the security of its managers. It may also increase the well-being of the staff by reducing the need for service cutbacks when revenues decline (Tuckman and Chang, 1990). Moreover, a strong equity position is helpful if a nonprofit wishes to leverage its operations using a financial institution as the funding source (Tuckman, 1991).

Increases in equity are also sometimes taken as indicators of financial success by a nonprofit's board of directors. Although a nonprofit's mission is not to make profits, businesspeople serve on the boards of directors and many carry the criteria of the for-profit sector to the board table. To the extent that a manager's performance is judged by business standards, increases in the net worth of the nonprofit may be interpreted as indicators of efficient operation. In addition, in markets where nonprofits face competition, large equity balances can have strategic value and this provides further encouragement for managers to accumulate surpluses. Finally, equity accumulation may be an end in itself for nonprofit managers who take pleasure in conducting a serious fundraising campaign, from seeing trust funds grow, and/or from the power that heading a campaign creates. Moreover, since financial strength provides insurance against the premature demise of a nonprofit, some managers may take pleasure from seeing equity grow because they feel that it ensures the long-term continuity of the organization.

The Positive Social Effects of Equity Accumulation

Perhaps the most persuasive argument for why nonprofits should be allowed to accumulate equity is that a strong nonprofit sector is an important asset to a society. When the sector builds its finances, society benefits both because the desire to accumulate equity creates a greater incentive to be efficient than would otherwise prevail and because less public subsidy is required to finance the sector than otherwise. Earnings from assets are a source of revenues that both strengthen nonprofits and enable them to engage in autonomous decision making.[9] For those who value diversity and independence of the sector, the creation of a pool of assets that yield earnings can have great social value and is to be encouraged. Society benefits when nonprofits provide services that would have otherwise been subsidized by government, that would otherwise have been produced at lower-quality levels, and/or that would not have been produced at all.

Consider the case of the nonprofit housing program that builds homes through the use of volunteer labor. The homes benefit those who cannot otherwise obtain a mortgage, and owners' monthly mortgage payments can be put into a trust fund to be used to finance additional building. Similarly, society gains when a clinic uses the earnings from its endowment to purchase a new Magnetic Resonance Imaging (MRI) machine that improves its diagnostic ability or when a large symphony orchestra funds several concerts from the revenues that it earns on its endowment fund. In these cases, society receives benefits that would otherwise have had to be financed from donations and/or tax revenues, or not received at all. Society also gains when equity can be drawn down to protect existing levels of service provision. Consider the case of the mental health organization that continues to treat its indigent patients by selling liquid assets after a funding cut from state or local government. In this case, the program's beneficiaries receive services that would otherwise have been cut. Similarly, many colleges and universities continue to provide financial aid from the proceeds of their endowment funds when their regular operating budgets have been cut.

In spite of these important advantages, we must recognize that nonprofit equity accumulation incurs costs to society. These take the form of forgone benefits because the accumulated funds are not available for use elsewhere in the economy. Because records on these opportunity costs do not exist, it is easy to ignore them. For efficiency to prevail, the social benefits from the use of these funds in the nonprofit sector should equal or exceed the benefits from the use of these funds in the for-profit sector. At present, we do not know whether this is the case.

Equity accumulation also provides nonprofits with the internal capital that they need for expansion, diversification, and/or creation of new ventures that may benefit society. At present, the vast majority of nonprofits rely on internal accumulation and fundraising campaigns as primary sources of capital funds (Tuckman, 1991). The banks are reluctant to lend to nonprofits because of the difficulties involved in laying claim to specialized assets when a venture fails and the adverse publicity that surrounds the reclaiming of these assets. Foundations are an alternate source of venture capital, but they tend to favor established and well-known nonprofits over small, new, or untested organizations, and their resources are not large enough to meet the needs of the nonprofit sector. Thus, most nonprofits create internal funds that can be used for expansion. For example, many nonprofit hospitals rely on internal funds to finance home health care and lifeline services, after-hours local emergency care, and other health care delivery activities. Similarly, many higher education institutions rely on internal funds to fund new programs and/or research institutes. Society benefits to the extent that these new activities reduce production costs, improve access, and/or raise quality to a point where the social benefits exceed the social costs.

Equity accumulation has several noteworthy macroeconomic impacts. An important one is the stabilizing effect that a large equity base has on the economy. Nonprofit drawdowns of equity to forestall cuts in services and job layoffs cushion the effects of a recession on employment and income. In the recession of 1990, one of the few sectors of the economy that continued to grow was the health care industry, an industry heavily populated by nonprofit hospitals with large equity balances. Similarly, the Memphis Arts Council cushioned severe cutbacks in Tennessee state government funding for the arts in 1991 by drawing down liquid assets. In this case, the programs of ten organizations most favored by the community were protected from funding declines through the dissipation of the accumulated equity of the funding organization. However, limits exist on the willingness of some nonprofits to tap into equity. For example, Hansmann (1990) notes that Yale did not draw down its endowments during the financial crisis of the 1970s, despite its straitened circumstances.

Nonprofits dampen the business cycle in several other respects. (1) Because the real estate holdings of nonprofits are less likely to be bought and sold for speculative purposes, increases in the holdings of these organizations decrease the volatility of this market. (2) Some of the largest nonprofits (measured in terms of assets and/or revenues) are in industries that usually do not react directly to the business cycle, such as education and health care. Demand and employment in these sectors are somewhat resistant to economic downturns, which helps to stabilize the economy. For example, the evidence suggests that adverse economic conditions cause students to extend the length of time that they spend pursuing a degree, and many educational institutions are either nonprofit or in the public sector (Tuckman, Coyle, and Bae, 1990). Similarly, economic stress can increase health care utilization. (3) Nonprofits do not engage in a large amount of inventory accumulation and liquidation. Their presence in an economy helps to dampen the effects that changes in inventories have on economic growth and decline. (4) Because volunteer labor is not as dependent on the economic cycle as paid labor, the services supported by volunteer labor are less vulnerable to budget cuts than the services offered on a quid pro quo basis.

A second macroeconomic impact relates to society's ability to develop an asset base dedicated to highly specific uses. Many assets required by nonprofits are specialized to their needs; alternative uses for a museum, an aquarium, a bloodmobile, and/or a botanical garden are difficult to find. Because nonprofit managers have a vested interest in seeing these organizations succeed, they will invest in assets that other investors find too risky or speculative because of their specialized nature. Furthermore, equity accumulation is a form of saving that benefits society when used for productive investment that produces services for both current and future generations. Funds invested by the nonprofit sector can improve not only its productivity but also that of the larger economy. Funds spent for a nonprofit medical research laboratory can give rise to new technologies that reduce the costs of treating disease. Similarly, investments in nonprofits that improve the level of worker education can increase productivity of many firms in the economy and raise the private incomes of the retrained workers. Funds donated to a nonprofit that develops new environmental technologies can improve the quality of the environment for everyone, and nonprofits that develop new varieties of seeds may benefit unborn generations. The critical issue is not whether nonprofits save but rather how their savings are used.

Contract Failure: A Negative Effect of Equity Accumulation

The potential for contract failure arises when nonprofits accumulate equity over periods of time. To understand this, consider Hansmann's (1981, 1987) argument for the existence of nonprofit organizations. Certain services (for example, health care and education) are of such a nature that an information asymmetry exists between the providers of the service and its purchasers. In these cases, both the users of the service and the donors who subsidize it must rely on the trustworthiness of the service providers to ensure that the latter deliver services at the levels and quality explicitly or implicitly contracted for. Because nonprofit managers cannot profit financially if they violate the contract they make with users and donors, Hansmann reasons that they will have the incentive to fulfill its terms in the specified manner. In contrast, for-profit firms have an incentive to underperform because they can directly profit from providing services at levels less than those specified in their contracts. The nonprofit organization becomes the preferred provider of services where information asymmetry is present because it is the institutional form most likely to fulfill its contract in the presence of this asymmetry. This theory has been widely accepted as a raison d'être for nonprofit organizations and as the critical feature that distinguishes this legal form. It has also been used to explain the prevalence of nonprofit institutions in, for example, the health care and education industries.

Although we agree with Hansmann's contract failure explanation of the existence of nonprofit organizations, we contend that contract failure is not limited to the for-profit sector but can happen in the nonprofit sector as well. Consider the case of a donative nonprofit supported primarily by donations and bequests. Because of the difficulty in gaining access to capital market, the nonprofit may want to save some of the funds to accumulate equity (Hansmann, 1981, 1990). However, the donors may wish the organization to use the funds immediately to provide certain services; they would not have donated or would have donated a different amount if they knew their contributions would be saved rather than spent. The question then arises as to whether there is sufficient incentive for nonprofit managers to deviate from the wishes of donors so that contract failure occurs. In other words, is equity accumulation sufficiently rewarding to cause managers to trade off higher levels of service delivery (or quality) in favor of higher levels of equity accumulation.[10]

The following discussion considers several forms of contract failure in the nonprofit sector: (1) when a donor provides a gift that is saved into perpetuity, (2) when a donation is initially saved but eventually spent for the intended purpose, (3) when a donation is used to finance diversification, and (4) when the purpose for which a donation is intended becomes obsolete.

Accumulation into Perpetuity

An information asymmetry exists if a donor provides funds to a nonprofit with the expectation that these will be immediately spent to provide services to the organization's beneficiary group. Consider, for example, a state heart association that raises funds to cure heart disease and then accumulates 50 percent of the donated funds in a trust fund. The donor believes that his or her funds are being used for research although in reality a significant portion is used to raise the level of the trust fund. Similarly, suppose that a nationally known university chooses to raise funds from its alumni with the expectation that these will be used to improve the quality of existing campus buildings. Over 60 percent of the donations are then placed in a perpetual endowment. In both cases, a difference exists between what the donor expects the funds to be used for and what is actually done with them. Because the donor is unaware that his funds are saved rather than spent, information asymmetry gives rise to contract failure. Such a failure can be avoided if a nonprofit makes explicit the portion of the funds that it expects to accumulate and how these will eventually be used.

Eventual Spending Out of Equity

Under state and federal statutes, accumulated funds must ultimately be spent on program services. It can be argued that the failure to notify donors that funds are saved is of little practical importance since the funds will eventually be spent in support of mission, which is the implicit assumption of most state and federal laws.[11] Unfortunately, it ignores the time value that the donor places on his money. A donor may receive a different level of satisfaction from seeing a service delivered today than on one carried out in ten years. Consider the donor who contributes large amounts to an asthma foundation hoping that these funds will be used to provide relief for his own lung problem. He is not indifferent if the foundation holds his funds for several years before expending them, for at least two reasons: first, he continues to experience pain that he had hoped to avoid; second, he has lost the chance to use his funds for other purposes during the period that the nonprofit held them. Given the circumstances, he may well have preferred to spend the funds elsewhere and to contribute only in the year in which the funds were expended for the intended purpose. Similarly, suppose that a woman with cancer donates to a cancer society expecting that the funds will be used to research a cure before she dies. If the funds are spent ten years later, she may not be around to benefit and the nonprofit has failed her. Under these circumstances she may decide that the benefits of donating are no longer worth the cost. In both instances, the fact that a nonprofit's equity is ultimately used in fulfillment of its mission does not satisfy donors with a high time value of money.

As the time value of money rises, the discount placed on the benefits of future services rises. Consequently, one might expect that informed donors with a high time preference would reduce the contributions that they make to charities that save their donations. It is also reasonable to assume that these donors might change the organizations they donate to, substituting those with lower benefits but shorter realization times for those with a higher personal payoff but a longer realization time. One can propose that donors do not factor time into their thinking (a dubious proposition, particularly for the wealthy), but this does not negate the fact that information asymmetries can distort the donation process. To the extent that the passage of time reduces the benefits of a contribution, the fact that the donor's contribution is saved and that he or she is not told this fact represents a contract failure. Of course, even if a nonprofit told the donor that the funds would be saved, it could not provide a definitive time when the donation would be spent. Thus, the donor would still not be able to determine the value of the benefit. Once again, this argument does not negate the fact that the donor may make a different contribution if the service will not be delivered until an unspecified future time.

Equity and Diversification

Contract failure can also arise if accumulated equity is used to provide services different from those intended by the donors. A hospital employs funds donated for research to acquire a free-standing nursing home without telling its donors. In this case, the nonprofit's mission is the same (contributing to the health of the community) but the type of service that it provides has been changed. A different situation arises if a public radio or TV station uses local contributions to acquire a station in another city, or a museum acquires a facility located in an adjacent city. In these situations, the service is the same but the population benefiting from the donations has been altered. Yet a third situation arises if donated funds are used for a purpose not understood to be part of the organization's mission, as in the situation where funds donated to help the members of a specific religious group are used instead to feed Vietnamese boat people who settle in a community. In each of these scenarios, the contract failure does not rest with what the organization does but rather with its failure to inform donors as to the purpose for which these funds were used. Diversification may make sound business sense to the organization in question, but it represents a change in the terms under which a contract was negotiated.

Contract Failure and Obsolescence

When funds are allowed to accumulate for long periods, the possibility of obsolescence of purpose arises. Consider a university that accepts an endowment to be used to educate electrical engineers who study vacuum tubes. As time passes, it is inevitable that the presssure will grow to use these funds for the education of students in a more contemporary technology, such as semiconductors. Similarly, consider an endowment to a zoo to be used to improve the quality of iron cages for animals. Since many zoos now emphasize the natural habitat as the environment of choice, a question arises as to when it is in society's interest to alter the terms of the original contract. In some cases, the contract may be written broadly enough to encompass changes in technology; in others, it is necessary to change the intent of the original donor. The courts can intervene under the doctrine of *cy pres,* but this may happen at a cost of violating the original contract between donor and nonprofit.

In all of these cases, the passage of time increases the likelihood of contract failure, which has led to some hostility on the part of students of nonprofits to perpetual restraints on gifts (Hansmann, 1990). However, it has not caused many practitioners to recognize the potential for contract failure that accompanies the accumulation of donations over time. Clearly, greater attention should be paid to the information that is provided to donors who contribute to those nonprofits that accumulate rather than spend their donations.

Additional Negative Effects: Market Power and Economic Inefficiency

At least two additional major concerns arise about nonprofit equity accumulation. The first deals with concentration of market power and the second with economic inefficiency.

Concentration of Market Power

When equity accumulation occurs, some nonprofits obtain disproportionate economic and political power because of their command over a large asset base. These nonprofits may influence the behavior of for-profit firms anxious to obtain their business, and they may also exercise control over a large number of investment dollars that provide them with broad leverage over the for-profit sector. This might occur, for example, if they bought large blocks of for-profit stock and sought to influence the direction of the companies they owned. A related concern is that the substantial assets of these nonprofits might cause banks and other financial institutions to invite their managers to serve on corporate boards or in other advisory positions. In these situations, nonprofit managers might reap indirect financial gain as a consequence of the decisions they make regarding the investment of nonprofit assets.

Large equity accumulations also pose a threat to competition in those sectors where commercial nonprofits currently operate, or where they might choose to compete in the future.[12] This accumulated equity can deter potential competitors from entering a market and can provide the wherewithal for commercial nonprofits to engage in predatory behavior. For example, a nonprofit hospital may choose to underprice a particular surgical procedure to keep a for-profit competitor out of the market, using earnings from equity to subsidize the costs of this action. Similarly, a nonprofit nursing home might use earnings from equity to provide nonmedical amenities that for-profits find difficult to match, making it the preferred provider. In the commericial realm, it is not easy to distinguish between decisions designed to improve the quality of a nonprofit's service offerings and those designed to provide competitive advantage. Similarly, it is hard to distinguish between lower prices as a charitable service and those that represent predatory behavior. Although the behavior of private foundations has been subject to substantial public scrutiny in the last four decades, surprisingly little analysis has been done on the misuse of power by operational nonprofits and support organizations.

Economic Inefficiency

The possibility arises that nonprofits will not put their accumulated equity to its best use. When nonprofits raise funds from the private sector and use them to purchase assets with a lower return than these funds would have earned elsewhere, society experiences a loss. In the for-profit sector, competition ensures that funds are invested in their best use. There are several reasons to be concerned about the efficiency of nonprofit investment. First, no mechanism exists to ensure that nonprofits with inefficient investments will be driven out of business. Indeed, a nonprofit that invests poorly may continue to receive donations for long periods because data are not available to evaluate its performance. Second, some donors fund their favored charities based on limited information as to how their donations will be spent or how accumulated surpluses are invested. There is no direct link between investment performance and the amounts donated. Third, since nonprofit managers are not rewarded for sound investment decisions, limited incentives exist for them to ensure that they are obtaining the highest yield from their investment portfolio.[13] Fourth, existing tax laws restrict the types of investments that nonprofits can make. Consequently, these organizations do not have the same opportunities to diversify as for-profit enterprises. Taken together, the above arguments suggest the need for greater public disclosure of the financial performance of nonprofits with sizable equity accumulations.

Should Governments Subsidize Nonprofits That Accumulate Equity?

A question also arises as to whether governments should subsidize nonprofits through tax exemption and direct grants when their own budgets are in deficit. The answer partially depends on where these governments get the greatest benefits from their expenditures. If efficiency is the only consideration, government should subsidize the nonprofit sector to the point where the benefits per dollar of subsidy just equal the benefits per dollar of expenditure spent for any other government purpose (Chang

and Tuckman, 1991). In such a world, and assuming no transaction costs, subsidies to nonprofits should fall whenever nonprofits put funds into investments with lower social benefits and
rise whenever funds are put into a higher use. In the real world,
informational constraints preclude the realization of this goal
because it is impossible to accurately measure and compare the
social benefits of alternative government expenditures. Hence,
there is limited linkage between the benefits that society receives
from nonprofits and the subsidies it provides to them.

Efficiency considerations are only part of the problem,
however. An issue arises as to whether it is fair to ask governments to subsidize organizations able to generate surpluses from
their operations, particularly if the surpluses are large. Moreover, the contract failure argument applies to government subsidies to nonprofits. To the extent that subsidies are provided
to augment the quantity or quality of services of nonprofits, contract failure arises when nonprofits choose to accumulate funds
for future use. If it is known that governments would not subsidize nonprofits if they were aware that these organizations were
accumulating large amounts of equity, a need exists for better
mechanisms for providing public disclosure of nonprofit equity.

This issue has emerged in recent legislation and court actions. In 1990, for example, tax challenges and/or increased
regulatory activities threatened the exempt status of nonprofit
hospitals in twenty-three states (Hudson, 1990). The health care
industry provides an example of what is at stake in the resolution of this issue. Nonprofit hospitals, clinics, nursing homes,
and other institutions receive large implicit and explicit subsidies from various government entities (Herzlinger and Krasker,
1987). The governmental entities that fund them face enormous
demands for funds to treat the medically needy (Lewin and Lewin, 1987). It can be argued that the equity accumulated by
nonprofit institutions should be drawn down to finance treatment of charity cases but, at some point, this would seriously
impede their operation. Hence, a need exists to identify when
equity accumulation becomes excessive. The political process
is moving toward greater scrutiny of the actions of nonprofits,
which may be seen in the introduction of a recent bill dealing

with the measurement of the benefits and costs of nonprofit hospitals by Congressman Roybal (D-Calif.) and in the works of several researchers (for example, Herzlinger and Krasker, 1987; Tuckman and Chang, 1991).

Excess Accumulation

Policies that prohibit equity accumulation will ultimately discourage cost-saving behavior, limit the ability of the nonprofit sector to deal with financial downturns, and inhibit growth. Alternatively, policies that ignore the potential problems posed by equity accumulation can have serious negative long-term consequences for the economy. The challenge is either to find a way to identify when nonprofits have excess accumulation or to find a way to avoid excess accumulation from occurring. We discuss both approaches below. The analysis begins with a discussion of existing laws.

Existing Laws

Section 4942 of the Internal Revenue Code requires that private foundations distribute approximately 5 percent of the fair market value of their investments annually; it does not prevent foundations from accumulating amounts above 5 percent. Moreover, this limitation applies only to one class of nonprofits — the private foundations. The courts have not specified useful criteria for determining when excess accumulation exists. Several court cases challenge the right of nonprofits to accumulate large amounts of equity. Thus far, the decisions in these cases suggest that while the existence of substantial equity accumulation can be construed as indicative of commercial intent, it is not a sufficient indicator of malevolence of purpose to warrant removal of a nonprofit's exempt status. What constitutes an acceptable level of accumulation remains to be defined.

Criteria for Identifying Excess Accumulation

It is in society's interest to provide nonprofits with guidelines as to the maximum rate at which equity can be accumulated and when the level of equity they hold may be excessive. This section offers five criteria that might be used if the goal is to examine the performance of nonprofits to determine which ones might be engaged in excess accumulation. Unfortunately, space limitations require that these be discussed briefly.

1. Do a nonprofit's surpluses exceed those of other nonprofits in its industry by a wide margin? The data needed for applying this criterion are available from Form 990, but several issues must be resolved. At present, a lack of consensus exists as to how broadly to define an industry and what is meant by "a wide margin."[14]

2. Has a nonprofit accumulated large surpluses over several consecutive years? The term "large" must be defined and a database created that allows consistent comparisons of equity across years. At present, no such database exists, but data are available to develop this information.

3. Does a nonprofit's equity level exceed its reasonable programmatic needs? One way to operationalize this criterion is to examine whether the return on a nonprofit's equity is greater by a wide margin than that needed to fund its program operations. Once again, a number of definitional issues arise concerning how to measure return on equity, how to determine the funding level needed for program operations, and what period of time to base the comparison on.

4. Does a nonprofit have specific plans to use its equity within a reasonable time frame? If an organization consistently accumulates equity with no concrete plans for how to use these funds, it is likely to be engaged in excessive accumulation. Specific goals should exist regarding how accumulated equity will be used in support of the mission of the organization. A problem arises in how to determine whether a nonprofit has such a plan without actually inspecting its documents. Hence, this criterion is more invasive than others.

5. Does a nonprofit have a rate of accumulation disproportionate to the rate of growth of its program service expenditures over a period of years? If so, a question arises as to whether the organization is more interested in increas-

ing its equity than its service offerings. In the situation where a nonprofit is rapidly accumulating equity to build a new facility or to begin a new program, the existence of a plan for the use of new equity within a reasonable time frame constitutes reasonable evidence that excess accumulation is not taking place.

Ways to Preclude Excess Equity Accumulation

An alternative approach to the problem is to establish payout rates for all charitable nonprofits similar to those proposed by the Filer Commission in 1977. These could require each non-profit to pay out a portion of its donated revenue each year or it could be levied on all of the revenue that nonprofits receive. Precedent exists in other countries for such a rule. For example, until 1985 Germany required its endowed institutions to either pay out or spend their total revenues. After 1985, the rule was changed to allow up to 25 percent of investment income to be added to equity. In Canada, charitable organizations must spend at least 80 percent of the tax deductible donations made to them each year (Scrivner, 1986). After 1983, the law was changed to allow the accumulation of funds restricted to the use of endowments free of the 80 percent rule (Hansmann, 1990).

The main purpose of these rules is to ensure that excess accumulation does not take place. Their key advantage is that they avoid the need for detailed public scrutiny of nonprofit finances while reducing the ability of nonprofits to accumulate equity in excess of their needs. The key problems in adopting this approach are to determine whether to apply it solely to investment income or to total revenue and how to establish a ratio that is fair to the nonprofit but that avoids large buildups of funds. Additional discussion of these issues would be productive.

Additional approaches can also be adopted, but these require the use of criteria for determining when excessive equity accumulation exists. One proposal involves removing tax deductibility for donations to nonprofits that have equity accumulation beyond those deemed reasonable by society. An alternative requires identified nonprofits to reduce their accumulations or risk losing their tax status. A third involves increasing the amounts spent in support of the beneficiaries of these organizations. An advantage of this alternative is that it seeks to reduce the accumulation levels of organizations with very large equity levels that cannot justify them. Thus, existing excesses are corrected, in contrast to the payout alternative, which is solely concerned with future accumulations. The main disadvantage is the increased administrative costs and government interference .with nonprofit decisions that this alternative creates.

Conclusions

Although the data do not currently exist to provide quantitative measures of the extent to which equity accumulation is a serious problem, we have identified the various issues that equity accumulation can raise. Questions regarding how contract failure in the nonprofit sector can be avoided, what can be done to avoid inefficient uses of saved funds, and how to prevent excess equity accumulation from interfering with the mission of the organization have not been adequately dealt with in the literature. It is clear that they should be. Our goal has been to demonstrate that a need exists for both scholars and practitioners to consider the prevalence of equity accumulation and to explore its consequences. Through such a process of inquiry and suggestion, the nonprofit sector can be made more efficient and more responsive to the needs of its constituents.

Notes

1. It is important to recognize that if the use of the funds is understood in advance of the donation, no failure occurs.
2. The laws are also explicit with respect to the effects of dissolution. For example, Oleck (1988) notes that if the purpose of a charitable organization cannot be achieved, "the assets must be applied as directed by the court in an action brought for that purpose by the trustees or the corporation, with the attorney general being joined as a party in the action" (p. 1191).

3. State law differs on this point. See, for example, New York Not-for-Profit Corp. Law §513.

4. It should be noted that society can affect the inputs used in production through its regulatory powers, however. For example, the requirement that hospitals must be accredited affects the ratio of professional staff to patients in both nonprofit and for-profit hospitals.

5. Illinois General Not-for-Profit Corporation Act, §4, Ill. Ann. Stat. ch 32, §163a3.

6. The federal government does seek to regulate saving by that class of nonprofits set up as foundations, as we shall discuss below.

7. For a description of the weighting procedure, see Hilgert and Mahler (1989, p. 59).

8. For those unfamiliar with financial concepts, a short explanation is needed of why we talk of net earnings on assets in this section. Equity is essentially an accounting concept defined as assets less liabilities. Although equity can be thought of as net assets, it does not earn income; assets do. A nonprofit earns income from its assets and incurs liabilities in the form of interest payments and other expenses. To be strictly accurate, net earnings on assets are the source of income for nonprofits, not earnings from equity.

9. Lest the argument be overstated, it is important to note that the prospects for building large revenue streams from assets are limited for most nonprofits. For example, a $1 million endowment that yields a 7 percent return produces only $70,000 in revenue. If a portion of the revenue is needed to preserve capital, then the actual amount available to fund operations may be in the neighborhood of $50,000. Thus, relatively large endowments are needed to finance a large portion of the costs of a moderately sized nonprofit.

10. Hansmann (1990) recognizes the case where persons will only donate if their gifts are placed in an endowment. However, he fails to consider the possibility that donors would not donate if they knew that their contributions would be saved rather than spent.

11. It can also be argued that if a charitable nonprofit abuses its rights of accumulation, the courts can step in to remedy the situation. But since it takes time for the courts to respond, the argument in this section applies.

12. Commercial nonprofits are nonprofit firms whose income derives primarily or exclusively from sales of goods or services (Hansmann, 1987).

13. Nonprofits who have members of their boards of directors with financial backgrounds may have an incentive to invest efficiently because of pressure from their boards.

14. INDEPENDENT SECTOR has developed a new classification scheme that attempts to provide a more rational approach to identifying the activities of nonprofits than previously existed in the literature. The National Taxonomy of Exempt Entities does not resolve the problems identified here, however.

References

Chang, C. F., and Tuckman, H. P. "Why Do Nonprofit Managers Accumulate Surpluses and How Much Do They Accumulate?" *Nonprofit Management and Leadership,* 1990, *1,* 117–135.

Chang, C. F., and Tuckman, H. P. "Vulnerability, Optimality, and Attrition in the Nonprofit Sector." *Annuals of the Nonprofit Sector,* 1991, *62*(4), 655–672.

Hansmann, H. B. "Reforming Nonprofit Corporation Law." *University of Pennsylvania Law Review,* 1981, *129,* 497–625.

Hansmann, H. B. "The Role of Nonprofit Enterprise." In S. Rose-Ackerman (ed.), *The Economics of Nonprofit Institutions.* New York: Oxford University Press, 1986.

Hansmann, H. B. "Economic Theories of Nonprofit Organization." In W. W. Powell (ed.), *The Nonprofit Sector: A Research Handbook.* New Haven, Conn.: Yale University Press, 1987.

Hansmann, H. B. "Why Do Universities Have Endowments?" *Journal of Legal Studies,* 1990, *19,* 3–42.

Herzlinger, R. E., and Krasker, W. S. "Who Profits from Nonprofits?" *Harvard Business Review,* Jan.-Feb. 1987, pp. 93–105.

Hilgert, C., and Mahler, J. "Nonprofit Charitable Organizations, 1985." *Statistics of Income Bulletin*, 1989, *9*, 53–65.

Hudson, T. "Not-for-Profit Hospitals Fight Tax-Exempt Challenge." *Hospitals*, Oct. 20, 1990, pp. 32–37.

James, E. "How Nonprofits Grow." *Journal of Policy Analysis and Management*, 1983, *2*, 350–366.

Lewin, L. S., and Lewin, M. E. "Financing Charity Care in an Era of Competition." *Health Affairs*, 1987, *6*, 47–60.

Oleck, H. L. *Nonprofit Corporations, Organizations, and Associations.* (5th ed.) Englewood Cliffs, N.J.: Prentice-Hall, 1988.

Scrivner, G. N. "Accumulations of Income by Charitable Organizations: How Much Is Too Much." *Tax-Exempt Organizations.* Englewood Cliffs, N.J.: Prentice-Hall, 1986.

Tuckman, H. P. "How Nonprofit Organizations Obtain Capital." Paper presented at the Mandel Center Conference on Nonprofit Organizations in a Market Economy, Cleveland, Ohio, Nov. 1991.

Tuckman, H. P., and Chang, C. F. "A Methodology for Measuring the Financial Vulnerability of Charitable Nonprofit Corporations." *Nonprofit and Voluntary Sector Quarterly*, Winter 1991, *20*(4), 445–460.

Tuckman, H. P., and Chang, C. F. "A Proposal to Redistribute the Cost of Hospital Charity Care." *Milbank Quarterly*, 1991, *69*, 113–142.

Tuckman, H. P., and Chang, C. F. "Nonprofit Equity: A Behavioral Model and Its Policy Implications." *Journal of Policy Analysis and Management*, Winter 1992, *11*(1), 76–87.

Tuckman, H., Coyle, S., and Bae, Y. *On Time to the Doctorate.* Washington, D.C.: National Academy Press, 1990.

14.

How Should Antitrust Laws Apply to Nonprofit Organizations?

Richard Steinberg

It's hard to tell whether the antitrust lawyers from Justice are leftover lefties, for whom big is always bad, or Reaganite righties, for whom "nonprofit" is a dirty word.

> —"Hospital Case: . . ."
> 1989, A8

This is the arrogance of an elite which is absolutely certain it knows what is best for everybody. Colleges feel folks shouldn't be making price decisions when it comes to deciding where to go to college. And even if they want to, [the colleges] won't let them.

> —Chester E. Finn, Jr.

Antitrust laws have traditionally been used to fight alleged abuses of market power by for-profit firms. More recently, arguing

Note: This chapter is drawn from a much longer paper entitled "Antitrust and the Nonprofit Sector" (unpublished), available from the author for those readers seeking further detail.

more by analogy than careful economic analysis, the legal system has scrutinized market power in the U.S. nonprofit sector. In this chapter, I survey current applications of the law to nonprofit organizations, then analyze some of the underlying policy issues, examining whether nonprofit organizations should receive distinctively different treatment under antitrust laws.

Current antitrust laws prohibit anticompetitive actions by nonprofit organizations, regardless of whether cooperation is in the social interest. Borrowing from the analysis of for-profit enterprises, the law apparently presumes that "anticompetitive" and "against the public interest" are near synonyms. However valid this identification is for for-profits (and there is controversy here), it appears far less valid for nonprofits. I conclude that although nonprofits should be covered by antitrust regulations, the standards of proof, allowable defenses, and regulatory remedies should be modified by statute, so that appropriate regulation does not depend upon semantic contortions (such as labeling collaboration as "procompetitive") or the good will of prosecutors.

My arguments fall into three categories. First, the structure of control in nonprofit organizations is distinctive. Certain control structures common to the sector are more likely to foster socially valuable collaborations, and organizations with these governance structures should not be subject to the same presumption that collusion is pernicious. Second, restricted competition is a prerequisite for the distinctive functioning of the sector. Too much competition can keep nonprofits from remedying the defects of the broader market system; it can also keep nonprofits from contributing their own defects. Whether good deviations or bad deviations predominate depends upon the governance structure; the possibility of good deviations suggests that a bias in favor of prosecuting can do real harm. Finally, I argue that competition in commercial activities is different from competition for donations. Some forms of collusion in fundraising can help society, and the laws ought to make exceptions for these acts.

Applications of Antitrust to the Nonprofit Sector

Hospital Mergers

The first case ever decided on the legality of nonprofit hospital mergers is *U.S. v. Carilion Health System and Community Hospital of Roanoke Valley* (1989). In this case, defendant Carilion (owner of Roanoke Memorial Hospitals) and defendant Community Hospital, both nonprofit corporations, wished to merge, arguing that this would allow them to cut costs by eliminating unnecessarily duplicative facilities. The Justice Department filed suit to block this merger, noting that the postmerger hospital would control roughly 70 percent of the hospital beds in the Roanoke metropolitan area (the remaining 30 percent are owned by Lewis-Gale Hospital, a for-profit corporation) and arguing that the merger would hurt consumers by allowing the hospitals to raise prices. The Justice Department lost, both in trial and in appeal, and the merger process is now under way.

The second case, *U.S. v. Rockford Memorial Corporation and the SwedishAmerican Corporation* (1989), is quite similar. Once again, two nonprofit hospitals wished to merge and face a single for-profit competitor, arguing that the merger would allow them to reduce costs by $40 million through elimination of duplication of services. However, in this case the Justice Department prevailed, and the merger has been blocked pending appeal. Commenting on this decision, Roger McCann, a lawyer in the Roanoke case, stated: "The biggest impact of the Rockford decision will be on merger cases in the future. Had the government lost in Rockford, too, it would have been forced to re-evaluate its position. I suppose now the government will press on in opposing other hospital mergers" (Hite, 1989, p. A1). Although there appear to be unsettled issues of jurisdiction over nonprofits, the FTC has also moved against hospital mergers [*Adventist Health Systems/West* (1989); *Ukiah Valley Medical Center v. FTC* (1990); *FTC v. University Health, Inc.* (1991)].

Colleges and Universities

Over fifty-five private colleges and universities have been investigated by the Justice Department for collusion in the granting of financial aid (and, according to press reports that Justice has neither confirmed nor denied, collusion in the setting of tuition and faculty salaries as well). Justice filed suit against nine universities on May 22, 1991 (*United States v. Brown, et al.*); the eight Ivy League defendants signed a consent decree, while M.I.T. is actively defending against the suit. Following Justice's example, a student filed a private antitrust suit (which provides for treble damages) against the Ivies, Wesleyan, Amherst, Williams, and Stanford [*Kingsepp v. Wesleyan, et al.* (1991)]. Kingsepp alleges conspiracies with respect to both tuition rates and financial aid policies and has moved to certify a class of present and former students to join in the complaint.

   The issue in *Brown* was the activities of the "overlap group," a group of twenty-three schools which, for years, has met in the spring of each year to exchange information on common applicants seeking financial aid. Following this meeting, financial aid packages were extended that were designed to cancel out the differences in tuition and other charges so that financial considerations would no longer play a role in the student's decision about which school to attend (Barrett, 1989). In the settlement decree, the Ivies agreed to stop participating in the overlap group, although they are specifically allowed to publicize their financial aid policies and to use a common form to determine the financial needs of common applicants according to their specified policies. Thus, the decree apparently allows the same outcomes as before and only changes the appearance and logistics of the financial aid process. Presumably, more severe sanctions will be sought against M.I.T.

   The universities are also under investigation for colluding in setting tuition rates, although no charges have been filed to date. Universities defend their similar increases in tuition, noting that they face similar increases in costs. Further, information about proposed tuition increases is often public, so the sharing of such information does not constitute collusion. But the most interesting defense here is that of snob appeal. Educational consultant Jan Krukowski argues that price increases are not evidence of collusion, for "colleges often raise charges to avoid being the least expensive among their peers. They're afraid of raising suspicion about why they're so low." Arnold Weber, president of Northwestern, adds: "Whereas businesses hold down prices to compete, many schools raise prices to meet the competition" (paraphrase of reports in Putka, 1989, p. A6).

That the cases should be brought at all is not surprising. Price fixing by for-profits has long been illegal per se (that is, the act is illegal regardless of its consequences), and educational institutions are not exempt from the relevant antitrust statute (Johnston, 1989; Swords, 1989; Bartlett, 1982; "Antitrust and Nonprofit Entities," 1981). The practice has long been public, so the timing of the investigation, coming on the heels of the hospital suits, may indicate a changing legal climate for nonprofits.

United Fundraising Organizations

Bartlett (1982) notes several practices of united fundraising organizations (hereinafter UFOs) that have been or may be found to be illegal. First, UFOs (such as United Way) typically restrict membership to a group of charities that appeal to shared values and meet standards of accountability and viability. Membership restrictions may be challenged under current antitrust law because they amount to monopoly control of a valuable common facility. Sullivan (1977, p. 131) summarizes the relevant case law: "If a group of competitors, acting in concert, operate a common facility and if due to natural advantage, custom, or restrictions of scale, it is not feasible for excluded competitors to duplicate the facility, the competitors who operate the facility must give access to the excluded competitors on reasonable non-discriminatory terms." Under this standard, Bartlett notes that a court may scrutinize whether a charity is lawfully excluded from membership and determine whether opposition is motivated by legitimate concerns or by a desire to suppress competition for limited funds.

Restrictions on supplemental fundraising are clearly necessary to obtain the efficiencies of a UFO. Yet the requirement that each member agree to restrict its own solicitation activities in exchange for a share of the funds raised by the group seems to constitute a horizontal market division that would be a per se violation of section I of the Sherman Act if practiced by a for-profit firm. Defendants seeking relief by arguing that collusion in fundraising is no different from collusion to avoid socially wasteful advertising by for-profit firms will find little solace in the law as currently constituted. For example, in *National Society of Professional Engineers v. U.S.* (1978), the Court rejected the defendant's claim that competitive bidding would cause engineers to cut costs in the area of safety, holding that "the Rule of Reason does not support a defense based on the assumption that competition itself is unreasonable" (p. 696). Although I know of no cases brought against UFOs under this argument, the potential for future cases should spur us to carefully analyze how to rewrite the law in this area.

Typically donors are unable to affect the allocation of gifts among UFO members. Bartlett suggests that this leaves UFOs susceptible to challenge for offering an illegal "tie-in" arrangement. Finally, Bartlett (1982) noted that some UFOs refuse to solicit in workplaces where other charities are also allowed to solicit. He persuasively argues (p. 1610): "If a united charity demands exclusive access to an employer's workplace, its goal must be to deny competitors the advantages of payroll deductions. . . . Such conduct constitutes a per se violation of section I of the Sherman Act." Similar issues arose in the case of *Associated In-Group Donors v. United Way, Inc.* (1978) (settled out of court), where plaintiffs alleged that United Way of Los Angeles threatened member agencies with a cutoff of funds if they accepted funds from a rival UFO. Arguably, such actions would constitute attempts to monopolize under section II and would be a per se violation under section I of the Sherman Act ("Antitrust and Nonprofit Entities," 1981).

Price Discrimination and Sliding-Scale Fees

Price discrimination (charging different prices to different customers) by for-profit firms is regarded with suspicion under the antitrust laws, especially when price differentials cannot be justified by differential cost of provision (Blair and Kaserman, 1985). Luckily, charities that seek reduced-cost office equipment, housing, or food and clothing for the poor need not fear that their for-profit suppliers will be prosecuted for their benevolence. Although the 1936 Robinson-Patman amendments to the Clayton Act contained a proscription on price discrimination, this law was itself amended by the Nonprofit Institutions Act of 1938 to exempt supplies purchased for their own use by "schools, colleges, universities, public libraries, churches, hospitals and charitable institutions not operated for profit" [current version at 15 U.S.C. section 13(c) (1976)]. However, this exemption does not apply to sales *by* nonprofit organizations, so that (in theory if not in practice) sliding-scale fees based on ability to pay could be challenged as an illegal attempt to maximize receipts from the public. More likely, charges of price discrimination will arise in the investigation of university financial aid policies. Variations in financial aid cause variations in the effective price of attending college, so collusion on financial aid is collusion in support of price discrimination.

Speculative Applications — Day Care, Nursing Homes, Research Charities

It is not too far-fetched to imagine further government incursions into the free functioning of the nonprofit marketplace. If nonprofit hospitals can be prohibited from merging, so can nonprofit day-care centers and nursing homes. Emergent medical research charities could one day sue the established giants (such as the American Cancer Society or the American Heart Association) under private antitrust statutes that provide triple damages, arguing perhaps that the established giants have attempted to monopolize government research grants or workplace solicitation rights, or have harassed their competitors through rumor-mongering. Even the Aspen Fund for Nonprofit Sector Research could one day find itself challenged by disgruntled researchers denied funding for their work if their coordinated grant-allocation process grows too prominent.

Rationales for Treating Nonprofit
Organizations Differently

In this section, I evaluate three interrelated rationales for treating nonprofit organizations differently from other institutional forms, finding merit in some of these. (1) The nondistribution constraint (which defines the sector), combined with the resulting structure of board control, mitigates the incentives for harmful anticompetitive practices. (2) Anticompetitive practices by nonprofits are not socially harmful; they are necessary to support the distinctive and socially beneficial outputs of the sector and to support desirable income redistribution. (3) Whereas competition is socially beneficial among commercial organizations (those deriving revenues principally from sales of goods and services), it is socially harmful for donative organizations (those deriving revenues from fundraising activities). I neglect a fourth rationale for reasons of brevity (see Steinberg, 1990a): nonprofit hospitals deserve distinctive treatment because of peculiarities of the hospital industry such as third-party payments and the dynamics of consumer health care choice.

The Nondistribution Constraint

The essential defining characteristic of the nonprofit sector (at least in the United States) is what Hansmann (1980) has called the "nondistribution constraint." Nonprofit organizations are allowed to generate surpluses (profits) in any year, but any excesses cannot be distributed to those controlling the firm (typically a board of directors). This is unlike for-profit firms, which typically distribute a portion of their surplus to owners through dividend checks.

Does the nondistribution constraint eliminate motives for abuse?
In *Rockford Memorial*, defendants argued that the nondistribution constraint insulated them from prosecution. The Court summarized their position (at 60,543), stating: "Defendants contend that they have no incentive to act anti-competitively because their decision-makers cannot personally gain from the monop-

oly profits derived from the exercise of market power." Commenting on *Carilion,* a newspaper editorial argued: "There are no shareholders to keep happy, no dividends to be paid out. Under the tax laws, any operating surpluses must be plowed back into hospital-related activities. If through merger a widget-maker could dominate its market, its incentives to maximize profits for its owners could lead it in the absence of competition to drive prices through the roof. But with nonprofit hospitals, that particular antitrust concern does not apply: Who is there to benefit from higher profits?" ("Merged Hospitals Would Benefit Area," 1988, p. A8).

Although the argument has merit, there are several reasons to limit its applicability. First, it is quite difficult to enforce the nondistribution constraint. Managers and board members could operate the firm as a "for-profit-in-disguise," obtaining private benefits through excessive salaries, purchases of inputs at inflated prices from other firms controlled by the board members, and self-grants of managerial perks. When this occurs, nonprofits have the same financial incentive to act against the public interest as for-profits. One might object that the appropriate remedy is better enforcement of the nondistribution constraint, rather than application of antitrust statutes, but this objection overlooks the very real difficulties forestalling improved enforcement.

A second objection is that personal financial gain is not the only motive for anticompetitive acts in either the for-profit or nonprofit sectors, and nonprofit managers may share the same other motives possessed by for-profits. In particular, altruistically motivated nonprofit entrepreneurs may possess subtle biases that lead them to cooperate with their nominal competitors. Judge Posner, in *Hospital Corporation of America* (1986), observed (at 1390) that:

> The adoption of the nonprofit form does not change human nature [citation omitted], as the courts have recognized in rejecting an implicit antitrust exemption for nonprofit enterprises [citation omitted]. . . .
> Nonprofit status affects the method of financing the

enterprise (substituting a combination of gift and debt financing for equity and debt financing) and the form in which profits . . . are distributed, and it may make management somewhat less beady-eyed in trying to control costs [citation omitted]. But no one has shown that it makes the enterprise unwilling to cooperate in reducing competition (some contrary evidence is presented in Hersch, 1984) — which most enterprises dislike and which nonprofit enterprises may dislike on ideological as well as selfish grounds.

The judge in *Rockford Memorial* was even more explicit (at 60,543): "A not-for-profit company's fund balances, enlarged through monopoly profits, are a means to an end. The end may not be the personal wealth of the decisionmaker but could be for an objective held in nearly as great esteem. The not-for-profit decisionmaker may desire more money for a new piece of equipment or to hire a new specialist or for a better office, salary or title, or just to keep the firm afloat in particularly lean or dangerous times. . . . Simply put, decisionmakers need not be solely interested in the attainment of profit to act anti-competitively." What detrimental actions would follow such incentives to collude? Judge Roszkowski suggested that the merged hospitals might stymie cost containment action by third-party payers. In addition, he argued (at 60,543) that "[t]hrough a collusive exercise of market power the hospitals in the relevant market could also eliminate 'quality' competition that has been a major drain on the hospitals' budgets." What was lacking in his investigation was a careful analysis of whether these collusive actions would result in efficiency losses or other detrimental effects. In particular, the judge complained first that collusion allows hospitals to keep prices high by resisting third-party proposed cutbacks, then that collusion allows hospitals to cut costs by coordinating their own cutbacks without ever considering which cutbacks (if either) are more appropriate. Clearly, laws need to be refined following careful economic analysis, and detrimental collusion should be distinguished from socially valuable cooperation.

Does the nondistribution constraint increase the costs of monopoly power? Even nonprofit firms must break even on average, and nonprofits in competitive markets must run efficiently to survive in the face of price cuts and quality enhancements by the competition. When protected from competition, one must rely on other forces to ensure efficiency, and the nondistribution constraint removes two of the forces that ensure productive efficiency among for-profits. Most obviously, the nondistribution constraint limits the use of financial incentives for efficiency (such as profit-sharing plans), although recent IRS decisions seemingly allow limited use of incentives (Steinberg, 1990b). On the other hand, there are nonfinancial incentives for productive efficiency that are stronger in the nonprofit sector, so the balance is unclear. Many nonprofit managers and boards are fanatically devoted to a charitable mission (feeding the poor; finding a cure for a childhood disease) that can best be accomplished if costs are held down.

Far more important is the absence of financially motivated hostile takeover bids in the nonprofit sector. When a publicly traded for-profit firm is inefficiently run, stock prices are low. Raiders who take control and improve the functioning of management are well rewarded for their efforts by the resulting increase in the value of the stock they hold. Even though the for-profit monopoly may possess power in marketing their product, ownership of the market is competitively traded, ensuring efficiency. In contrast, hostile takeover bids are virtually impossible in the nonprofit sector (and, when possible, cannot be motivated by financial gain to the bidder). Thus, if a particular nonprofit monopoly is run by an incompetent or ill-motivated board, there are no evolutionary correctives.

For reasons such as these, Blair and Fesmire (1987) argue against special treatment for nonprofit hospital mergers. They worry that competitive pressures are the chief spur to productive efficiency, which would suffer if nonprofit firms are allowed to merge. Further, they argue that any cost efficiencies associated with merger will be dissipated when the merged firm loses the incentives to control costs. For two reasons, I find their case plausible but overstated. First, despite the theoretical arguments above and a plethora of attempts, there is little empirical evidence persuasively documenting that such inefficiencies are important. Second, I will argue that nonprofits can offer important social benefits when protected from competition, and these benefits weigh against productive inefficiencies.

Can the structure of board control ensure against abuses? For-profit boards are selected from among the largest stockholders, who have a clear incentive to utilize monopoly power to the detriment of consumers. The incentives of nonprofit boards are less clear cut. As a general rule, board members are selected according to procedures set out in a corporate charter filed under the rules of the state in which the nonprofit is incorporated. Hansmann (1980) categorizes nonprofits according to two polar selection mechanisms. "Mutual" nonprofits are those in which the power to select the board of directors inheres in the patrons (donors and customers) of the organization. Common Cause, Consumers Union, the National Audubon Society, and many country clubs are clear examples of mutual nonprofits. "Entrepreneurial" nonprofits are those in which the board is either self-perpetuating or selected by an outside agent who is not a patron. Most hospitals, nursing homes, and art museums are organized as entrepreneurial nonprofits, as are the National Geographic Society and the March of Dimes. Private universities are typically a mixture of these polar types, with some board members elected by alumni and some self-perpetuating.

The structure of board control can provide some protection against abuse. Although some patrons could collude against the interests of other patrons, the selection of board members from the patron class by mutual nonprofits would eliminate the much clearer collusion incentives found elsewhere. Thus, if a mutual nonprofit sought approval for a merger, the claim that they would use their postmerger costs to reduce consumer prices is more credible than the claim that they would extract monopoly rents. One should be more suspicious of the activities of entrepreneurial nonprofits, but even here, the legal structure of the board could provide some assurances against pernicious intent. For example, although self-perpetuating, the corporate charter could require that a large share of board members be selected from relevant patron groups. Weaker protection would be provided by an analysis of the current makeup of the board — weaker because without structural requirements, there is no assurance of continued patron control. Finally, other details of committee structure, board power, and board/management relations might prove relevant. For example, the nominations committee controls the makeup of self-perpetuating boards. If patron control of the nominations committee is structurally ensured, appropriate functioning of the board as a whole can be presumed.

Board structures play many roles, and one should not expect many entrepreneurial nonprofits to reorganize as mutuals in order to strengthen patron control and minimize risks of successful antitrust prosecution. Board members are often selected for the prestige, political connections, or likely donations they bring to the position, and boards are reluctant to incorporate many patron groups (Middleton, 1987). Finally, although boards are nominally in control, real power often resides more generally with the manager or staff. In her survey of the literature, Middleton (1987) concluded: "Most of the data indicate that boards do not formulate policy but rather ratify policy that is presented to them by staff. . . . For many important decisions, the board is the final authority. Yet it must depend upon the executive for most of its information" (p. 152).

Board-structure defenses, based on the current composition of entrepreneurial boards, were raised in both hospital cases, with conflicting outcomes. Board functioning and board-staff relations appear to be legitimate subjects for judicial inquiry. Prosecutorial claims that the staff dominated the board were rejected by the judge in *Carilion*. In *Rockford Memorial,* the judge was not persuaded that the board's fiduciary duty to the community was sufficient to ensure against abuse, given the history of behavior by this particular board.

The fiduciary-duty defense might be more viable if breach-of-duty laws were given more teeth. Hansmann (1981) noted that donors and beneficiaries generally lack standing to sue nonprofit trustees for breach of fiduciary duties, and state authorities have rarely exercised their right to bring such suits. Enhanced enforcement against breach-of-duty violations may constitute an alternative to antitrust for improving the functioning of nonprofits.

What is the overall impact of the nondistribution constraint on antitrust policy? There is a frequent presumption in antitrust law that errors of omission (failure to prosecute the guilty) are far more serious than errors of commission (successful prosecution of the innocent), justifying the "per se violation" standard. I will argue that errors of commission against nonprofits are far more serious, justifying a "rule of reason" approach. Nonprofit organizations should possess a rebuttable presumption of lack of intent by virtue of the nondistribution constraint. This defense would be strengthened if the board were structurally constituted to ensure appropriate membership and control and could be countered by specific demonstrations of past self-dealing, excess compensation, or cooperative behavior by the defendants that was detrimental to social welfare.

The Outputs of Nonprofit Organizations

Is imperfect competition necessary for socially beneficial outputs? One hopes that nonprofit organizations provide goods and services with unique social benefits. Three such benefits assume particular importance. First, nonprofits may redistribute goods and services to the poor, offering reduced cost or charity provision. Second, nonprofits may produce public goods that are underprovided by for-profits and governments (Weisbrod, 1980). Public goods are those consumed in a nonrival fashion (that is, when one individual consumes the good, this does not restrict others from also consuming the good). Third, nonprofits may market trustworthiness (Hansmann, 1980). Profit-maximizing firms have incentives to profit from their informational advantages over their patrons, and such mechanisms as warranties, quality certification, reputation, and public regulation are inherently limited in their ability to control such behavior (Weisbrod and Schlesinger, 1986).

Nonprofit organizations cannot serve any of these beneficial functions without both the ability and the motivation. In turn, nonprofits lack the ability to provide unique social benefits if they lack a revenue "cushion" (White, 1979; Steinberg, 1987, 1988), and imperfect competition is an important source of such cushions. To see this point, imagine first that a nonprofit organization receives no donations or tax or regulatory subsidies and faces competition from for-profit firms with no barriers to entry or exit. Further, assume that consumers have no preferences for sector per se, in that they are not willing to pay more to buy a service from a nonprofit than from a for-profit. Then, any nonprofit firm that attempts to provide unique social benefits will have higher costs than its competitors who do not, and these costs will not be recoverable from sales revenue (if they were recoverable, they would already have been provided by for-profits). A few "for-profits-in-disguise", masquerading as nonprofits degrade the consumer's ability to reward trustworthy behavior by paying a higher price for nonprofit output. Thus, any nonprofit that tries to provide unique social benefits will not be able to break even and will be forced out of business.

Revenue cushions can be provided in three ways: through donations, through special tax and regulatory advantages, and through imperfect competition. The first two are quite limited (Rose-Ackerman, 1982; Steinberg, 1990a). Thus, nonprofits must receive some protection from competition if they are to have any hope of fulfilling their promise. Imperfect competition is necessary, but not sufficient, for revenue cushions may be devoted to productive and allocative inefficiencies instead of to correcting market failures (Steinberg, 1988; Eckel and Steinberg, 1991; Tuckman and Chang, ch. 13). Whether a nonprofit chooses to devote its cushion to "good" or "bad" deviations from profit maximization depends upon the motives of managers and boards, which in turn depend upon structural considerations detailed above.

Few studies are directly on point, but one (Shortell and others, 1987) provides a bit of suggestive evidence about the impact of competition on unique social benefits. An econometric analysis of over 1,100 hospitals finds that competition significantly deters the proportion of services for which charity care is provided. Further, hospitals that offer a high percentage of services involving high market shares also provide significantly more services involving charity care.

In sum, imperfect competition is a necessary condition for the unique social benefits possible from nonprofit organizations. The implications for antitrust policy are far from clear, however. We know little about the determinants of entry by nonprofit firms, and natural entry may be so limited that no special treatment is necessary under antitrust laws to ensure the persistence of imperfect competition.

What about redistribution through cross-subsidization and price discrimination? Price discrimination occurs when different customers (or classes of customers) pay different prices for the same service in a fashion unrelated to the differential costs of providing that service. Examples include American Association of Retired Persons (AARP) discounts or sliding-scale fee schedules for social services. Cross-subsidization occurs within multiproduct firms, when profits from the sale of one product are used to subsidize the price of a loss-making product, a practice common in the hospital and education industries. Neither practice survives perfect competition. A firm that wished to charge prices above costs (for either some customers or some product lines) would find itself undersold by a competitor with a smaller markup, until all firms were forced to charge identical prices that just cover opportunity costs.

Cross-subsidization pervades the nonprofit sector. James (1983) provides many examples, including university education (where revenues from the undergraduate program subsidize graduate education and research), hospitals (who may use profits from appendectomies to finance research and to maintain expensive, prestigious, and underutilized facilities such as those for open heart surgery), and art museums (who use profits from gift shops and special exhibitions to pursue activities "of more artistic value").

Cross-subsidization and price discrimination are suspect under antitrust laws because they may transfer the potential gains to trading from consumers to producers. For example, a for-profit monopoly that is prohibited from price discrimination charges a price that is just equal to the willingness to pay of the last (marginal) consumer making a purchase. All inframarginal consumers obtain surplus, as their willingness to pay exceeds the required price. In contrast, a monopoly that practices perfect price discrimination would charge each consumer a price infinitesimally below willingness to pay, capturing the entirety of potential consumer surplus as its profits.

Thus, there is a clear presumption that price discrimination by for-profit firms is motivated solely by profit considerations. Whether such a presumption should extend to nonprofit organizations is unclear, but the evidence weighs strongly in favor of alternative motivations. If Harvard were conducting its tuition and financial aid programs to maximize profits, it would be far less selective in its admissions decisions. No student would be admitted with financial aid as long as there were some applicant (regardless of academic qualifications) willing to pay full tuition. Tuition (net of aid) would differ across students so that every student wishing to attend after hearing his or her aid decision would be admitted, regardless of academic qualifications. It is quite impossible to rationalize free care provided to the very poor under a sliding-scale system if profit is the only motive for price discrimination.

If the goal of universities is not to maximize tuition revenues, what is it? The most favorable interpretation, argued by some university officials, is that the goal is to improve access to quality education. Areeda notes that "colleges could argue that by saving money on some students, they can aid others and thereby expand access to college—to the public's benefit" (Putka, 1989b, p. A6). Without collusion, bidding wars in the form of merit scholarships would impede the offering of need-based aid. Fiske (1989) notes that "critics . . . say the practice [of offering merit scholarships] is the academic equivalent of a gasoline war—one that diverts scarce resources from those who need them to attend colleges to others whose only problem is which institution to attend" (p. A11).

The argument seems sensible but exaggerated. If universities were prohibited from colluding to ensure that aid is need based, individual schools would have incentives to make inappropriately large awards for the most "desirable" students, and this would drain some resources from financial aid for the most needy. However, the goals of ensuring access to the poor and admitting a diverse student body for cross-fertilization purposes are quite ingrained at the schools accused of collusion and would not be wholly abandoned. A minimum level of need-based aid would likely be maintained at all costs, and resources to support merit-based aid would largely come from other programs.

A different and more troubling rationale has been offered by some university officials. Arnold Weber caricatured this paternalistic argument: "[Many colleges think that] we know what's best for you because we aspire to something called excellence in higher education. We don't want to cloud the student's mind by putting him in a position where he'd have to make trade-offs between prices and quality" (Putka, 1989b, p. A6). Defenders of the practice are less bald-faced but seem to quite agree. Sheldon Steinbach, general counsel for the American Council on Education, argued: "A few hundred dollars should not be a swaying factor in deciding which institution offers the best fit" (Fiske, 1989, p. A11). Whether money should or should not sway students, it hardly advances the educational mission to take the mature responsibility for choices away from students.

Harris (1979) notes the potential for using cross-subsidization to improve economic efficiency. He shows (p. 225) that this pricing practice tends to compensate for significant distortions and inequities in existing health insurance coverage. As long as there is shallow insurance coverage for catastrophic illness, or excessive coverage for routine hospital care, or inadequate insurance for the working poor, or regressive financing of insurance premiums, the hospital's practice of cross subsidization can perform a prominent corrective pricing function" (citations omitted).

Most other analysts have focused on the equity issues. Clark (1980, pp. 1439, 1468) was most emphatically opposed to price discrimination by hospitals:

> Those who control the nonprofit hospital exploit the vulnerability of consumers as potential taxpayers. They charge for hospital services at rates that allow some funds to be directed toward research,

teaching, favored patients, and favored departments of the hospital; they do not advertise or fully disclose this practice; and they do not give consumers any choice in the matter. . . . The point is simply that the controlling group constitutes an undemocratic ruling class with respect to the hospital's minigovernmental functions. . . . [And] in acting as minigovernments, they employ an unjust method of taxation. . . . If it should happen that the latter (taxpayers) are taxed according to a plausible ideal of tax policy, the result would be fortuitous. It is far more likely that the nonprofit's method of taxation will violate principles of horizontal and vertical equity.

Colleges are no less vociferous about defending price discrimination in financial aid on equity grounds, noting that "the poor, as well as the rich ought to be free to choose a college on the basis of which one best suits their academic, not economic needs" (Fiske, 1989, p. A11). It is difficult to resolve the competing claims. Turning first to the idea that these pricing practices are deceptive or unfair to consumers, James (1983) notes that nonprofits should hold themselves to a higher standard of accountability because they represent themselves as uniquely trustworthy. On the other hand, she points out practical difficulties with disclosure and also argues (p. 358) that "it is not at all clear that students would change colleges or patients hospitals upon learning that the colleges or hospitals were earning a profit from the services they provided." Nor is it clear to which patrons the nonprofits should be held accountable: to donors and overcharged customers or to beneficiaries of charitable services. Competition ensures accountability to the former at the expense of the latter.

Equity is further complicated by third-party payments. Patients in hospitals typically bear (directly) only a small share of their costs. If insured, should they complain that their insurers were overcharged? If uninsured, they are more likely to be the beneficiaries than the victims of price discrimination and cross-subsidization. Do the third parties have a valid complaint against these pricing patterns? Perhaps not, for pricing practices tend to cancel out at the aggregate level of insurers, who may be victimized by cross-subsidization patterns when reimbursing one policyholder but benefit from being undercharged on other policyholders.

Swords (1989) suggests that tuition rates are typically set below the cost of education (although James, 1983, reports some contrary evidence) and presents a hypothetical case study (clearly modeled on the Justice Department case) in which, even after collusion on tuition and financial aid levels, students continue to pay less than the costs of their education. Do those potential students wishing to engage in bidding wars have a valid ethical objection that although they are undercharged, they would be undercharged more in a free market?

Clark's (1980) argument that cross-subsidies amount to unfair taxes imposed by undemocratic ruling classes does not persuade me in the least. First, unlike taxes, all transactions between patrons and nonprofits are voluntary. Even an absolute monopoly in the private sector must offer prices acceptable to consumers; taxing authorities face no such constraint as citizens can be (and sometimes are) forced to "purchase" more national defense than they would like. Second, redistribution should not be entirely centralized. Our pluralist system applauds voluntary redistribution mechanisms; indeed, that is one of the principal reasons why charities have been granted favorable tax and regulatory treatment, as have donations themselves. Volumes have been written about the limitations of redistribution through the state, and it is hard to characterize existing state redistribution as consistent with "principles of horizontal and vertical equity." Third, much of the redistribution is consistent with state directives. Barrett (1989) notes that "the schools have contended that sharing financial information is proper because federal statutes establish a basic formula for determining applicants' financial need for scholarships. The schools have said they discuss why, using the same formula, they frequently come up with different assessments of what a family can afford" (p. B1).

The Structure of Funding

Although many nonprofits are essentially commercial, relying principally on revenues from sales, others receive distinct sources of revenue—donations, grants, and dues. In addition, commercial nonprofits may receive revenues from activities consistent with their exempt purpose (for example, health care receipts for nonprofit hospitals) or from unrelated business income (for example, receipts from a gift shop). These funding sources present distinct considerations for antitrust policy. Competition between commercial for-profit enterprises leads to dissipation of profits in favor of consumer surpluses. In contrast, in a purely donative market, competition tends to obliterate consumer and donor surpluses, as each new charity makes it more difficult for preexisting charities to obtain funds, until, in the limit, the net returns from fundraising are zero (Rose-Ackerman, 1982). Unfettered competition is no longer in anybody's interest, and antitrust law should recognize the special character of donative nonprofits.

Feigenbaum (1987) provided some evidence on the effect of competition on one kind of donative nonprofit—the medical research charity. She found that concentration significantly reduced the share of solicitation costs in gross receipts, supporting the analysis above. However, she also found that charities in concentrated markets spent more on administration and less on research itself (both measured as shares of gross receipts). This result can be interpreted in one of two ways. It can illustrate that although concentration allows a charity to avoid competitive fundraising, it also allows the charity to avoid making exempt-purpose expenditures, diverting resources instead to managerial perks. Alternatively, administration expenditures can be devoted to ensuring that research expenditures are of particularly high quality. For example, administrative expense can largely represent payments to outside reviewers of grant proposals. In such a case, donor wishes and the exempt purpose may both be served by concentration despite the lower share devoted to research. Regardless, no one has examined whether similar findings apply to other industries, although one would expect that concentration would always reduce fundraising share. Whether it would also reduce the service share or increase the administrative share would depend upon the structures of information and control.

Hansmann (1989) suggests that there may be a policy distinction worth drawing between unrelated and related activities of nonprofits: "Suppose, for example, that each of the Ivy League colleges owned a macaroni factory. And suppose that the presidents of these colleges got together to fix the price of macaroni in order to increase the amount of unrelated business income each college receives. We should have no difficulty deciding that this is an antitrust violation. . . . The harder question is whether a conspiracy among nonprofit organizations to eliminate competition concerning their *principal* activities should be treated more leniently than a similar conspiracy among for-profit firms" (p. 12).

The point is worth further analysis in future research. Differential treatment under the antitrust laws will presumably encourage the migration of activities to the nonprofit sector on inappropriate grounds, impairing economic efficiency. However, if one decides that it is important to protect nonprofit organizations from competition in order to allow them to cross-subsidize one of their exempt purposes, then it is an empirical question whether the better approach is to protect exempt-purpose sales or unrelated business income from competition.

Summary and Conclusions

It seems clear that nonprofit organizations will have to become more cognizant of antitrust law. As cases are increasingly brought against hospitals, colleges and universities, united fundraising organizations, amateur athletics groups, day-care facilities, nursing homes, and research charities, nonprofit managers will need to structure their cooperative activities more carefully. More important, as antitrust law is extended to nonprofit organizations by analogy rather than careful analysis, it becomes more important for legislatures to consider reforms. Nonprofits should not be exempt from antitrust, but the standards of proof, allowable defenses, and regulatory remedies probably ought to be distinct from the treatment accorded to for-profit firms.

The nondistribution constraint provides one rationale for treating nonprofit firms distinctly. However, the distribution of financial surpluses does not constitute the only incentive for harmful collusion. In determining the appropriate burden of proof, the structure of board control becomes critical. One should give greater presumption that the collusive activities of mutual nonprofits (those with patron-elected boards) are in the public interest, lesser presumption to entrepreneurial nonprofits (those with appointed and self-perpetuating boards).

In order for nonprofits to behave in a distinctive fashion, they must be cushioned from competitive forces to act as profit maximizers. Cushions allow both good and bad deviations from perfectly competitive behavior by for-profit firms. Bad deviations include productive and allocative inefficiencies, as managers have little incentive to hold down costs and need not ensure that product mixes accord with the desires of consumers. Good deviations include provision of public goods and trustworthiness and (arguably) decentralized income redistribution. The structures of board control, managerial contract form, and tax and regulatory advantages determine the relative proportion of good to bad deviations. Nonprofit organizations that are structured to ensure a predominance of good deviations should receive more favorable treatment under antitrust law.

Cross-subsidization and price discrimination are the mechanisms whereby nonprofits redistribute income. Both mechanisms require immunization from competition. Although some object that such redistribution constitutes fraud or is otherwise unfair or antidemocratic, I argue against these conclusions, particularly in light of the prevalence of third-party payers. However, in light of wrong-way redistribution through price discrimination by for-profit firms, the actual patterns of redistribution supported by nonprofit firms deserve far more study.

Donative nonprofits are distinct from commercial nonprofits. Competition among commercial organizations has a tendency to dissipate profits and promote consumer surpluses; in contrast, competition among donative organizations tends to

dissipate consumer and donor surpluses. Thus, donative organizations (especially united fundraising organizations) should
receive limited exemption from antitrust law.

Regulatory authorities are ready to apply antitrust statutes to nonprofit organizations. It is time for policy analysis
to develop appropriate models that account for the distinct aspects
of the nonprofit sector. In this survey, I have made a start, but
many research paths remain open and inviting.

Cases Cited

Adventist Health Systems/West, FTC Dkt. 9234 (issued Nov. 7,
1989).
Associated In-Group Donors v. United Way, Inc., No. C. 23112 (Cal.
Super. Ct. Los Angeles County, filed March 28, 1978).
FTC v. University Health, Inc., 1991-1 Trade Cas. 69, 444 (S.D.
Ga.), reversed in part in *FTC v. University Health, Inc.,* 1991-
1 Trade Cas. 69, 424 (11th Cir. 1991).
Hospital Corporation of America v. FTC, 807 F. 2d 1381, 1386 (7th
Cir. 1986).
Kingsepp v. Wesleyan, et al., Civil Action No. 89-6121 (S.D. N.Y.
1991).
National Society of Professional Engineers v. U.S., 435 U.S. 679
(1978).
Ukiah Valley Medical Center v. FTC, 911 F. 2d 261 (9th Cir. 1990).
U.S. v. Brown, et al., Civil Action No. 91-3274 (E.D. Pa. 1991).
*U.S. v. Carilion Health System and Community Hospital of Roanoke
Valley,* 707 F. Supp. 840 (W.D. Va. 1989).
*U.S. v. Rockford Memorial Corporation and the SwedishAmerican Cor-
poration,* 1989-1 Trade Cases Para. 68,462 (N.D. Ill.).

References

"Antitrust and Nonprofit Entities." *Harvard Law Review,* 1981,
94, 802–820.
Barrett, P. M. "U.S. Investigates Prestigious Universities, Colleges for Possible Antitrust Violations." *Wall Street Journal,*
Aug. 9, 1989, p. B1.

Bartlett, R. "United Charities and the Sherman Act." *Yale Law Journal*, 1982, *91*, 1593–1613.

Blair, R. D., and Fesmire, J. M. "Antitrust Treatment of Nonprofit and For-Profit Hospital Mergers." In R. Scheffler and D. Rossiter (eds.), *Advances in Health Economics and Health Services Research*, Vol. 7. Greenwich, Conn.: JAI Press, 1987.

Blair, R. D., and Kaserman, D. L. *Antitrust Economics*. Homewood, Ill.: Irwin, 1985.

Clark, R. "Does the Nonprofit Form Fit the Hospital Industry?" *Harvard Law Review*, 1980, *93*, 1416–1489.

Eckel, C., and Steinberg, R. "Competition, Performance, and Public Policy Towards Nonprofits." Paper presented at the Mandel Center Conference on Nonprofit Organizations in a Market Economy, Cleveland, Ohio, Nov. 1991.

Feigenbaum, S. "Competition and Performance in the Nonprofit Sector: The Case of US Medical Research Charities." *Journal of Industrial Economics*, Mar. 1987, *35*, 241–253.

Fiske, E. B. "Colleges and Costs: Price-Fixing Inquiry Turns Spotlight on the Ethical Issues in Financial Aid." *New York Times*, Aug. 11, 1989, p. A11.

Hansmann, H. "The Role of Nonprofit Enterprise." *Yale Law Journal*, 1980, *89*, 835–901.

Hansmann, H. "Reforming Nonprofit Corporation Law." *University of Pennsylvania Law Review*, 1981, *129*, 500–623.

Hansmann, H. "'Trouble Spots' in the Law Affecting Nonprofit Organizations." In *Research Agenda: Legal Issues Affecting Nonprofit Corporations*. New York: Program on Philanthropy and the Law, New York University School of Law, 1989.

Harris, J. E. "Pricing Rules for Hospitals." *Bell Journal of Economics*, 1979, *10*, 224–243.

Hersch, P. L. "Competition and the Performance of Hospital Markets." *Review of Industrial Organization*, 1984, *1*, 324–340.

Hite, C. "Illinois Judge Blocks Merger." *Roanoke Times and World News*, Feb. 28, 1989, p. A1.

"Hospital Case: In Rockford, a Different Outcome." *Roanoke Times and World News*, Mar. 5, 1989, p. A8.

James, E. "How Nonprofits Grow: A Model." *Journal of Policy Analysis and Management*, 1983, *2*, 350–366.

Johnston, D. "Top Colleges' Scholarships Under Scrutiny." *New York Times,* Aug. 10, 1989, p. B1.

"Merged Hospitals Would Benefit Area." *Roanoke Times and World News,* May 28, 1988, p. A8.

Middleton, M. "Nonprofit Boards of Directors: Beyond the Governance Function." In W. W. Powell (ed.), *The Nonprofit Sector: A Research Handbook.* New Haven, Conn.: Yale University Press, 1987.

Putka, G. "Do Colleges Collude on Financial Aid? Elite Schools Compare Notes on Applicants." *Wall Street Journal,* May 2, 1989a, p. B1.

Putka, G. "Educated Moves: Elite Private Colleges Routinely Share Plans for Raising Tuition." *Wall Street Journal,* Sept. 5, 1989b, pp. A1, A6.

Rose-Ackerman, S. "Charitable Giving and Excessive Fundraising." *Quarterly Journal of Economics,* 1982, *97,* 193–212.

Shortell, S. M., and others. "Diversification of Health Care Services: The Effects of Ownership, Environment, and Strategy." In R. Scheffler and L. Rossiter (eds.), *Advances in Health Economics and Health Services Research,* Vol. 7. Greenwich, Conn.: JAI Press, 1987.

Steinberg, R. "Nonprofit Organizations and the Market." In W. W. Powell (ed.), *The Nonprofit Sector: A Research Handbook.* New Haven, Conn.: Yale University Press, 1987.

Steinberg, R. "Regulating the Competition Between the Nonprofit and For-Profit Sectors." In U.S. House of Representatives, Small Business Committee, *Hearings on Nonprofit Competition.* Washington, D.C.: U.S. Government Printing Office, 1988.

Steinberg, R. "Antitrust and the Nonprofit Sector." Paper presented at the annual conference of the Association of Voluntary Action Scholars, London, England, July 1990a.

Steinberg, R. "Profits as Incentives Within Nonprofit Firms." *Nonprofit Management and Leadership,* 1990b, *1,* 137–152.

Sullivan, L. *Handbook of the Law of Antitrust,* St. Paul, Minn.: West Publishing, 1977.

Swords, P. "Other Legal Issues Affecting Nonprofit Organizations." In *Research Agenda: Legal Issues Affecting Nonprofit Corpo-*

rations. New York: Program on Philanthropy and the Law, New York University School of Law, 1989.

Weisbrod, B. "Private Goods, Collective Goods: The Role of the Nonprofit Sector." In K. Clarkson and D. Martin (eds.), *The Economics of Nonproprietary Organizations.* Greenwich, Conn.: JAI Press, 1980.

Weisbrod, B., and Schlesinger, M. "Public, Private, Nonprofit Ownership and the Response to Asymmetric Information: The Case of Nursing Homes." In S. Rose-Ackerman (ed.), *The Economics of Nonprofit Institutions: Studies in Structure and Policy.* New York: Oxford University Press, 1986.

White, W. D. "Regulating Competition in a Nonprofit Industry: The Problem of For-Profit Hospitals." *Inquiry,* 1979, *16,* 50–61.

Conclusion

Developing a
Research Agenda
for Nonprofit Management

Robert M. Hollister

This chapter reflects on the emerging themes discussed in Dennis R. Young's introduction. Next it highlights the special importance of two topics discussed in the essays: the boards of directors of nonprofits and program evaluation. A third section focuses on what is missing in this book and advocates priorities for future research. There is an urgent need for more study of nonprofits' advocacy roles, the functioning of smaller organizations, the leadership as well as the management of nonprofits, and the behavior of religious organizations. The final section looks at how future research will be done and by whom, arguing for more participatory and action research and for greater collaboration between academics and practitioners.

What Are the Emerging Issues
and Where Do They Lead?

Dennis R. Young's introduction predicts that the 1990s will be a period of more comprehensive and organized research about leadership and management of the independent sector. This book certainly supports his claim. Young identifies four emerging themes that are explored by the authors: the incomplete implementation of management and governance practices, variation in the types of nonprofits and the contexts in which they operate, strategies of inclusiveness, and the role of values. These broad categories chart out both terrain covered to date by researchers and that which is unexplored in any depth. In addition, the themes also define areas of choice and conflict. Therefore, the chapters should be read not only for their specific contents but also for how they may shape and direct the general themes that Young identifies. Yes, we have an opportunity to follow through vigorously on the growing body of research about the leadership and management of nonprofits. But there is an equally compelling need to make a transition to a new period for dealing with the leadership and management of nonprofits. This book contains work that is stuck in the dominant present paradigms and a few that point beyond them.

As his first theme Young states, "Nonprofit organizations do not seem to have taken the implementation of sophisticated management and governance practices completely to heart." His central point is prescriptive: nonprofits would do better to adopt modern management techniques. Contrary about his contention, the issue facing the sector is not so much the incomplete implementation of management and governance practices but rather our still limited notions about what constitutes effective management of nonprofits and what tools and approaches will in fact enhance their administration. Young's subsequent qualification is more persuasive, that "nonprofits must . . . develop their own management practices and must adapt these practices to widely diverse contexts." The problem here is that, by focusing on nonprofits' failure to use sophisticated management and governance practice, we are less likely to remedy our inadequate knowledge of what is and what could be good leadership and management of nonprofits. In each of the chapters — from Te'eni and Speltz's discussion of cultural institutions' limited use of information system technologies to Abhay's description of the tensions between the boards and staffs of mutual assistance associations — useful information is offered about why particular management issues exist. In order to address these problems effectively, we need to confront aggressively the obstacles to more effective practice *and* to be open to new approaches to leading and administering nonprofits that may not fit conventional concepts of good management.

Young's second theme is the wide variation among nonprofits. It is, of course, important to acknowledge the broad diversity that exists in the types of nonprofits and the contexts in which they operate and to support research that adds to our knowledge of the full range of types and contexts. But on this point a pair of challenges is not addressed by this book: Which types and contexts are of highest priority for adding to our knowledge base and for guiding more effective practice? And when will this evolving community of scholars and practitioners begin to organize its work and discourse in terms that distinguish more systematically among types and among contexts? It is not enough to celebrate the fact of variation, for we continue to lump together research about nonprofits that are vastly different in their sizes, missions, and environmental situations. This refusal to distinguish and to disaggregate severely restricts the development of knowledge about the sector and its component parts. These chapters cover very distinct kinds of nonprofits that are important in their own right but in many instances have very little to say to one another. The hospitals and universities discussed by Steinberg are in an entirely different realm than the voluntary development organizations studied by Hunt.

We must move beyond calling for more and better studies that cover the waterfront. The next period of research needs to be organized according to a much more clearly delineated set of subtopics that permit comparability and accumulation of knowledge. Ten years ago the challenge was to encourage more serious study of a broad range of topics, drawing upon the many different disciplinary traditions and their respective analytical tools. That task has been accomplished very well. Now it is time to move on to more focused inquiry that builds knowledge about, for example, small nonprofits, nonprofits involved in social change efforts, large service delivery nonprofits, and so forth.

Young notes that inclusiveness is a third theme common to several of the chapters. This feature is a real strength of the collection because so many different kinds of nonprofits are being pressured from within and without to achieve greater racial and ethnic diversity in their boards and staffs, to involve their clients and constituencies more substantially in their governance, and to work with other organizations in new forms of cooperation. Yet applauding inclusiveness as a general goal is only a first step. The difficult challenge that lies ahead for both researchers and practitioners is to make progress on the *several* distinct goals that march under the broad banner of "inclusiveness," and to ask and act on these questions: inclusiveness of whom? for what purposes? and how?

The role of values, underscored by Young as the final theme common to several of the chapters, is again a point of departure. The next stage requires that we ask: Which values and value conflicts are most important? How are nonprofits handling these dilemmas and why? And what new approaches hold promise?

In order to be intellectually productive and to contribute to more effective practice, the coming period of research about the leadership and management of nonprofits will need to be more disciplined about disaggregating and segmenting the field while not steering away from the quest for knowledge about the sector as a whole.

Within this collection of very useful chapters, two subjects merit special attention by readers with a broad set of interests and backgrounds: boards of directors and program evaluation.

Boards of Directors: A Key
Point of Leverage for Change

An especially satisfying feature of this book is that it includes significant attention to the role of boards of directors (see the chapters by Abhay, Harris, Ostrander, and Saidel). After years of being ignored and taken for granted, of being treated as add-ons rather than as integral features of nonprofit organizations, boards are really beginning to come into their own — as a subject for inquiry and as a focus for efforts to strengthen nonprofits. With the establishment of the National Center for Nonprofit Boards and many local sources of training and assistance, we are starting to invest in the effective functioning of this vital dimension of the sector. Furthermore, the expanding research about boards by Middleton Stone (1987), Herman and Van Til (1989), Carver (1990), and others is building a solid knowledge base to guide these support efforts.

A great deal more remains to be done because in the next several years the functioning of boards will be the most promising point of leverage for strengthening the sector. Although there has been an impressive and rapid increase in the volume of good written materials and of sources of training and assistance about board development and board-staff relations, fundamental problems remain. The pervasive weakness of many boards and dysfunctional board-staff relations are a major problem both for individual organizations and for the sector as a whole. At a time when U.S. electoral participation is at a low ebb and citizen involvement in the voluntary sector is robustly alive, nonprofit boards are especially important because they can be a key vehicle for strengthening and channeling the popular will to participate and to assume community responsibility.

It remains a root problem that nonprofit managers are not sufficiently committed to supporting the board role. This aspect of the problem is much more central than the lack of adequate training materials. We are operating with an enlightened view of the role of boards, but we are still functioning within the perspective that the boards of directors of nonprofits are somehow a separate, detachable concern. Both practitioners and academics are guilty of this fallacy. Our overall conception of the structure and the functioning of nonprofits relegates the functioning of boards to a kind of secondary status. This tendency limits the effectiveness of individual organizations and undercuts the potential of boards of nonprofits in combination to be a vital part of our democratic infrastructure.

Looking ahead, these are priority questions: How do boards manage the imperative to increase their racial and gender diversity? How and under what conditions do they function as stewards of community values as well as monitors of their organizations' well-being? How and why do board roles and functions change over time? What intraboard and board-staff dynamics are associated with different stages of development and varying contexts?

Judith R. Saidel's analysis in Chapter Two of the role of nonprofit boards in managing the relationships between nonprofits and the governmental agencies that fund them is a strong contribution. She shows that at present the balance is "precariously tipped toward the power of government." She urges more work on "the conditions under which different board roles are more likely to be performed." Therefore, future research and action can learn from examples of nonprofit boards that function effectively as buffers between their organizations and government funders and regulators, and from situations where they do not. A related opportunity would be to design and assess interventions that seek to enhance the role of boards in mediating the nonprofit-government relationship.

Toward a Greater Commitment
to Program Evaluation

Nonprofit managers, foundation officials, and providers of technical assistance should read with special interest Chapter Five, by Martha E. Taylor and Russy D. Sumariwalla. By reaching beyond the tired plea for more and better evaluation, they lay out a promising agenda for renewed attention to program evaluation. They document key barriers to more extensive evaluation and to evaluation that yields outcome measures and measures of participant satisfaction rather than just counting the number of participants and the volume of services provided. Because the field of program evaluation is dominated by research methods that are hopelessly out of sync with the workaday realities of nonprofit managers, Taylor and Summariwalla are to be congratulated for calling for the development of evaluation approaches and tools that are practical in terms of their cost, availability of data, and staff capabilities. They advocate that "a new paradigm of program evaluation, separate from that of rigorous evaluation research models, needs to be developed for nonprofit organizations," an approach that is not "so prohibitively expensive and sophisticated that it is beyond reach." This is an area of particular opportunity for joint efforts between researchers and practitioners.

Previewing New Issues

Another good way to use this book is as a preview of coming attractions. Some of the essays explore issues that are only dimly visible to most managers and academics today but that may become pressing concerns in the future. Richard Steinberg, for example, in Chapter Fourteen, reviews the application of antitrust laws to hospital mergers and universities' granting of financial aid, asking whether nonprofits should be treated differently under these statutes. He speculates that antitrust laws may be applied increasingly to day-care services, nursing homes, and research charities. His forward-looking legal and economic analysis provides a thoughtful rationale for differential treatment of nonprofits and lays a foundation for amending the antitrust statutes. Steinberg argues that nonprofits should receive different treatment than private firms under antitrust laws. He recommends that policy analysis "develop appropriate models which account for the distinct aspects of the nonprofit sector." A research opportunity suggested by his work is to observe whether antitrust statutes are applied increasingly to kinds of nonprofits beyond hospitals and universities, which have been the focus of such application to date. If this trend does occur, then a related need will be to measure the impacts of antitrust laws on additional types of nonprofits. Similarly attentive to problems that may become larger issues for the sector, Howard P. Tuckman and Cyril F. Chang examine in Chapter Thirteen why nonprofits seek to accumulate equity and the potential of "contract failure" posed by this phenomenon. Although the future significance of excessive equity accumulation is far from clear, the authors develop five criteria for determining whether such accumulation is excessive and offer suggestions on how to avoid it.

Upon completing Chapter Ten by Susan A. Ostrander, one wonders whether the principles of diversity and democratization that are central to her account of the Haymarket Peoples' Fund can be extended to other philanthropic groups and to other types of organizations. Her chapter suggests the importance of doing more work on the question of how recipients can be effectively involved in philanthropic decision making. One can easily dismiss the Haymarket Fund as too unusual in its objectives and its operating style to provide useful lessons for more mainstream foundations. This would be unfortunate, however, because the issues of diversity and democratization that are a special concern to Haymarket will continue to grow in importance for other organizations as well. The experience of any philanthropy seriously grappling with these issues is thus worth trying to capture.

Robert W. Hunt's analysis in Chapter Eleven of emerging approaches to promoting development abroad and at home notes the growing importance of regional voluntary agencies that work as mediators and facilitators among other development organizations. Because they are expanding so rapidly in their numbers and their influence, these intermediary or bridging organizations—in the development area and in several other fields as well—demand more attention from both nonprofit administrators and academics. How are the regional mediating organizations developing and changing, and why? What particular leadership and management dilemmas are they facing? How are these needs being addressed and what alternative approaches might be productive?

Priorities for Future Research

A number of issues notable for their relative absence in this book are also receiving insufficient attention in the field as a whole. Four topics that are largely ignored here are prime candidates for increased research. First, the elements and performance of leadership as distinct from management (or the leadership dimensions of management) demand more study. Second, the advocacy roles of nonprofits remain a central purpose of the sector

and continue to be neglected by researchers. Third, although
we acknowledge the importance of variation among nonprofits,
we persist in sliding by the critical variable of size—failing to
organize emerging knowledge in relation to the different sizes
of nonprofits. And fourth, religious organizations, which com-
prise a major portion of the sector but receive a miniscule amount
of study, require a dramatic increase in research.

Although conferences, projects, and books are typically
framed in terms of both "leadership and management," the
leadership side of the phrase tends to get short shrift, to be the
stepsister of the pair. Although it has been for the most part
a positive movement, the professionalization of the management
of nonprofits has been accompanied by a relative neglect of the
dynamics of leadership. There is a tendency, evident in this
volume and in the field as a whole, to speak glibly of "leadership and management" but not to distinguish clearly the separate
as well as intertwined elements of both. Cynthia S. McCauley
and Martha W. Hughes explore in Chapter Eight the leadership challenges facing human service administrators in a fashion
that attends well to true leadership functions. As many have
observed, good management includes effective leadership, yet
this volume speaks mostly in the vocabulary of management.
Issues of leadership thus demand additional study: leadership
to mobilize and sustain volunteers, to communicate effectively
with organizations' clienteles and constituencies, and to realize
the advocacy missions of many nonprofits.

Because we look to the nonprofit sector as a source of
change, as an instigator or incubator of new approaches to intractable social ills, there is an urgent need for more research
about the advocacy roles of nonprofits and how these functions
are led and managed. This is a particularly troubling gap at
a time when the advocacy functions of nonprofits are under political attack. Furthermore, painful social and economic problems demand the vigorous involvement in public policymaking
by nonprofits, which are uniquely able to give voice to the needs
of the disenfranchised. The chapters in this book include very
little attention to nonprofits' social change missions, such as lobbying for and against abortion, promoting protection of natural

resources, and building support for public policies to combat homelessness. The predominant focus on management tends to deflect attention away from the advocacy mission of nonprofits. Important questions include: How do advocacy roles change over time and why? What are boards' roles in planning and carrying out advocacy goals? What are the roles of associations and coalitions as vehicles for advocacy? What are the tensions between advocacy and the delivery of services, especially when the latter role involves funding relationships with the targets of advocacy for change?

Although smaller nonprofits have received insufficient attention in research about the sector, they are somewhat better represented in this book. The accounts analyze a social-change-oriented foundation (Ostrander), indigenous development groups (Hunt), Southeast Asian mutual assistance associations (Abhay), and cultural institutions (Te'eni and Speltz), all of modest size. Research about smaller nonprofits must increase greatly until it becomes proportional to their cumulative scale and impacts.

This book serves as a reminder about the importance of distinguishing among different types of nonprofits, particularly in terms of their various sizes. The smallest nonprofits often have more in common with small businesses than they do with large nonprofit universities or hospitals. In this book the objects of study range from tiny in terms of numbers of people involved and budget to quite large, from self-help groups that are entirely volunteer or barely staffed to major hospitals with vast budgets and complex organizational structures.

Thomas H. Jeavons's thoughtful discussion in Chapter Three of management in a religious context concludes with a forceful reminder of how little research has been done on religious organizations, although they make up a large portion of the voluntary sector. This area of work, which needs to become a much higher priority for the doers and supporters of research, would be helped along by the development of a clearer statement of the actual questions that demand attention. There is encouraging progress on this front in the work of Wuthnow and Hodgkinson (1990) and others, but given the scale and importance of the challenge we are still at a very early stage. Because it both criticizes current practice and offers useful suggestions for reforming it, one hopes that Jeavons's chapter will help to stimulate more research on a woefully neglected part of the sector. He asks: "Does appropriate management practice vary according to the type of beliefs or values a group wishes to promote?" "Are different types of religious groups, or different denominations, inclined to put together organizations in different ways?" "How have religious organizations planned?" "What kinds of planning are really helpful in the context of religious management?"

The Need for More Participatory and Action Research

From the perspective of managers, this book shows the benefits of independent analysis but also the limitations of the role of outside observer. Academics can ignore topics that speak to managers' practical needs, but left to their own devices, managers are preoccupied with immediate pressures and demands (for example, how to raise more funds, how to shore up sagging staff morale, or how to respond to escalating demands for services). They thus tend to ignore or argue against questions that may challenge the assumptions and policies of current organizational leaders and managers (for example, whether dependence on government service contracts undercuts an organization's advocacy role, whether a religious organization's personnel policies conflict with the religious ideals that drive its mission, or whether present concepts of an organization's purposes hamper its prospects for serving an increasingly diverse community population).

In order to maximize their contributions to knowledge about the field and to provide practical guidance to the staff and boards of nonprofits, researchers should sustain their present range of techniques but also make increasing use of direct observation and of action research approaches. There are also attractive unrealized opportunities for collaboration between researchers and practitioners, as is discussed in the following section. Many of the chapters in this book are of limited use to practitioners because they do not provide specific practical recommendations for improving organizational leadership and management. One way for the authors and their colleagues to really assist practitioners is to help design and study new tools and techniques for strengthening nonprofit administration.

Although the authors do not always fully describe their research methods, their methods display considerable diversity. They include mail surveys, personal interviews, examination of documents, literature review, laboratory experimentation, analysis of tax returns, some direct observation, and case studies, although they tend not to involve much participant observation or extensive direct observation. With but one or two exceptions, they are independent, arms-length studies rather than interventions to assist nonprofits that also include a research component.

The potential of less distant styles of research is demonstrated in a few of the foregoing chapters. Each illustrates an approach to learning about organizations and their management that edges beyond more prevalent social science research models. Susan A. Ostrander's study of the Haymarket Foundation is based on extensive observation, on an approach of virtually living with the organization. This method yields a very different account than she would have constructed if she had written a case study based on multiple interviews and an examination of selected documents. In another example, Krisna Abhay's study of mutual assistance associations is informed not only by a survey of such groups but also by working with these organizations, presumably providing forms of technical assistance. And Margaret Harris's chapter on Total Activity Analysis reflects a depth of acquaintance with the role of boards and the relationships between boards and staffs that comes from having worked with and for many organizations.

Building New Bridges
Between Research and Practice

The preceding chapters highlight basic dilemmas about the connections between research and practice—divergent views about the purposes and uses of research, about who does it and how it is done, and about approaches to better connecting these two worlds. The realms of research and of practice have much to gain from strengthening relationships between the two. Strategies for enhancing these working ties include heightening collaboration on all aspects of research activity, enabling researchers and practitioners to experience each other's realities more directly, and reinforcing the mixed constituency for research. We are at a point of real opportunity in this regard precisely because a truly mixed base of support for research in this field is beginning to grow.

Researchers and practitioners are guided by different interests and espouse divergent goals for research about the leadership and management of nonprofits. Practitioners typically complain that the research is irrelevant to their needs and academics complain that practitioners fail to use findings that could in fact enhance their work and that the questions practitioners advocate as research priorities are mundane and uninteresting. The mutual railing has become a kind of tired ritual that leads nowhere; they go through the motions, but the ritualistic steps are more an end in themselves than a route to addressing the problem. To deal with this situation, we need to do two things: first, to reframe the issues about the research-practice connection and second, to take specific steps to strengthen the exchange. There are a few clear-cut activities that would make a real difference, that would make research more useful to practice and would enhance the quality of research by incorporating the interests and insights of practitioners. The issue here is not only the *relevance* of the research but more fundamentally its *quality*. Sustained dialogue and true collaboration will generate not only more studies that can be more readily applied but also higher-quality research.

A limiting feature of this book is that for the most part the work remains trapped in the conventional separation of the production and the consumption of research. In this as in other fields, discussion of the research-practice linkage focuses mostly on the need to translate research more effectively to nonscholarly audiences, to try new ways to overcome the barriers to use by practitioners (the form and specificity of publications, practitioners' capabilities, and so forth). Mark Rosenman argued at the 1991 Research Forum that the research production/consumption distinction is a false and unstrategic dichotomy. Susan A. Ostrander elaborates this point, arguing in Chapter Ten that the dominant research models "assume that 'application' of research findings and implementation of recommendations will automatically enable practitioners to more effectively accomplish already established ends." She advocates an alternative approach of research as an "ongoing dialogue" based on the "premise that practitioners already have a substantial base of knowledge that guides their practice." Although much good research will continue on terms that isolate its production and its consumption, there is great potential in experimenting with approaches that merge the two. This can mean engaging the skills and interests of both academics and practitioners in all aspects of research activity: framing questions and determining study priorities, designing methodologies, gathering and analyzing data, reporting and using results, and building theory.

The research-practice nexus hinges in part on the identity of the researchers. Not surprisingly, most of the authors in this book are academics, yet it is a strength of our emerging field that the list of authors includes some practitioners and some scholar-practitioners. Their writing integrates insights from practice with concepts from the research literature. Krisna Abhay is a leadership and management consultant to the Indochina Resource Action Center and a self-employed entrepreneur. Thomas H. Jeavons is associate director of program for the Association of American Colleges, and his chapter draws upon his previous executive experience in nonprofit service organizations. Nike F. Speltz is program associate at the New Hampshire Charitable Foundation and has been a consultant to nonprofit organizations. Martha E. Taylor is director of market research at United Way of America, and her previous work includes state government experience. Margaret A. Duronio and Bruce A. Loessin are both senior administrators of university development divisions and accomplished researchers. Their analysis of why some university fundraising efforts are more successful than others is informed by their extensive practical experience as well as their academic backgrounds.

The practitioners' role in the research enterprise is still relatively undeveloped. With the exception of studies that aim to examine practitioners' expressed needs and perceptions, the questions framed by the authors come primarily from academics' interests, not from practitioners' concerns. Furthermore, the implications for the actual management of nonprofits in some chapters have an overly speculative quality and are not informed fully by interaction with practitioners. On the positive side, these chapters do provide a potential basis for real exchange, dialogue, and collaboration. By offering recommendations on how to strengthen the management of nonprofits, they set the stage for more extensive give and take between researchers and practitioners. In the context of these issues, there are several promising avenues to bridging the research-practice gap.

1. Enable more practitioners to do research and encourage joint research efforts by researchers and practitioners. The nonprofit sector is blessed with a cadre of managers who have in abundance the intellectual resources that equip them to contribute more robustly to our collective research endeavor. As Pablo Eisenberg has argued, it is naive to expect large numbers of practitioners to become productive researchers, but it is also dead wrong to suggest that only the rare practitioner has a potential research contribution to make. They need the time, encouragement, and resources to enable them to do research, to collaborate with scholars, and also to reflect on their practice. Encouraging reflective practice can contribute effectively to building theory in professional fields (Schön, 1983). Promising recent developments in this regard include the MacArthur Foundation's commissioning of research by community development organizations in Chicago and the establishment of the Nonprofit Research Fund administered by the Aspen Institute, which includes practitioners as well as scholars on its selection panel and whose research agenda and selection criteria balance basic and applied objectives for research.

2. Provide more opportunities for researchers to take sabbaticals in the world of practice — not just to study practice but to do it, and to gain the insights and perspectives that can come from this experience.

3. Take a broader view of what constitutes research, elevating the importance of documenting approaches and experiences that seem promising. Where the functioning of non-

profits is changing rapidly, a first order for research is to clearly record what is happening and why. For example, the initial priority for research about burgeoning growth of nongovernmental organizations in countries around the world is to accurately record the phenomenon.

4. Involve practitioners as well as researchers in framing the questions to be studied. Bridging the research-practice divide requires that we devote more energy to an earlier stage in the research process — to involving practitioners in setting the agenda for research, in defining the questions that guide studies. How can this be done? Polling practitioners about their needs and concerns is an important step but is hardly sufficient. A more promising approach is to promote dialogue in relation to specific issues, including responding critically to research reports. The point here is that the conversation typically stops with the complaint. So the challenge is to make the practitioners' response the start of a real exchange, to ask practitioners, "Okay, what is missing? What additional questions should be asked? Where would you take this inquiry next?"

5. Organize task forces of academics and practitioners to synthesize and translate currently available research into guidance on how to handle selected issues. This idea has been advanced by Bradford Gray, director of the Program on Nonprofit Organizations at Yale University, drawing upon the analogous experience of the National Research Council.

As was suggested above, involving practitioners in responding to these chapters is an immediate opportunity for building real dialogue. For example, if asked what they would like Tuckman and Chang to do next in studying excess equity accumulation by nonprofits, practitioners would likely advocate developing action research that tries out the authors' criteria for determining what is "excessive" equity accumulation, and asking: How useful are these guides in practice? Do they need to be refined and if so, how? Many practitioners would argue that for a large portion of the sector, the converse of excess accumulation is of greater interest — that is, how to secure rather than to avoid equity accumulation. What approaches have nonprofits used in order to accumulate equity? What are barriers to this goal and how have they been successfully surmounted? How do they use surpluses?

To take a second example, McCauley and Hughes identify and rank the leadership challenges faced by human service
administrators and probe the competencies essential for successfully addressing these challenges. The competencies are broad
general qualities such as "resourcefulness" and "flexibility." Practitioners would respond, "Fine, we agree, but how does this help
us to manage better? Can't you define more precisely what these
general abilities mean in relation to specific issues? For instance,
what does it mean for us to be resourceful and flexible in a context of the kinds of challenges that you document — uncertainty
about funds and operating under stressful time pressures?" We
need to know further what the components and ingredients of
these qualities are and how they can be engendered and supported. Otherwise, McCauley and Hughes's framework will be
yet again another prescriptive checklist of desirable traits or steps
that is sensible but difficult for practitioners to apply (or for researchers to study in greater depth).

The prospects are bright for building wider, firmer bridges
that connect research and practice about the leadership and management of nonprofits, because the need for better linkages is
great and because there are promising initiatives already under way. To an extent that is unusual in applied research circles, the study of nonprofits has a relatively mixed base of support that INDEPENDENT SECTOR has so skillfully nurtured.
Participants at the March 1991 Research Forum were impres-
sively diverse — including both academic and practitioner communities. This mixed auspice and audience gives us an opportunity to make that very diversity a distinctive strength of research
about the voluntary sector — to continue to build an informed
constituency for research that is a robust alliance of academics
and administrators, of studiers and doers.

References

Carver, J. *Boards That Make a Difference: A New Design for Leadership
in Nonprofit and Public Organizations.* San Francisco: Jossey-Bass,
1990.
Herman, R. D., and Van Til, J. (eds.). *Nonprofit Boards of Direc-*

tors, *Analyses and Applications*. New Brunswick, N.J.: Transaction, 1989.

Middleton Stone, M. "Nonprofit Boards of Directors, Beyond the Governance Function." in W. W. Powell (ed.), *The Nonprofit Sector: A Research Handbook*. New Haven, Conn.: Yale University Press, 1987.

Schön, D. A. *The Reflective Practitioner*. New York: Basic Books, 1983.

Wuthnow, R., Hodgkinson, V. A., and Associates. *Faith and Philanthropy in America: Exploring the Role of Religion in America's Voluntary Sector*. San Francisco: Jossey-Bass, 1990.

Name Index

324

Subject Index